Freedom and Resentment

'Prime philosopher of Oxford's golden age, and champion of both the richness of ordinary language and of natural beliefs' *The Guardian*

'Distinguished Oxford philosopher whose spare, elegant work made sense of Kant's metaphysics' *The Independent*

'A stimulating and wide-ranging book.' *A.J. Ayer, New Statesman*

'. . . this collection enabled one to appreciate the great versatility Professor Strawson has. We have here, under one cover, valuable contributions to the most diverse and broad ranging problems in philosophy.' *Philosophical Books*

At the time of his death in 2006, Sir Peter Strawson was regarded as one of the world's most distinguished philosophers. First published thirty years ago but long since unavailable, *Freedom and Resentment* collects some of Strawson's most important work.

Broadly conceived as analytical philosophy, the essays in this collection demonstrate the vitality of Strawson's thinking on such topics as the philosophy of language, metaphysics, epistemology and aesthetics. Beginning with the title essay, *Freedom and Resentment*, which has been called the most influential philosophical article of the twentieth century, this invaluable collection demonstrates the great range of Strawson's thought as he discusses free will, ethics and morality, logic, the mind-body problem and aesthetics.

This reissue includes a substantial new foreword by Paul Snowdon and a fascinating intellectual autobiography by Strawson, which together form an excellent introduction to his life and work.

T0386376

Freedom and Resentment
And other essays

P.F.
Strawson

Routledge
Taylor & Francis Group

LONDON AND NEW YORK

First published in 1974
by Methuen & Co Ltd.

This edition published 2008
by Routledge
2 Park Square, Milton Park, Abingdon, Oxon OX14 4RN

Simultaneously published in the USA and Canada
by Routledge
711 Third Avenue, New York, NY 10017

Routledge is an imprint of the Taylor & Francis Group, an informa business

© 1974, 2008 P.F. Strawson
© 2008 Foreword Paul Snowdon

'Intellectual Autobiography' by P.F. Strawson first published by Open Court
in *The Philosophy of P.F. Strawson* (1999). Reprinted with kind permission.

Typeset in Aldus and Scala by RefineCatch Limited, Bungay, Suffolk

British Library Cataloguing in Publication Data
A catalogue record for this book is available from the British Library

Library of Congress Cataloging in Publication Data
A catalog record for this book has been requested

ISBN10: 0–415–44850–6 (pbk)
ISBN13: 978–0–415–44850–5 (pbk)

CONTENTS

FOREWORD

By Paul Snowdon
University College London, UK

Strawson published two collections of papers in the 1970s. *Freedom and Resentment and Other Essays* was the second of these collections, coming out in 1974. The first, *Logico-Linguistic Papers*, contained many of Strawson's most famous papers on the philosophy of language.[1] This second collection covers a broad range of topics: moral philosophy, perception, philosophy of language, aesthetics, the metaphysics of mind, and Wittgenstein's *Philosophical Investigations*. Further, one paper about perception deals with Kant, and the essay on mind engages with Descartes. The collection, therefore, exemplifies one of the striking aspects of Strawson's philosophical output – its breadth. His writing touched virtually every branch of philosophy. The collection also reveals two other aspects of his writings. Each essay contains and develops a bold and novel hypothesis (not necessarily only one). Strawson's originality stands out. In each, also, the ideas are developed, without exception, with intelligence, subtlety and care. One can liken reading these papers to listening to a succession of performances by a virtuoso of pieces of contrasting complexity, but where the control and the quality are always manifest. The most important paper in this collection is undoubtedly 'Freedom and Resentment', which gives its name to the volume itself, and I shall talk about it at the end of this foreword. Before that I wish to introduce the other papers.

STRAWSON ON WITTGENSTEIN

It was a measure of Strawson's status in Oxford in the early 1950s, that Ryle chose him to review *Philosophical Investigations* for the journal *Mind*. Strawson's deeply considered review contains a perspicuous division into a number of areas of the topics covered by Wittgenstein. The chief characteristic of the review is balance. It attempts to formulate the leading ideas sympathetically but also to maintain a critical distance, and it is in the critical responses that I feel there is most to learn. I shall select one example. Wittgenstein thought that the role of proper philosophy is basically negative, to eliminate philosophical errors, arising, as he thought, from misuse of language. On his conception this is to be done by basically re-acquainting the thinker with his or her language. This is sometimes called philosophy as *therapy*. About this Strawson points out that if one's dominant purpose is the elimination of traditional error and this is the most effective method by which to do it, then there may be some justification to limit one's own procedures as a philosopher to regenerating such acquaintance. But it is quite another matter to claim that this is the sole purpose of good philosophy.

Moreover, no reason has yet been given to suppose there are no general interesting truths discoverable by philosophical methods. As Strawson puts it, 'could not the activities we call "doing philosophy" also form a family?'[2] In these few remarks, I believe, Strawson brings out as well as anyone the sheer arbitrariness of Wittgenstein's official philosophy of philosophy. Similarly, when engaging with Wittgenstein's thought on language and most other matters Strawson's touch is sure. The only point on which it is less sure is when he considers Wittgenstein's approach to the idea of private experience. Strawson's interpretation of these famous passages is that Wittgenstein is saying, amongst other things, that 'no words name sensations (or private experiences); and in particular the word "pain" does not'. It seems better to think that

Wittgenstein himself would agree that 'pain' designates pain, and so names a sensation. Wittgenstein's purpose is, rather, to uproot a *misconception,* as he saw it, of what sensations, including pain, are. This misconception is supposed to be captured in talk of pain as *essentially private.* Strawson is right, though, to suggest that when Wittgenstein develops his supposedly myth-free conception of sensations he says much that is hard to accept and, indeed, to understand.

STRAWSON ON DESCARTES

Strawson sought to define his conception of persons by, as it were, bouncing off the conception provided by Descartes. Descartes thought that each of us is an individual, non-spatial ego, which is causally linked to a body in space. As Strawson puts this approach, '. . . the history of a human being is not the history of one two-sided thing, it is the history of two one-sided things.'[3] In 'Self, Mind and Body' Strawson highlights an anti-Cartesian objection, different from the famous one in Chapter 3 of *Individuals.* The central problem is that the Cartesian hypothesis requires that we can understand the notion of a single enduring consciousness, an ego, including such aspects as the contrast between one and another at a time, and of a single one continuing over time. Strawson suggests that no such understanding can exist once we cut our understanding of subjects of consciousness from our normal conception of ourselves as physical and embodied persons. The question raised, though, is not whether such an understanding is required – it obviously is – but by what *standards* it can be shown that the Cartesian notion is *not* intelligible.

Earlier in the paper Strawson develops another anti-Cartesian problem. His idea is that the analysis of our lives into the lives of two different substances, the ego and the body, requires that statements about us must be reducible to statements about the body conjoined with statements about the ego. Strawson suggests that 'there might be very considerable difficulties in effecting' such a reduction.[4] Strawson himself suspects this impossibility might reflect inadequacies in extant language, and so he discounts the objection. But there is another weakness. Surely, a chair, for example, consists of a seat plus back, but the property of being a *comfortable* chair can hardly be reduced to a conjunction of claims about the seat and others about the back. It depends rather on the relation between seat and back. Similarly, if people are egos with bodies, properties of people do not have to be analysable into conjunctions.

Whatever the merits of these objections, one of Strawson's greatest achievements is to have characterized how we *do* think of ourselves, and that is, as he says, as a 'human being, a man, a type of thing to which predicates of all those various classes I distinguished earlier can be ascribed'.[5]

STRAWSON ON PERCEPTION

Three of the essays discuss perception. In the first one, 'Imagination and Perception', Strawson combines two tasks. One is historical, to make as much sense as one can of the tendency to appeal to imagination in theorizing about perception, as evidenced in the writings of Hume, Kant, and Wittgenstein. But that task is linked to another – to specify, and explain the real character of perceptual experience. Strawson's claim is that it is impossible to characterize normal perceptual experience without employing objective concepts. Thus, I have to say something like: my visual experience is as of a *rock on a beach*. Strawson, himself, puts it by saying that 'the actual occurrent perception ... is, as it were, soaked with or animated by, or infused with ...' such concepts.[6] Strawson's examination of the historical figures is exemplary and his assertions about the objectivity of perception have proved very influential, but the question that remains is: wherein precisely is the link?

In 'Causation in Perception' Strawson asks: what is required for a physical object to be perceived? Strawson accepts and argues for the view propounded by H. P. Grice that the object must cause an experience in the subject.[7] Strawson endorses Grice's argument but, importantly, he suggests that it is also implied by the knowledge-giving role of perception. What else is required? Which causal chains qualify? Grice's answer is, in a nutshell, causal chains of this (indicated) sort, and not of that (indicated) sort. Strawson objects that this leaves the concept of perceiving quite un-illuminated. Strawson instead invokes certain requirements relating to the 'spatial and temporal positioning' of the subject and object. This is highly ingenious and has attracted considerable discussion.[8]

The third paper on perception and identification is a response to one by Hampshire. Hampshire was concerned with cases where a percipient cannot make out what he is seeing and gives a non-committal description, such as 'I can see a black patch.' Hampshire's point seems to have been that the existence of such cases does not mean that such a phenomenal description describes something that is omnipresent in perception, and Strawson, of course, agrees. He argues, though, that given how Hampshire defines 'non-committal', such descriptions are possible only of visual experience. The other issue can be introduced by asking whether, when the subject who discriminates the black patch is in fact seeing a dark island, we should say that the black patch *is* the island, or that there is the island *and* the black patch. Strawson proposes that we can say either. Again, this is interesting, but as Michael Hinton later argued, in an important paper directly inspired by Strawson's, we may not quite have that much freedom.[9]

ESSAYS ON LANGUAGE

Three of the essays can be counted as about language. In 'Is Existence Never a Predicate?' Strawson aims to support the answer 'No'. At the time he wrote this essay, most philosophers held that the answer is 'Yes' because of some supposed paradoxes the idea of existence as a property of an individual raised.[10] Strawson identifies two contexts in which it seems that 'exists' is a predicate of individuals. Others after him attempted to tear up the orthodoxy root and branch, which they did so successfully that the orthodox answer nowadays would be 'certainly it is a predicate'.[11] The essay 'Categories' can also be counted as being about language. Gilbert Ryle talked often about category mistakes without giving a general explanation of them. Strawson proposes that given, roughly, the ideas of picking out an object in an adequate way and of *a priori* derivations from such modes of reference, the notion has a chance of being explained. Significantly, despite this, it is not a notion employed nowadays. The third essay about language, 'On Understanding the Structure of One's Language', raises, it seems to me, a very important question. In a certain way of thinking about natural language, associated with Davidson, the attempt is made to say what the words of ordinary language are doing, by assigning them a logical form. The assignment is effected by pairing ordinary language sentences with formulae in the predicate calculus. What does it mean to propose that a certain formal sentence 'gives the logical form' of a natural language sentence? Strawson shows that to answer this is not straightforward, and his discussion of alternatives is highly illuminating.

Eventually he suggests a satisfactory account can be given. However, what that leaves is the question as to why we should accept such proposals. Strawson's idea is that such a proposal, which reads into the relatively simple grammar of English a highly complex semantic structure, needs a strong reason to be accepted. Strawson suggests that there is no evident reason that forces us to accept it. Obviously Strawson is not able to survey all possible replies to his question, but his paper forces anyone inclined to play the logical form assignment game in this way to justify their practice.

VALUES – AESTHETIC AND MORAL

Two of the essays might be said to relate to issues in the general theory of value. In 'Social Morality and Individual Ideal', Strawson develops a distinction between two aspects of the ethical. The first is the way in which forms of life or pursuit strike individuals as attractive or even compulsory – say, the life of the artist or the soldier or the great lover – attractions which can change within a single life, and attractions which may or may not lead to action. The second is the idea of the moral, the idea of constraints and obligations acknowledged in our social lives. Strawson's approach is not to attempt to establish value claims but rather to illuminate the social and psychological sources of moral thought, the aim being to contribute to an understanding of moral thought as we have it and not to justify it. What is, for me, particularly impressive about the essay is the vividness of his description of ideals and the tensions that one can feel under their influence, conveying a strong sense that Strawson's description reflects aspects of his own inner life. Whether the perspective he adopts in thinking about morality is the most illuminating one is, perhaps, the main question the essay prompts.

The second essay about value is 'Aesthetic Appraisal and Works of Art'. Strawson's question is whether there is a way to capture what is distinctive of aesthetic appraisal (as opposed to other sorts of appraisal). Strawson's answer is that with aesthetic appraisal there are no such things as properties which make the work good or bad – there are no such things as 'aesthetic merit conferring properties'. By contrast, with moral evaluation we can locate such properties, say cruelty or kindness. This claim about the aesthetic certainly has the ring of truth. One might push the question further and ask why there are no such properties. One might also ask whether the absence of such properties is unique to aesthetic appraisal. And, indeed, whether it is the sole mark of aesthetic evaluation.

FREEDOM AND RESENTMENT

Delivered as a lecture to the British Academy in 1962 'Freedom and Resentment' has become one of Strawson's most discussed papers. Strawson's goal is to resolve a debate where the two sides are simply jammed. What implications does the possible truth of determinism have for our status as agents susceptible of moral evaluation? Strawson calls one side which claims that determinism does not impugn that status the 'optimists', the other side, which thinks it does, or would, the 'pessimists'. The aim of the reconciliation is to defend optimism, avoiding any temptation to endorse what Strawson calls the 'obscure and panicky metaphysics' of libertarianism, while at the same time providing a better characterization of our moral attitudes than optimists normally manage. How does Strawson try to do this? He initially focuses on certain participant reactive attitudes that are central to human life. Examples are resentment and gratitude. As Strawson characterizes them, these are feelings we get in response to our sense of the attitudes towards ourselves of those around us. We feel resentment if we think that in their actions they wish us harm or display no concern. Gratitude is felt where we sense their actions are expressions of liking or regard. Strawson's idea is that such responses can be moderated and affected by excuses and justifications, and, moreover, it is in our power to suspend such reactions where the agents are perceived as under a mental abnormality, say excessive stress, or if they are, in virtue of their nature, unfit for such responses. However, it is, according to Strawson, impossible to maintain such an objective attitude towards normal people most of the time, since these attitudes are inevitable and central. This would remain impossible even if we were convinced of determinism. Moreover, our involvement with such reactions clearly does not flow from any general metaphysical belief in the falsity of determinism. Strawson concludes that it cannot be said that the rationality of such attitudes depends on the falsity of determinism. He then isolates certain parallel reactions which are moral and vicarious, rather then participant, such as the disgust or anger one feels on hearing of the slaughter of innocents. Strawson notes that such responses are like the participant ones in that they can be modified by excuses and justifications, and that they can be suspended in special cases, and also towards certain people who are abnormal or immature in certain ways. His claim is, though, that the same impossibility of a general suspension applies here, and there is a similar lack of dependence of such responses on a rejection of determinism. Determinism similarly cannot impugn their rationality either. Now, this is significant because these attitudes and feelings are constitutive of our moral views and they are what blaming and punishing and praising are expressive of. Strawson is stressing two things. First, that there is no rational dependence of our responses on the falsity of determinism. Second, that in recognizing our moral attitudes for what they are, and our practices as expressive of them, we avoid treating our practice of holding responsible as simply instruments of control, justified by their efficacy. This attitude towards our moral attitudes which optimists often appeal to, fails to give an account of their true character, and is what pessimists sense as inadequate in the optimists' defence. Strawson's account avoids that distortion. Strawson hopes that this offering of a more realistic account of our thinking will remove the problems that pessimists have with optimism.

Why has Strawson's proposal attracted such attention? I conjecture that it is because the attitude that Strawson calls 'optimism' and which he is defending is the attitude that most of us wish to believe in. Strawson is right, surely, that social life as we know it must include what we might describe as living and regarding others as living under the idea of responsibility for their actions. It would, therefore, be highly inconvenient should it be true that falling under the idea of responsibility requires something that we lack. Naturally, a novel attempt to ground optimism attracts attention. Further, there is considerable interest in Strawson's attempt because, although he does not put it this way, the framework of his approach is the idea of morality and moralizing as essentially sentiment and feeling involving. That conception is one that has considerable appeal and lasting attractions.

Despite these attractions the crucial question is whether Strawson has done enough to really persuade us that the pessimist is wrong. What precisely does Strawson offer? The crucial page is 19. Strawson points out, first, that when we do suspend moral attitudes to an individual it is never because we think of them as simply determined in their behaviour. The pessimist will reply that my claim is not that people already do this, but that in fact if we are determined then we do not qualify as responsible. Strawson next points out that we cannot envisage abandoning holding each other responsible. The pessimist will reply that this simply means that we are bound to treat each other in ways that are not merited, but why is that impossible? Finally, Strawson remarks that if the psychological necessities he identifies do obtain then it is simply *useless* to pursue the philosophical issue about determinism. It remains unclear though quite what this uselessness means as far as the pessimist's programme is concerned. That is the fundamental question.

My aim has been to highlight some of the features of, and issues raised by, Strawson's essays as I see them. My response is a personal one and quite other aspects would have been highlighted by others. But what anyone would share is a sense that more or less all of Strawson's essays remain as important and as relevant for the subject now as they were when published in the 1970s.

NOTES

1 Strawson used to say that the best title for it would have been 'Language, Truth and Logic', but unfortunately that had already been taken. Part of the point of this joke was, I believe, to imply or insinuate, with some justice, that the title was not quite such a good one for Ayer's famous book!

2 F & R p. 158.

3 F & R p. 187.

4 F & R p. 189.

5 F & R p. 188.

6 F & R p. 59.

7 Grice's famous paper is reprinted in (ed.) J. Dancy, *Perceptual Knowledge* (Oxford: OUP, 1988) pp. 66–78.

8 For critical discussion see Christopher Peacocke *Holistic Explanation* (Oxford: Clarendon Press, 1979) pp. 95–9, and P. Snowdon 'Strawson on the Concept of Perception' in (ed.) L. E. Hahn *The Philosophy of P. F. Strawson* (Chicago: Open Court, 1998) pp. 293–310. See also Strawson's reply to the latter paper in the Hahn volume, pp. 311–14.

9 See Michael Hinton 'Perception and Identification' in *Philosophical Review* Vol. LXXVI 1967, pp. 421–35.

10 A very clear exposition of the orthodox view is D. F. Pears, 'Is Existence a Predicate?' in (ed.) P. F. Strawson *Philosophical Logic* (Oxford: OUP, 1967) pp. 97–102.

11 Opponents of the view that Strawson in a smaller way opposed have been Saul Kripke, in his unpublished John Locke Lectures, Gareth Evans, in *Varieties of Reference* (Oxford: Clarendon Press, 1982) ch. 9, and Michael Woods in 'Existence and Tense' in (eds) Evans and McDowell, *Truth and Meaning* (Oxford: Clarendon Press, 1976) pp. 248–62.

INTELLECTUAL AUTOBIOGRAPHY TAKEN FROM
THE PHILOSOPHY OF P. F. STRAWSON

The Library of Living Philosophers Volume XXVI
Edited by Lewis Edwin Hahn

I was born, on 23 November 1919, in one London suburb, Ealing, and was brought up in another, Finchley. I was the second child, with two brothers and one much younger sister. My parents were both school teachers, though my mother gave up teaching on marriage. They had met when studying English literature at Goldsmith's College, London. My mother retained an excellent memory for verse, which I inherited. My father's parents came from Lincolnshire and Yorkshire, my mother's from Hampshire and Gloucestershire. Unlike many English people, I know of no Scottish, Welsh, or Irish ancestry. After my first year's secondary education at the Finchley County School my parents transferred me to the boys-only Christ's College, Finchley (motto: '*Usque proficiens*'), where academic standards were higher and where my elder brother, four years my senior, was already being educated. Unlike him, I declined to join the Cadet Corps. I still feel grateful to the French teacher (Miss Jacobi) at the earlier school, who required us to learn the phonetic alphabet and strove to inculcate a correct pronunciation of the language she taught.

At Christ's College I had good teachers and flourished academically. When the time came to choose specialist subjects for what was then called 'Higher Certificate' (modern 'A-Level') I chose

English, French, Latin, and History, to the disapproval of my maths master who claimed, incorrectly, that mathematics was my best subject. In fact, my best subjects were the literary ones, and especially English, in which an excellent teacher, J. H. Taylor, gave me much encouragement. I developed a liking for grammar and a devotion to English poetry and prose, neither of which has left me. With Mr Taylor's support I entered for and won an open scholarship in English at St. John's College, Oxford. My Higher Certificate examination results had additionally secured for me a State Scholarship, and an anonymous benefactor had undertaken to supplement my undergraduate income. So I went up to Oxford in October 1937, at the age of 17, with adequate financial provision. This was necessary, since my father's salary, as Headmaster of a poor London school, had been modest, and his early death in 1936 – he had suffered bad health ever since the 1914–18 war – had left my mother a widow. So we were rather poor.

Before I joined my college, I had decided to change my course, if possible, from the Honour School of English to that of Philosophy, Politics and Economics (PPE); and when I arrived in Oxford I succeeded, against some mild resistance, in persuading the Fellows to allow me to do this. My motives for wishing to change were various. One was the perhaps rather priggish thought that since, at that period, the political future and the civilization of Europe seemed threatened, I ought to be better equipped than I was with understanding of politics and economics. More important was the fact that I had already begun to feel the intellectual pull of philosophy. This was partly due to my having read Rousseau's *Du Contrat Social* and been captivated by its combination of passion with what I then mistook for rigour; partly because I had already discovered in myself some capacity for argument and for detecting the flaws, confusions, and inconsistencies in the discourse of others; and partly to reading some popular books on philosophy (notably by the not contemptible C. E. M. Joad) and being taken with the irresistible fascination of the questions, problems, and theories there recorded. It was not that my love of literature had in any way diminished. On the contrary. I had read much, including modern, poetry (particularly T. S. Eliot); and I thought and continue to think of great poetry as the greatest of human achievements. I had contributed poems myself to issues of an anthology of schoolboy verse, called *The Threshold*, published in the 1930s. I am, or was, a competent versifier, and if I had been able to choose my talents, I would have chosen to be a poet. But of course I could not, and am not. So it was rather the assurance, perhaps mistaken, that my enjoyment and appreciation of good writing would not be enhanced – might even be injured – by making a profession or a career of it.

After one preliminary term of eight weeks at Oxford, concluding with a simple examination, for which I read with enjoyment some Tacitus and Pliny, Tocqueville and Corneille, the serious work of the P.P.E. school began. Economics, I found, interested me hardly at all, the historical part of politics much more; philosophy I found congenial and absorbing from the start. Besides the required subjects of moral and 'general' philosophy I chose the only two options then allowed to P.P.E. students specializing in philosophy, viz. Logic (broadly understood to include what would now be called Philosophy of Language, and some metaphysical and epistemological questions) and the philosophy of Kant (*The Critique of Pure Reason* and the *Grundlegung*). My principal philosophy tutor throughout was J. D. Mabbott, a very reasonable, courteous, and helpful teacher, whose main interest was in moral and political philosophy and who subsequently became an excellent head of the college. But I also enjoyed one term's tuition by H. P. Grice, the other philosophy tutor at St. John's and one of the cleverest and most ingenious thinkers of our time. Tutorials with him regularly extended long beyond the customary hour, and from him I learned more of the difficulty and possibilities of philosophical argument than from anyone else. His resourcefulness seemed inexhaustible.

By the end of my three undergraduate years in Oxford I knew that, of all the world's possible occupations, the one I most desired was that of a Fellow and Tutor in Philosophy in a college of that University. But the result of my final examination, though it did not greatly surprise me, was a disappointment both to myself and my tutors; so I had no very high hopes of achieving such an ambition.

In any case, by then, we were in the summer of 1940. The war was going badly. I was duly called up into the army (the Royal Artillery), and sent for basic training to a territorial searchlight battery in Sussex, where, in between learning to drill and to shoot I had an excellent view of the aerial Battle of Britain during the day, and, at night, of the red glow of the Northern sky where London was undergoing bombardment by the Luftwaffe. Fairly soon I was selected for instruction in the mysteries of radar and attended a number of courses, in London and elsewhere, at which I learned a great deal, now forgotten, about electronics. Having no difficulty with examinations in this subject, I was, to the reasonable surprise of senior NCOs, fairly rapidly promoted through the ranks, briefly commanded a small radar station near the Sussex shore, and in 1942 was commissioned in the newly formed corps of the Royal Electrical and Mechanical Engineers.

I eventually attained the rank of captain; but my military career was in no way distinguished. The only part of it in which I took much satisfaction was that of discharging the duty of defending officer at the courts martial of putatively delinquent soldiers, where, though I only once secured an acquittal (of a senior NCO charged with a serious offence of disobedience to orders) I flatter myself I may often have reduced the severity of sentences by the persuasive power of my 'pleas in mitigation'. In 1945, before being posted abroad to the occupying army in Italy, and then Austria, I had the great good fortune of persuading Grace Hall Martin, my girlfriend of some years' standing – whom I had renamed 'Ann' – to marry me: probably the most judicious action of my life.

In the summer of 1946, having unhesitatingly declined the bait of further promotion, I was demobilized. I had served for six years, thinking a little, but not much, about philosophy and devoting most of such private leisure as I had enjoyed to reading the greater French and English novelists. My ambitions, however, for a career as an academic philosopher, had not changed. I contemplated returning to Oxford to read for a further degree (a B.Phil. in philosophy); but there were difficulties in the way of that; and my future was in effect decided by the intervention of my former tutor, John Mabbott – in this my guardian angel – who suggested that I apply for the post of Assistant Lecturer in Philosophy at the University College of North Wales, Bangor, where he himself had taught for a short time before becoming a Fellow of St. John's. It was no doubt largely due to his support that, when I did apply, I was elected on interview. So I set myself to some hard reading in subjects on which I was to lecture – particularly philosophy of logic (for which I read Russell, Moore, Ramsey, C. I. Lewis, and an introductory book by Susan Stebbing) and Kant's moral philosophy. In the course of my year at Bangor I also lectured on the philosophy of Leibniz (studied mainly in the Gerhardt edition) and on ethics in general; and wrote two papers, one an attempt to solve the problem of the 'paradoxes of entailment', the other an attack on ethical intuitionism. The first I submitted to *Mind*, where it appeared, as 'Necessary Propositions and Entailment Statements', my first published article, in 1948. Though it contained the germ of a fruitful idea, it also contained a serious mistake and so failed in its declared aim. The second was much too long and too involved, therefore tedious; so I later recast it in the crisper, dialogue form in which it appeared as 'Ethical Intuitionism' in *Philosophy* 1949.

During the same academic year I visited Oxford, where Ann and I shared a flat – she having entered St Anne's College to read English as an undergraduate – to take the competitive examination for the John Locke Scholarship, as it was then called. My success in winning this had two beneficial results: first, the prize of £80, then worth many times its present value, was extremely welcome to an impoverished couple; second, my papers sufficiently impressed Gilbert Ryle, one of the examiners, for him to recommend me to University College, then in need of a second teacher of philosophy. So, in 1947, I returned to Oxford as, in effect, a philosophy tutor, though bearing the inappropriate title of 'College Lecturer' until, in the following year, I was elected a Fellow. Ann and I were then fortunate enough to be able to leave our North Oxford flat and take up residence in an apartment in the College itself, where we lived until we moved, in 1950, on the birth of our first child, to an elegant College house of the 1840s.

Having thus achieved, at the age of 28, my prewar ambition, I set seriously to work at the two tasks of tutorial teaching and of thinking my own thoughts. They are not unconnected tasks, for the first is of immense benefit to the second, as the second is to the first. Indeed I think there is no better or more mutually profitable method of philosophical instruction than the one-to-one tutorial exchange. The pupil, who brings and reads to his tutor a weekly essay, prepared on the basis of recommended reading, gains from the attention and criticism of his more experienced listener. The tutor, striving to understand and clarify his pupil's thoughts, will frequently succeed in clarifying his own. This admirable system, like many good things, is under threat.

My colleague, George Paul, and I divided the tutorial teaching between us in a way satisfactory to both. He undertook the teaching of moral and political and ancient philosophy (Plato and Aristotle), while logic and general modern philosophy from Descartes onwards fell to me. The questions which at the time most seriously engaged my attention were questions in the philosophy of logic and the philosophy of language. While still at Bangor, lecturing on these matters, I had become deeply concerned with the matter of singular reference and predication, and their objects – a topic which has remained central in my thought throughout my working life. Now in Oxford I proceeded, beginning in 1948, to supplement my college teaching with a series of University lectures under the title 'Names and Descriptions', in which I referred to and criticized the work of Russell, Moore, Kneale, and some few others. From these I extracted two lectures, given to an American Summer School, in which I concentrated on my critique of Russell's Theory of Descriptions; and the report of these induced Gilbert Ryle, then editor of *Mind*, to say, bluntly, that he wanted them as an article for that journal. Hence 'On Referring' (*Mind*, 1950), which remains, probably, the best known of my writings.

Russell's theory, elegant and ingenious as it is – a 'paradigm of philosophy' according to F. P. Ramsey – seemed to me then, and still does, to misrepresent the true character and function of singular definite descriptive phrases, as, for the most part, we actually use and understand them. It does so by overlooking or neglecting the pragmatic, contextual, and communicative aspects of their use. To the objection that this is to introduce merely pragmatic considerations into what is essentially a semantic question, the answer must be that no serious semantic theory can afford to ignore the points – and their consequences – to which I drew attention. I think my view, with variations, is now generally accepted by linguists, though the issue remains, to some extent, controversial among philosophers. I should add that I had not at the time read Frege and was, regrettably enough, completely ignorant of the work of that great figure; so subsequent references to the 'Frege-Strawson' view of the matter I found, at first, surprising, though in no way disturbing.

I had, after all, jumped straight, with six years military service intervening, from undergraduate to university teacher; so serious gaps in my knowledge were perhaps pardonable. My major influences remained Russell and Moore, whom I viewed, and still view, as the founding fathers of contemporary analytical philosophy. Other influences, of course, were soon to be added: locally Ryle, whose verve and brilliance might excuse, if they sometimes masked, a certain lack of rigour in thought, and Austin, consistently clear, precise, witty, and formidable; more remotely, Wittgenstein, whose Blue and Brown Books began to circulate in pirated copies at the beginning of the 1950s, at once breathtakingly impressive and profoundly enigmatic; and Frege himself, whose articles on Sense and Reference and Concept and Object were made available in English translation by Geach and Black in 1952. Nor should I fail to mention A. J. Ayer whose *Language, Truth and Logic* I had read, enthralled, in the gardens of St. John's as an undergraduate – even though, by now, I no longer found satisfying his undiluted classical empiricism.

Austin did me the honour of proposing that I should reply to his paper on Truth at the Joint Session of the Mind and Aristotelian Society in 1950. I was already convinced that Ramsey had got the matter essentially right a long time ago, and hence thought that Austin had got it essentially wrong. Though I tried to convey as much in my reply, I also spoiled the effect, and diverted general attention, with a gratuitous flourish of my own, which was itself due in part to Austin's own observation of the 'performatory' function of speech. That little flourish had itself formed the substance of a short article in *Analysis* the year before (*à propos* of which I remember fatuously announcing to George Paul that I had a new theory of truth; to which he sensibly and characteristically replied: 'Come on now, which of the old ones is it?'). The issue, of course, persists; and, much later, I was able to make my considered position clear and to finalize my critique of Austin in the two articles 'A Problem about Truth: A Reply to Mr. Warnock' (1964) and 'Truth: A Reconsideration of Austin's Views' (1965), both of which were reprinted in *Logico-Linguistic Papers* (1971).

Meanwhile, I had been invited to give regular introductory lectures on logic in the University for the benefit of undergraduates studying for the Preliminary Examination in PPE. This I did, and as a result was further invited by a publisher, again, I think, at Ryle's prompting, to write a book on the subject. It duly appeared as *Introduction to Logical Theory* in 1952 and received the accolade of a lengthy review in *Mind* by Quine, in which he deplored my use of the notion of analyticity but pleased me by his slightly ironical reference to my 'lucid vernacular'. My double concern in the book was to explain the nature of standard elementary logic while at the same time emphasizing the point that, perspicuous, powerful, and elegant as it is, modern formal logic is not an adequate instrument for revealing clearly all the structural features of language as we use it. Rather, it is an idealized abstraction of great power and beauty, an indispensable tool indeed for clarifying much of our thought, but not, as some are tempted to suppose, the unique and sufficient key to the functioning of language and thought in general.

The early 1950s in general were a busy and productive time. For a few years in the first half of the decade Grice and I together held a graduate seminar at which we took it in turn to read papers, some of them (e.g. that which surfaced later as 'In Defence of a Dogma' (1954)) actually produced in collaboration. Among those at different times attending the seminar were a number of senior members, including, on his first visit to Oxford, Quine. At about this time I was charged by Ryle with the task of reviewing Wittgenstein's *Philosophical Investigations* for *Mind*, a task to which I devoted a considerable amount of time and effort, with results (1954) which, though they recorded my sense of the work's genius, also recorded some perplexity, even dissatisfaction, and was accordingly not received with entire approval by the committed disciples. It might not be quite coincidental that Norman Malcolm, as an epigraph to his own review, quoted Lichtenberg: 'Ein Buch ist ein Spiegel. Wenn ein Affe hineinguckt, dann kann freilich kein Apostel heraussehen'.

The birth of my daughter, Julia, in 1950 was followed by the birth of my two sons, Galen (named after his uncle who was named after his) in 1952, and Robert in 1954. Soon after the publication of 'Logical Theory' I ceased to give the introductory lectures on formal logic and began instead to think and lecture on the lines which led, ultimately, to *Individuals*. This was a natural development from my already established concern with the operation, fundamental in thought and speech, of reference and predication; an operation fundamental also, as many, from Aristotle to Quine, have thought and stressed, in ontology or metaphysics. So it was natural to address the question of what the most basic or primitive or fundamental objects of reference, or subjects of predication, are. In the first part of *Individuals* I argued that they are – and necessarily are – relatively enduring space-occupying individuals, falling under substance-concepts. Here was an at least partial echo of Aristotle. In the same part I speculated on the theoretical possibility of reproducing the essential structure of our scheme with a greatly attenuated ontology (sounds); sought, perhaps by then unnecessarily, to deliver a *coup de grâce* to Cartesianism and to dispose of the pseudo-problem of other minds; and concluded by examining the brilliantly conceived and finally impossible Leibnizian ontology of monads.

All of this and more I made the topic of one of the seminars I conducted at Duke University, North Carolina, throughout the fall semester of 1955. This was my first visit to the United States. The other seminar I conducted there was devoted to a series of papers in the philosophy of logic and language: on such topics as reference again, propositions, the constants of logic and their analogues in natural language, necessity, etc. While at Duke, I had the opportunity of visiting and reading papers at a number of other

American Universities, on the West and East coasts and in between. The visit which stays most vividly in my mind, and that for a bizarre reason, is the one I paid to Seattle, Washington State. The paper I read there contained the substance of what became the chapter on Persons in *Individuals*; and one member of my audience stood throughout, with his back turned to me, evidently more willing to hear what I had to say than to contemplate the sight of me saying it.

Another event which occurred, I think, earlier in the 1950s was an assembly of French and Anglophone philosophers at one of the Colloques de Royaumont, which was designed to bring about a meeting of minds between representatives of the continental and analytical traditions. Whether this desirable result was actually achieved remains uncertain. But Austin at least made an impression with his paper, delivered in French on 'Performatifs'. In a paper entitled 'Analysis, Science and Metaphysics' I gave an account of the relations between these three, as I then conceived of them; and this, later published in French in *La Philosophie Analytique* (Cahiers de Royaumont, 1962), appeared later still in English in *The Linguistic Turn* edited by Rorty in 1967. At about this time I wrote my contribution to the Schilpp volume on Carnap, under the title 'Carnap's Views on Constructed Systems versus Natural Languages in Analytical Philosophy'. Completed to a deadline in 1954, it did not appear until the volume was published, nine years later, in 1963.

Philosophical disagreements with Quine – which have in no way impaired a personal friendship of some forty years' standing – surfaced again in 'Propositions, Concepts and Logical Truth' (1957). The disagreements, both then and later, turn on my more than permissive attitude towards a whole range of intensional notions which Quine is unable to countenance; and of which, I then argued, his own account of truths of logic compelled recognition. My next major undertaking was that of getting my lectures on Individuals into shape as a book. This did not take me very long, since the lectures were already pretty complete; but I did rewrite the first chapter and add an introduction about the general character of the enterprise, in which I introduced the term 'descriptive metaphysics'. In the second part of the lectures and of the book I sought both to explain the basic association of two distinctions – the logical or grammatical distinction between subject and predicate (reference and predication) on the one hand and the ontological distinction between spatio-temporal particular and universal on the other – and at the same time to show that and why this association, though fundamental, is not exclusive. Particulars indeed can never be predicated, but universals, and abstract and intensional objects generally, can certainly be objects of reference or subjects of predication; and given the acknowledged connection between being an object of reference and being an entity, we should abandon, if we suffer from them, any natural but ill-founded nominalistic anxieties and recognize such objects in our ontology.

Individuals was published in 1959, and in the same year A. J. Ayer was elected to the Wykeham Chair of Logic, for which I too, encouraged by colleagues, had applied. The result of the election, so far from being a disappointment to me, was a profound relief. I did not yet feel ready for an Oxford Chair, and was perfectly satisfied to continue with undergraduate tutorial teaching. The weekly discussion group for selected dons which Ayer established replaced, in a totally different but equally stimulating style, the Saturday morning meetings over which Austin, before his untimely and much lamented death, had so brilliantly presided. With Austin, proceedings were informal and no standard philosophical issues were tackled head-on; instead, particular specific concepts or concept-groups (words or word-groups), and the conditions of their use, were examined in detail, with results that were always fascinating, and often philosophically suggestive or illuminating. With Ayer, a different member of the group each week would read a paper on a philosophical topic of his choice; then drinks would be served by the host for the term and discussion, usually spirited, never acrimonious, would begin. 'Freddie's Group', as it was and is called, survived and survives the death of its founder.

1960 was a full year. I was elected to the British Academy and delivered there a lecture, 'Freedom and Resentment', which is one of my very few ventures into moral philosophy. Another such venture, written about the same time, and published in 1961 (the year of the birth of my younger daughter, Virginia), I entitled 'Social Morality and Individual Ideal'. Between them, these two papers effectively embody all I have thought or have to say in a philosophical area which, important as I recognize it to be, I have never found as intellectually gripping as those to which I have given more attention. The 1961 paper I had previously given as a public lecture in Princeton University, where I had been invited for the fall semester of 1960. There I conducted a seminar attended by some extremely able graduates and, from time to time, by such teachers as Hempel, Benacerraf, and Vlastos. My subjects were, again, generally in the region of philosophy of logic and language, e.g. singular reference and predication, logical constants and logical form. Colleagues and students were friendly and the standard of discussion was high. While at Princeton I again visited and read papers at a number of other universities.

1960 also saw the publication, in the *Times Literary Supplement*, of a series of articles under the general heading, 'The British Imagination'. I contributed the article on philosophy. It was given the title 'The Post-Linguistic Thaw' – a title not chosen by me and which I deplored. The title was not without point in that, as I indicated in the article, concentration on the actual use of words in ordinary linguistic practice – a philosophical method largely inspired by Austin and cultivated by at least a substantial minority of British, and especially Oxford, philosophers in the postwar period – was already, before 1960, beginning to loosen its grip in favour of more systematic and 'theoretical' approaches. Yet the title metaphor was objectionable in its suggestion of emergence from a period of frozen sterility; whereas in fact the gains and advances in philosophical understanding made in that period were probably as great as any that have been made in a comparably short time in the history of the subject; and the intellectual pleasure and excitement of living through it were correspondingly intense.

In the immediately succeeding years, besides lecturing and writing papers in the philosophy of language – on truth, reference, speech-acts, etc. – I began to lecture on Kant's *Critique of Pure Reason*, a book on which I had regularly tutored those undergraduates, or supervised those graduates, who had chosen to study it, finding it, as most of them did, both baffling and profound. There was a link here, too, with *Individuals*. In that book I had found myself frequently enquiring into the conditions that make possible certain kinds of knowledge and experience that we in fact have, or certain kinds of distinction that we in fact draw; and Kant, in the Critique, addresses this kind of question in its most general form, investigating the conditions of the possibility of experience, or empirical knowledge, in general. My lectures on the Critique, given in alternate years from 1959 and modified or added to from year to year, finally formed the basis of my book, *The Bounds of Sense*, published in 1966. My endeavour, in that work, was to separate Kant's brilliant and profound account of the structure of necessarily interconnected ideas and concepts which form the limiting framework of all human thought about the world and experience of the world from the overarching theory which he saw as the explanation of the possibility of any such account; and at the same time to explain that explanation and to show why it should be rejected. But I am aware that the last word on what remains the greatest single work of modern Western philosophy has not yet been, and probably never will be, spoken.

This publication naturally did not end my concern with Kant. On the first Critique, over the next twenty years, I regularly conducted a graduate seminar which never failed to attract graduate students, many of whom made excellent contributions to it. In an article, 'Imagination and Perception', first published in 1970 and subsequently reprinted, I made some amends for my cavalier treatment of the notion of synthesis in *The Bounds of Sense*. In 1987 I contributed papers to conferences in both Stanford and Stuttgart ('Sensibility, Understanding and the Doctrine of Synthesis' at the former, 'Kant's New Foundations of Metaphysics' at the latter), the proceedings of which were subsequently published. In 1987 again I contributed a paper on Kant's Paralogisms to a volume in honour of Dieter Henrich on his sixtieth birthday. In 1992 I gave a talk on 'The Problem of Realism and the A Priori in Kant' at a conference in Florence on Kant and Modern Epistemology. More recently I paid tribute to his insight into the nature of aesthetic judgment (in the *European Journal of Philosophy*, 1993).

In 1968 I succeeded Ryle in the Waynflete Chair of Metaphysical Philosophy at Oxford. Before taking up my duties in October of that year I worked hard at preparing a set of introductory lectures on philosophy. My aims were, first, to explain the general nature of the discipline as I conceived and tried to practise it; then to demonstrate the interdependence of ontology, epistemology, and logic; and finally to show how certain central philosophical issues should, in my view, be resolved. I was incidentally concerned both to lay classical empiricism to rest and, in rejecting at least one favoured conception of analysis, to resist the reductive tendency in philosophy in general. I gave the same series of lectures, under the title, 'Analysis and Metaphysics: an Introduction to Philosophy', in almost every succeeding year until my retirement in 1987, keeping the earlier and more general parts substantially unchanged, while varying the choice of particular issues to be treated in more detail in the later parts.

The initial investment of effort in the preparation of these lectures has served me well. Much of a late version I translated into French and delivered as a course at the Collège de France in the spring of 1985; I delivered substantially the same lectures in English, with some variations, as the Immanuel Kant lectures in Munich in the summer of that year; in the Catholic University of America in Washington in September 1987; and as my contribution to the Sino-British Summer School in Philosophy in Beijing in 1988. The French version was published in Paris in 1985 as *Analyse et Métaphysique* and the final English version in Oxford in 1992.

It is customary, though not obligatory, for one newly elected to an Oxford Chair to give an Inaugural Lecture. I was glad of the opportunity to pay tribute to my predecessor, Gilbert Ryle, who, by reason of his energy, his authority and his vision – besides the brilliance and inventiveness displayed in his own philosophical writing – contributed perhaps more than any other single person to the flowering of the subject in England in the years after the war. I was glad, too, to return in the lecture, 'Meaning and Truth', to my abiding concern with language as an instrument of human communication. Although, in this lecture, I too blithely acquiesced, as John McDowell subsequently pointed out (1980), in an approach suggested by Grice's well-known article 'Meaning' of 1957, yet the centrality of the notion of fully overt communication-intention to any general understanding of the notion of linguistic meaning remains indisputable. Hence the failure of all inevitably self-frustrating attempts to expel all considerations dismissed as merely 'pragmatic' from the sacred area of semantic theory.

Philosophy of language was indeed a dominant, though not an exclusive, concern in the papers written about this time and in the next few years. Reading Chomsky's *Aspects of the Theory of Syntax* (and attending the John Locke lectures which he gave in the late 1960s) had led me to write 'Grammar and Philosophy', which I gave as the Presidential address to the Aristotelian Society in 1969, and in which I argued that no general explanatory theory of grammar was possible which did not intimately link semantic considerations to syntactic classifications and relations. At the conclusion of this essay I looked forward to the notion of a 'perspicuous grammar' which I developed, though only in a limited fashion, in my next book, *Subject and Predicate in Logic and Grammar* (1974). Though representing a new departure for me insofar as it was explicitly concerned, in its second part, with the theory of grammar, the book also showed its continuity with earlier work in that I began from the basic case of definite singular reference and predication and then proceeded, on this basis, to offer an explanatory account of the grammatical notions of subject and predicate in general. So a central theme of *Individuals*, further developed and exploited in 'The Asymmetry of Subjects and Predicates' (1970), lay at its foundation.

Asked to contribute to a volume of essays on the work of Gilbert Ryle, I chose as my topic the notions of category and category-mistake, which Ryle had frequently invoked and which had long interested me. I showed that the theoretical accounts he had earlier given of these ideas (and later viewed with distrust) were in fact indefensible and offered a less striking but, as it seemed to me, more plausible alternative ('Categories', 1970). I wrote other articles in a similarly critical vein: thus I argued that Austin, in *How to Do Things with Words*, had failed to give a consistent account of what he called the 'locutionary' aspect of speech-acts (1973);

anticipated my later contention that the Tarskian truth-theoretical model favoured by Davidson as a means of elucidating the semantically significant structural features of natural language was not adequate to the task (1974); and argued that the positions available for nonsubstitutional quantification were more than Quine allowed for, in that they included predicate-position ('Positions for Quantifiers', 1974). I later came to think that I had not fully understood at the time the full implications of this last article; and that a fully developed view would in fact bring me in one respect closer to Quine (all such positions being indeed referential), while in another leaving me equally remote from him (since properties and other intensional entities could properly occupy those positions). This development emerges implicitly in my 'Concept and Property or Predication and Copulation' (1987); but the most general defence of intensional or abstract entities is to be found in my 'Entity and Identity' (1976), 'Universals' (1979) and 'Two Conceptions of Philosophy' in *Perspectives on Quine* (1990).

In the winter of 1975–76 I made my first visit to India, where I already had friends, including Ramchandra Gandhi, who had written an admirably lucid doctoral thesis under my supervision in Oxford, and Roop Rekha Verma, who had spent a year in Oxford under the auspices of the British Council. While there, I lectured, read papers, and took part in discussions in Delhi, Lucknow, Santiniketan, and Calcutta. In general I was enchanted by this great and various country, by the beauty to be found there and by the warmth and vivacity of my hosts; and was delighted to repeat my visit, this time accompanied by Ann, in 1979–80.

Issues in the philosophy of language and ontology were not the only ones that occupied me in the 1970s. At a conference in Valencia, Spain, in the spring of 1973, I criticized foundationalist theories of knowledge ('Does Knowledge Have Foundations?', 1974); at the Joint Session of the Mind and Aristotelian Societies in 1975 I differed sharply from the antirealist views previously expounded by Dummett and there defended by Wright ('Scruton and Wright on Anti-Realism', 1976); for volumes in honour of Charles Baylis and Ayer I wrote two papers on the ever-challenging topic of perception ('Causation in Perception', 1975, and

'Perception and its Objects', 1979); at a high-powered conference held in Jerusalem in 1976 I delivered a paper on the concept of possibility, concentrating on its epistemic use, so frequently overlooked in discussions of modality in general ('May Bes and Might Have Beens', 1979); and on a second visit to Israel in 1977, at a conference commemorating the tercentenary of the death of Spinoza, I spoke on Liberty and Necessity, complementing the views I had advocated in 'Freedom and Resentment' by adding what I took to be a decisive demonstration that the thesis of determinism, in any form in which it was defensible, had no bearing on the issues of moral judgment and moral responsibility.

In 1977 I received the honour of knighthood; immediately after the investiture in December I departed for Yugoslavia, where I gave lectures in Belgrade, Sarajevo, and Zagreb. I registered a certain difference in atmosphere in the three places. At least in academic circles the intellectual style seemed relatively untrammelled in Belgrade and Zagreb, though the political tone was different. In Sarajevo, where I was only allowed to give one of my two scheduled lectures and had minimal contact with fellow academics, one perhaps time-serving young man in my audience suggested that my lecture revealed an essentially bourgeois outlook. I replied, 'But I *am* bourgeois – an élitist liberal bourgeois'. My interpreter commented, *sotto voce*, 'They envy you'.

In the early 1980s there appeared two collections of critical essays about my work, both of which elicited, and contained, replies by me. One was the book, *Philosophical Subjects* (Oxford, 1980), the other a special number of the Israeli journal, *Philosophia* (1981). Three articles in the first I must particularly mention: the one by John McDowell already referred to; an excellent piece by Gareth Evans, a Fellow of University College and formerly the brightest pupil I ever had there, whose early death can never be too greatly lamented; and that of Hidé Ishiguro, one of the most sensitive and discerning of philosophers. The topics discussed in these collections were as various as those I had myself previously written on. Later in the decade I published two more papers on singular reference, one a contribution to the Library of Living Philosophers volume devoted to the work of Quine ('Reference and its Roots', 1986), the other as summary a statement as I could make of my current views on the question ('Direct Singular Reference: Intended Reference and Actual Reference', 1986). The latter I had already delivered as my contribution to a round table on the subject, at which Quine and Kripke also spoke, at the World Congress in Montreal in 1983. In 1982 I also published two papers, written long before, but hitherto used only in lectures or seminars, one on logical constants, the other on conditionals. The latter ('If and ⊃') had been written many years earlier as a riposte to Grice's ingenious and long unpublished attempt to demonstrate that the meaning of the ordinary conditional was in fact identical to that of the material condition of standard logic – an application or anticipation of his later elaborated theory of conversational implicature, which, profound and fruitful as it is, is also capable, like most good ideas, of misapplication such as it suffered, I argued, in this case. The other article ('Logical Form and Logical Constants'), which aimed to give a general characterization of the constants of standard logic, I submitted as my contribution to a collection of essays, *Logical Form, Predication and Ontology*, published in India and edited by Pranab Kumar Sen, Professor of Philosophy at Jadavpur University, Calcutta, a leading Indian philosopher and my very good friend.

In the same decade, besides the travels, already mentioned, to France, Germany, Canada, the U.S.A., and China, I made a second visit to Spain, two more to America, spoke for the first time in Switzerland and went for the third time to India. At Valencia, in Spain, I repeated the arguments which formed the substance of the Woodbridge Lectures I gave at Columbia University in 1983 and of the book based on them which was published in 1985 as *Skepticism and Naturalism: Some Varieties*. In that book I had two different, though not unrelated aims. The first chapter was concerned with traditional philosophical scepticisms about, e.g. the external world and induction. In common with Hume and Wittgenstein (and even Heidegger) I argued that the attempt to combat such doubts by rational argument was misguided: for we are dealing here with the presuppositions, the framework, of all human thought and enquiry. In the other chapters my target was different. It was that species of naturalism which tended to discredit, or somehow to reduce to more scientifically acceptable, physicalistic terms, whole regions of ordinary human thought, language, and experience – in particular the regions of moral discourse, of the subjectively mental and of the intensional. Here my reaction, as well as my target, was different. I did not merely stress the inescapability of the natural or common human standpoint from which we normally take for granted all that is called in question by scientistic naturalism. I also allowed the latter its own validity from its own limited standpoint. Each standpoint could be called a form of naturalism – one with a pronounced bias towards natural science, the other of a more humanistic or, as I called it, 'liberal' variety. But to those – not few – in whom the drive for completely unified philosophical explanation is strong this tolerance may well seem unacceptable.

While in America for the Quine conference at St. Louis (1988) I also read papers elsewhere: at Vassar I distinguished and elaborated different senses or applications of the phrase 'the meaning of what was said'; at Columbia I repeated my views on 'Kant's New Foundations of Metaphysics', and also critically discussed that philosopher's treatment of the concept of substance; and did the same at Bloomington, Indiana, where I had the pleasure of renewing ties with old friends from Duke, more than thirty years before.

My third visit to India, in the winter of 1987–88, was occasioned by a conference on my work organized at Lucknow by the Indian Council of Philosophical Research. I prepared a paper on my own philosophical development, and there were several seminar meetings at which pertinent points were made. I also gave talks at Calcutta, Delhi, and Hyderabad. Privileged, in the company of Ann and an Indian philosopher from Delhi, to visit many of the great Indian sites in North, South, and Central India which I had not seen before, I was again struck by the inexhaustible variety and great cultural and artistic wealth of the country.

In the autumn of 1987 I retired, under the age limit, from my Chair at Magdalen; but because of the generosity of a former pupil at University College and of the College itself, I have a room there in which I can, and do, continue to work. As already indicated, retirement by no means brought an end to academic travel or to philosophical discussion and composition. My most protracted visit was to the University of Colorado at Boulder in the Fall semester of 1991. There I lectured twice a week to an undergraduate class and conducted a weekly graduate seminar. For the undergraduate class I drew partly on my Oxford lectures, which had already served me well elsewhere, and partly improvised on the basis of other papers of mine. For the first time in my life I had the invaluable help of a 'teaching assistant' – a highly intelligent graduate student who relieved me of much of the burden of grading papers and stood in for me when I was reading papers at other universities, as I did in Seattle, at Yale, and in two states, Wyoming and Wisconsin, which I had never visited before. This was my first experience of undergraduate teaching in the United States, having previously, on semester-long visits, been in contact only with graduate students and faculty members. I found the informality of the proceedings and the enquiring receptiveness of my audience most refreshing, though I was also struck by the surprising difference in level of literary and philosophical sophistication between the undergraduate and graduate students. At the graduate seminar I generally announced in advance which paper of my own was to form the topic of discussion at the next meeting, and then introduced the subject briefly myself; but on the last occasion I read a new paper, entitled 'Individuals', in which I attempted a synthesis of all the matters on the book of that name and subsequent writings, giving special prominence to the union of logic, epistemology, and ontology and to that realist view of universals and of abstract objects in general which I am ready to call a demythologized Platonism. My most abiding memory of Boulder, however, is of the perfection of the climate, the beauty of the mountains, and the courtesy and kindness of the inhabitants.

My most recent journeys, in 1992, were to the Kant conference in Florence in April and, in November, to Kingston, Ontario, where the Queen's University, in celebration of its sesquicentenary, had organized a series of philosophical lectures, My own was entitled 'Philosophy: a Personal View' and substantially followed the line traced in the account of my philosophical development which I had prepared for the 1987 Indian conference on my work. In the course of my career, academic occasions have taken me to all the world's continents except Australasia, to most of the countries of Western Europe, to about half the States of the Union, to Argentina, and to Mexico. These extensive travels, as others of my profession will agree, are among the uncovenanted benefits of an abiding passion for philosophy.

It remains to say something about my methods of work, the influences I am most aware of, my relations with other philosophers and, perhaps, my general conception of philosophy. I certainly did not initially approach the subject with any large general plan of campaign; and I have never achieved, or aimed at, any such comprehensive, integrated system as the great metaphysicians, e.g. Kant and Spinoza, have constructed. Rather I have been moved – often, as Moore reported, provoked by philosophical views that have struck me as preposterous or obviously false or one-sided – by the wish to understand better some particular concept or range of concepts, or the views of some particular philosophers; or by the rare exciting occurrence of one of those moments of what at least at the time seems like a blinding flash of insight into connections of which one had been previously but imperfectly, if at all, aware. Such moments as these are not altogether pleasant: mingled with exhilaration is a slightly disagreeable, even physical, sense of agitation or discomfort, only to be alleviated as the exhilaration also subsides into a cooler and more laborious consideration of how it is to be controlled and the truth, if there is one, conveyed. Such experiences are infrequent indeed. More often, it is a matter of arriving, without excessive excitement, at a reasonably clear idea of the general line one intends to follow and the setting about the task of organizing it, and working out the detail, in readily comprehensible and tolerably harmonious prose. Excitement or not, the working out sometimes requires a good deal of hard and continuous thinking which can keep one awake for hours. But this too I have found to be infrequent. Usually, when the general line is reasonably clear, the writing, though it calls for care, follows without much strain or is even attended with pleasure.

I have, of course, found philosophical discussion with others, in small groups, enjoyable and stimulating, even sometimes amusing. But except for a brief period in the early 1950s, when Grice and I collaborated in a seminar, I have found it best, indeed necessary, to think and work independently. In this, as in other ways, philosophy differs from natural science, where teamwork is apparently a quite regular thing. Austin, it is true, was attracted by this model, by the *idea* of cooperative endeavour; but what he actually *did* was as essentially individual as Ryle rightly held that all fruitful philosophical enterprise must be. Why this is so I tried to explain in a few lines in the preface to *Skepticism and Naturalism*. What, perhaps surprisingly, I have in the past found most helpful in the way of discussion is the one-to-one tutorial exchange with undergraduates – when one finds oneself obliged to clarify one's own half-formed thoughts in order to make things clear to one's pupil. Seeking a way past, or through, his or her mistakes and confusions, one may find a path past, or through one's own.

Many philosophers in the past – among them some of the greatest – have seen themselves as starting afresh, as setting out on a new path which they conceive to be the only sure one; and thus as freeing themselves, and us, from fundamental mistakes or misconceptions which have hitherto impeded the discovery of the true way. It is unlikely that any of us, in the second half of the twentieth century, will be buoyed up by any such glad, confident assurance – or, if you prefer, will be the victim of any such vainglorious delusion. Philosophers today tend to be more soberly and modestly aware of the greatness of the achievements of their illustrious predecessors and of the possibility of learning from them. Yet I think it is evident that there is a notable selectiveness in these appreciative responses. It is in no way surprising that this should be so; that each philosopher should respond most positively to those of his predecessors whose work is most in harmony with his own intellectual bent. And this in its turn will imply a certain further selectiveness within the domain of the favoured predecessor's teaching.

So at least I have found it to be. Thus in the case of Wittgenstein, an acknowledged philosophical genius – perhaps the only one in our century – it must be that I am influenced by, for I profoundly share, the view that our essential, if not our only, business is to get a clear view of our concepts and their place in our lives. Such a clearing of the view, freeing it from the seductive illusions of whose fascination he was himself so vividly aware, Wittgenstein in his later work did more than anyone to promote. Yet, at the same time, the very strength of his resistance to the myths and fictions of theory seemed to me to lead to a certain loss of balance in two ways. First, the most general concepts and categories of the human conceptual scheme do form, in their connections and interdependences, an articulated structure which it is possible to describe without falsification; and this possibility Wittgenstein's distrust of systematic theorizing in general seems to lead him to dismiss. Second, at the root of some of the false pictures which earned his particular animus there sometimes lie harmless, commonplace elements of truth which receive in him too little acknowledgement.

The cases of Aristotle and Kant – the two whom I see, without qualification, as the very greatest of our predecessors – are quite different. Neither shrank from systematic theory. If I found, in Kant in particular, much to discard, I also found much to embrace, as answering, with modification, to my own natural prejudices or half-formed ideas, which is why I am presumptuous enough to enrol them both under the banner of 'descriptive metaphysics'.

Finally, a few personal observations. I have no religious beliefs. When asked whether I believe in God, I am obliged to answer 'No'; I have difficulty with the concept. But I am sometimes tempted to add that I believe in grace – a quality which eludes precise description, but is sometimes manifested in the words and actions of human beings. My political views are centrist: I am conservative in my tastes, liberal in my sentiments (principles?). I am of a conciliatory temper – which sometimes extends, in philosophy, into an attempt to reconcile views which appear to be sharply opposed to each other. I am very little, perhaps too little, prone to anger.

I have sometimes criticized the views of other philosophers, dead or living. Such adverse criticism is a form of compliment. It is only the very best with whom it is worthwhile to differ. My own philosophical views I am prepared to defend, or modify, when required; but their neglect or rejection leaves me relatively indifferent. I enjoy applause, but have no expectation of, or wish for, disciples.

All in all I count myself extremely lucky. Above all, I am fortunate in my friends and my family; friends whom I made as an undergraduate and to whom I am still close, and others, of many nationalities, whom I have come to know since; a family of wife and four children, all variously gifted and all, to my mind, invariably charming. Philosophy, friends, and family apart, my life has been enriched by the enjoyment of literature, landscape, architecture, and the company of clever and beautiful women. So far every decade has been better than the one before, though I recognize that, in the nature of things, this cannot continue indefinitely.

Reproduction permission obtained from:

Open Court Publishing Co
315 Fifth St
PO Box 300
Peru
Illinois 61354–0300
ISBN 0–8126–9377–9

PREFACE

Of the eleven essays collected in this volume nine have been previously published and are here reprinted without, or with only minor, alteration. The exceptions are 'Causation in Perception' and 'On Understanding the Structure of One's Language'. The former of these two is to appear in a *Festschrift* for Charles Baylis edited by Paul Welsh. It is printed here by kind permission of the editor and of Duke University Press.

The essays deal with a variety of topics, though there are links between some of them. Three are devoted to different aspects of the concept of perception, and of these one, 'Imagination and Perception', may be thought to make some amends for the scant attention which I gave, in *The Bounds of Sense*, to Kant's doctrine of synthesis. My single venture into the field of aesthetics, 'Aesthetic Appraisal and Works of Art', though not published till 1966, was originally written for a seminar which the late G. A. Paul and I gave together, under the title 'The Language of Taste', in 1953.

Details of first publication of the papers are as follows:

'Freedom and Resentment', in *Proceedings of the British Academy*, vol. XLVIII, 1962.

'Social Morality and Individual Ideal', in *Philosophy*, vol. XXXVI, 1961.

'Imagination and Perception', in *Experience and Theory*, edited by Lawrence Foster and J. W. Swanson, University of Massachusetts Press, 1970.

'Perception and Identification', in *Proceedings of the Aristotelian Society*, supp. vol. XXXV, 1961.

'Categories', in *Ryle: A Collection of Critical Essays*, edited by Oscar P. Wood and George Pitcher, New York, Doubleday (© 1970 by Doubleday & Company, Inc.), and London and Basingstoke, Macmillan, 1970.

'Wittgenstein's *Philosophical Investigations*', in *Mind*, vol. LXIII, 1954.

'Self, Mind and Body', in *Common Factor*, no. 4, 1966.

'Aesthetic Appraisal and Works of Art', in *The Oxford Review*, no. 3, 1966.

'Is Existence Never a Predicate?' in *Crítica*, vol. 1, 1967.

I have to thank the editors and publishers in question for permission to reprint these essays.

OXFORD   P. F. S.
APRIL 1973

1

FREEDOM AND RESENTMENT

1

Some philosophers say they do not know what the thesis of determinism is. Others say, or imply, that they do know what it is. Of these, some – the pessimists perhaps – hold that if the thesis is true, then the concepts of moral obligation and responsibility really have no application, and the practices of punishing and blaming, of expressing moral condemnation and approval, are really unjustified. Others – the optimists perhaps – hold that these concepts and practices in no way lose their *raison d'être* if the thesis of determinism is true. Some hold even that the justification of these concepts and practices requires the truth of the thesis. There is another opinion which is less frequently voiced: the opinion, it might be said, of the genuine moral sceptic. This is that the notions of moral guilt, of blame, of moral responsibility are inherently confused and that we can see this to be so if we consider the consequences either of the truth of determinism or of its falsity. The holders of this opinion agree with the pessimists that these notions lack application if determinism is true, and add simply that they also lack it if determinism is false. If I am asked which of these parties I belong to, I must say it is the first of all, the party of those who do not know what the thesis of determinism is. But this does not stop me from having some sympathy with the others, and a wish to reconcile them. Should not ignorance, rationally, inhibit such sympathies? Well, of course, though darkling, one has some inkling – some notion of what sort of thing is being talked about. This lecture is intended as a move towards reconciliation; so is likely to seem wrongheaded to everyone.

But can there be any possibility of reconciliation between such clearly opposed positions as those of pessimists and optimists about determinism? Well, there might be a formal withdrawal on one side in return for a substantial concession on the other. Thus, suppose the optimist's position were put like this: (1) the facts as we know them do not show determinism to be false; (2) the facts as we know them supply an adequate basis for the concepts and practices which the pessimist feels to be imperilled by the possibility of determinism's truth. Now it might be that the optimist is right in this, but is apt to give an inadequate account of the facts as we know them, and of how they constitute an adequate basis for the problematic concepts and practices; that the reasons he gives for the adequacy of the basis are themselves inadequate and leave out something vital. It might be that the pessimist is rightly anxious to get this vital thing back and, in the grip of his anxiety, feels he has to go beyond the facts as we know them; feels that the vital thing can be secure only if, beyond the facts as we know them, there is the further fact that determinism is false. Might *he* not be brought to make a formal withdrawal in return for a vital concession?

2

Let me enlarge very briefly on this, by way of preliminary only. Some optimists about determinism point to the efficacy of the practices of punishment, and of moral condemnation and approval, in regulating behaviour in socially desirable ways.[1] In the fact of their efficacy, they suggest, is an adequate basis for these practices; and this fact certainly does not show determinism to be false. To this the pessimists reply, all in a rush, that *just* punishment and *moral* condemnation imply moral guilt and guilt implies moral responsibility and moral responsibility implies freedom and freedom implies the falsity of determinism. And to this the optimists are wont to reply in turn that it is true that these practices require freedom in a sense, and the existence of freedom in this sense is one of the facts as we know them. But what 'freedom' means here is nothing but the absence of certain conditions the presence of which would make moral condemnation or punishment inappropriate. They have in mind conditions like compulsion by another, or innate incapacity, or insanity, or other less extreme forms of psychological disorder, or the existence of circumstances in which the making of any other choice would be morally inadmissible or would be too much to expect of any man. To this list they are constrained to add other factors which, without exactly being limitations of freedom, may also make moral condemnation or punishment inappropriate or mitigate their force: as some forms of ignorance, mistake, or accident. And the general reason why moral condemnation or punishment are inappropriate when these factors or conditions are present is held to be that the practices in question will be generally efficacious means of regulating behaviour in desirable ways only in cases where these factors are *not* present. Now the pessimist admits that the facts as we know them include the existence of freedom, the occurrence of cases of free action, in the negative sense which the optimist concedes; and admits, or rather insists, that the existence of freedom in this sense is compatible with the truth of determinism. Then what does the pessimist find missing? When he tries to answer this question, his language is apt to alternate between the very familiar and the very unfamiliar.[2] Thus he may say, familiarly enough, that the man who is the subject of justified punishment, blame or moral condemnation must really *deserve* it; and then add, perhaps, that, in the case at least where he is blamed for a positive act rather than an omission, the condition of his really deserving blame is something that goes beyond the negative freedoms that the optimist concedes. It is, say, a genuinely free identification of the will with the act. And this is the condition that is incompatible with the truth of determinism.

The conventional, but conciliatory, optimist need not give up yet. He may say: Well, people often decide to do things, really intend to do what they do, know just what they're doing in doing it; the reasons they think they have for doing what they do, often really are their reasons and not their rationalizations. These facts, too, are included in the facts as we know them. If this is what you mean by freedom – by the identification of the will with the act – then freedom may again be conceded. But again the concession is compatible with the truth of the determinist thesis. For it would not follow from that thesis that nobody decides to do anything; that nobody ever does anything intentionally; that it is false that people sometimes know perfectly well what they are doing. I tried to define freedom negatively. You want to give it a more positive look. But it comes to the same thing. Nobody denies freedom in this sense, or these senses, and nobody claims that the existence of freedom in these senses shows determinism to be false.

But it is here that the lacuna in the optimistic story can be made to show. For the pessimist may be supposed to ask: But *why* does freedom in this sense justify blame, etc.? You turn towards me first the negative, and then the positive, faces of a freedom which nobody challenges. But the only reason you have given for the practices of moral condemnation and punishment in cases where this freedom is present is the efficacy of these practices in regulating behaviour in socially desirable ways. But this is not a sufficient basis, it is not even the right *sort* of basis, for these practices as we understand them.

Now my optimist, being the sort of man he is, is not likely to invoke an intuition of fittingness at this point. So he really has no more to say. And my pessimist, being the sort of man he is, has only one more thing to say; and that is that the admissibility of these practices, as we understand them, demands another kind of freedom, the kind that in turn demands the falsity of the thesis of determinism. But might we not induce the pessimist to give up saying this by giving the optimist something more to say?

3

I have mentioned punishing and moral condemnation and approval; and it is in connection with these practices or attitudes that the issue between optimists and pessimists – or, if one is a pessimist, the issue between determinists and libertarians – is felt to be particularly important. But it is not of these practices and attitudes that I propose, at first, to speak. These practices or attitudes permit, where they do not imply, a certain detachment from the actions or agents which are their objects. I want to speak, at least at first, of something else: of the non-detached attitudes and reactions of people directly involved in transactions with each other; of the attitudes and reactions of offended parties and beneficiaries; of such things as gratitude, resentment, forgiveness, love, and hurt feelings. Perhaps something like the issue between optimists and pessimists arises in this neighbouring field too; and since this field is less crowded with disputants, the issue might here be easier to settle; and if it is settled here, then it might become easier to settle it in the disputant-crowded field.

What I have to say consists largely of commonplaces. So my language, like that of commonplaces generally, will be quite unscientific and imprecise. The central commonplace that I want to insist on is the very great importance that we attach to the attitudes and intentions towards us of other human beings, and the great extent to which our personal feelings and reactions depend upon, or involve, our beliefs about these attitudes and intentions. I can give no simple description of the field of phenomena at the centre of which stands this commonplace truth; for the field is too complex. Much imaginative literature is devoted to exploring its complexities; and we have a large vocabulary for the purpose. There are simplifying styles of handling it in a general way. Thus we may, like La Rochefoucauld, put self-love or self-esteem or vanity at the centre of the picture and point out how it may be caressed by the esteem, or wounded by the indifference or contempt, of others. We might speak, in another jargon, of the need for love, and the loss of security which results from its withdrawal; or, in another, of human self-respect and its connection with the recognition of the individual's dignity. These simplifications are of use to me only if they help to emphasize how much we actually mind, how much it matters to us, whether the actions of other people – and particularly of *some* other people – reflect attitudes towards us of goodwill, affection, or esteem on the one hand or contempt, indifference, or malevolence on the other. If someone treads on my hand accidentally, while trying to help me, the pain may be no less acute than if he treads on it in contemptuous disregard of my existence or with a malevolent wish to injure me. But I shall generally feel in the second case a kind and degree of resentment that I shall not feel in the first. If someone's actions help me to some benefit I desire, then I am benefited in any case; but if he intended them so to benefit me because of his general goodwill towards me, I shall reasonably feel a gratitude which I should not feel at all if the benefit was an incidental consequence, unintended or even regretted by him, of some plan of action with a different aim.

These examples are of actions which confer benefits or inflict injuries over and above any conferred or inflicted by the mere manifestation of attitude and intention themselves. We should consider also in how much of our behaviour the benefit or injury resides mainly or entirely in the manifestation of attitude itself. So it is with good manners, and much of what we call kindness, on the one hand; with deliberate rudeness, studied indifference, or insult on the other.

Besides resentment and gratitude, I mentioned just now forgiveness. This is a rather unfashionable subject in moral philosophy at present; but to be forgiven is something we sometimes ask, and forgiving is something we sometimes say we do. To ask to be forgiven is in part to acknowledge that the attitude displayed in our actions was such as might properly be resented and in part to repudiate that attitude for the future (or at least for the immediate future); and to forgive is to accept the repudiation and to forswear the resentment.

We should think of the many different kinds of relationship which we can have with other people – as sharers of a common interest; as members of the same family; as colleagues; as friends; as lovers; as chance parties to an enormous range of transactions and encounters. Then we should think, in each of these connections in turn, and in others, of the kind of importance we attach to the attitudes and intentions towards us of those who stand in these relationships to us, and of the kinds of *reactive* attitudes and feelings to which we ourselves are prone. In general, we demand some degree of goodwill or regard on the part of those who stand in these relationships to us, though the forms we require it to take vary widely in different connections. The range and intensity of our *reactive* attitudes towards goodwill, its absence or its opposite vary no less widely. I have mentioned, specifically, resentment and gratitude; and they are a usefully opposed pair. But, of course, there is a whole continuum of reactive attitude and feeling stretching on both sides of these and – the most comfortable area – in between them.

The object of these commonplaces is to try to keep before our minds something it is easy to forget when we are engaged in philosophy, especially in our cool, contemporary style, viz. what it is actually like to be involved in ordinary inter-personal relationships, ranging from the most intimate to the most casual.

4

It is one thing to ask about the general causes of these reactive attitudes I have alluded to; it is another to ask about the variations to which they are subject, the particular conditions in which they do or do not seem natural or reasonable or appropriate; and it is a third thing to ask what it would be like, what it *is* like, not to suffer them. I am not much concerned with the first question; but I am with the second; and perhaps even more with the third.

Let us consider, then, occasions for resentment: situations in which one person is offended or injured by the action of another and in which – in the absence of special considerations – the offended person might naturally or normally be expected to feel resentment. Then let us consider what sorts of special considerations might be expected to modify or mollify this feeling or remove it altogether. It needs no saying now how multifarious these considerations are. But, for my purpose, I think they can be roughly divided into two kinds. To the first group belong all those which might give occasion for the employment of such expressions as 'He didn't mean to', 'He hadn't realized', 'He didn't know'; and also all those which might give occasion for the use of the phrase 'He couldn't help it', when this is supported by such phrases as 'He was pushed', 'He had to do it', 'It was the only way', 'They left him no alternative', etc. Obviously these various pleas, and the kinds of situations in which they would be appropriate, differ from each other in striking and important ways. But for my present purpose they have something still more important in common. None of them invites us to suspend towards the agent, either at the time of his action or in general, our ordinary reactive attitudes. They do not invite us to view the *agent* as one in respect of whom these attitudes are in any way inappropriate. They invite us to view the *injury* as one in respect of which a particular one of these attitudes is inappropriate. They do not invite us to see the *agent* as other than a fully responsible agent. They invite us to see the *injury* as one for which he was not fully, or at all, responsible. They do not suggest that the agent is in any way an inappropriate object of that kind of demand for goodwill or regard which is reflected in our ordinary reactive attitudes. They suggest instead that the fact of injury was not in this case incompatible with that demand's being fulfilled, that the fact of injury was quite consistent with the agent's attitude and intentions being just what we demand they should be.[3] The agent was just ignorant of the injury he was causing, or had lost his balance through being pushed or had reluctantly to cause the injury for reasons which acceptably override his reluctance. The offering of such pleas by the agent and their acceptance by the sufferer is something in no way opposed to, or outside the context of, ordinary inter-personal relationships and the manifestation of ordinary reactive attitudes. Since things go wrong and situations are complicated, it is an essential and integral element in the transactions which are the life of these relationships.

The second group of considerations is very different. I shall take them in two subgroups of which the first is far less important than the second. In connection with the first subgroup we may think of such statements as 'He wasn't himself', 'He has been under very great strain recently', 'He was acting under post-hypnotic suggestion'; in connection with the second, we may think of 'He's only a child', 'He's a hopeless schizophrenic', 'His mind has been systematically perverted', 'That's purely compulsive behaviour on his part'. Such pleas as these do, as pleas of my first general group do not, invite us to suspend our ordinary reactive attitudes towards the agent, either at the time of his action or all the time. They do not invite us to see the agent's action in a way consistent with the full retention of ordinary inter-personal attitudes and merely inconsistent with one particular attitude. They invite us to view the agent himself in a different light from the light in which we should normally view one who has acted as he has acted. I shall not linger over the first subgroup of cases. Though they perhaps raise, in the short term, questions akin to those raised, in the long term, by the second subgroup, we may dismiss them without considering those questions by taking that admirably suggestive phrase, 'He wasn't himself', with the seriousness that – for all its being logically comic – it deserves. We shall not feel resentment against the man he is for the action done by the man he is not; or at least we shall feel less. We normally have to deal with him under normal stresses; so we shall not feel towards him, when he acts as he does under abnormal stresses, as we should have felt towards him had he acted as he did under normal stresses.

The second and more important subgroup of cases allows that the circumstances were normal, but presents the agent as psychologically abnormal – or as morally undeveloped. The agent was himself; but he is warped or deranged, neurotic or just a child. When we see someone in such a light as this, all our reactive attitudes tend to be profoundly modified. I must deal here in crude dichotomies and ignore the ever-interesting and ever-illuminating varieties of case. What I want to contrast is the attitude (or range of attitudes) of involvement or participation in a human relationship, on the one hand, and what might be called the objective attitude (or range of attitudes) to another human being, on the other. Even in the same situation, I must add, they are not altogether *exclusive* of each other; but they are, profoundly, *opposed* to each other. To adopt the objective attitude to another human being is to see him, perhaps, as an object of social policy; as a subject for what, in a wide range of sense, might be called treatment; as something certainly to be taken account, perhaps precautionary account, of; to be managed or handled or cured or trained; perhaps simply to be avoided, though *this* gerundive is not peculiar to cases of objectivity of attitude. The objective attitude may be emotionally toned in many ways, but not in all ways: it may include repulsion or fear, it may include pity or even love, though not all kinds of love. But it cannot include the range of reactive feelings and attitudes which belong to involvement or participation with others in inter-personal human relationships; it cannot include resentment, gratitude, forgiveness, anger, or the sort of love which two adults can sometimes be said to feel reciprocally, for each other. If your attitude towards someone is wholly objective, then though you may fight him, you cannot quarrel with him, and though you may talk to him, even negotiate with him, you cannot reason with him. You can at most pretend to quarrel, or to reason, with him.

Seeing someone, then, as warped or deranged or compulsive in behaviour or peculiarly unfortunate in his formative circumstances – seeing someone so tends, at least to some extent, to set him apart from normal participant reactive attitudes on the part of one who so sees him, tends to promote, at least in the civilized, objective attitudes. But there is something curious to add to this. The objective attitude is not only something we naturally tend to fall into in cases like these, where participant attitudes are partially or wholly inhibited by abnormalities or by immaturity. It is also something which is available as a resource in other cases too. We look with an objective eye on the compulsive behaviour of the neurotic or the tiresome behaviour of a very young child, thinking in terms of treatment or training. But we *can* sometimes look with something like the same eye on the behaviour of the normal and the mature. We *have* this resource and can sometimes use it: as a refuge, say, from the strains of involvement; or as an aid to policy; or simply out of intellectual curiosity. Being human, we cannot, in the normal case, do this for long, or altogether. If the strains of involvement, say, continue to be too great, then we have to do something else – like severing a relationship. But what is above all interesting is the tension there is, in us, between the participant attitude and the objective attitude. One is tempted to say: between our humanity and our intelligence. But to say this would be to distort both notions.

What I have called the participant reactive attitudes are essentially natural human reactions to the good or ill will or indifference of others towards us, as displayed in *their* attitudes and actions. The question we have to ask is: What effect would, or should, the acceptance of the truth of a general thesis of determinism have upon these reactive attitudes? More specifically, would, or should, the acceptance of the truth of the thesis lead to the decay or the repudiation of all such attitudes? Would, or should, it mean the end of gratitude, resentment, and forgiveness; of all reciprocated adult loves; of all the essentially *personal* antagonisms?

But how can I answer, or even pose, this question without knowing *exactly* what the thesis of determinism is? Well, there is one thing we do know: that if there is a coherent thesis of determinism, then there must be a sense of 'determined' such that, if that thesis is true, then all behaviour whatever is determined in that sense. Remembering this, we can consider at least what possibilities lie formally open; and then perhaps we shall see that the question can be answered *without* knowing exactly what the thesis of determinism is. We can consider what possibilities lie open because we have already before us an account of the ways in which particular reactive attitudes, or reactive attitudes in general, may be, and, sometimes, we judge, should be, inhibited. Thus I considered earlier a group of considerations which tend to inhibit, and, we judge, should inhibit, resentment, in particular cases of an agent causing an injury, without inhibiting reactive attitudes in general towards that agent. Obviously this group of considerations cannot strictly bear upon our question; for that question concerns reactive attitudes in general. But resentment has a particular interest; so it is worth adding that it has never been claimed as a consequence of the truth of determinism that one or another of *these* considerations was operative in every case of an injury being caused by an agent; that it would follow from the truth of determinism that anyone who caused an injury *either* was quite simply ignorant of causing it *or* had acceptably overriding reasons for acquiescing reluctantly in causing it *or* . . ., etc. The prevalence of this happy state of affairs would not be a consequence of the reign of universal determinism, but of the reign of universal goodwill. We cannot, then, find here the possibility of an affirmative answer to our question, even for the particular case of resentment.

Next, I remarked that the participant attitude, and the personal reactive attitudes in general, tend to give place, and it is judged by the civilized should give place, to objective attitudes, just in so far as the agent is seen as excluded from ordinary adult human relationships by deep-rooted psychological abnormality – or simply by being a child. But it cannot be a consequence of any thesis which is not itself self-contradictory that abnormality is the universal condition.

Now this dismissal might seem altogether too facile; and so, in a sense, it is. But whatever is too quickly dismissed in this dismissal is allowed for in the only possible form of affirmative answer that remains. We can sometimes, and in part, I have remarked, look on the normal (those we rate as 'normal') in the objective way in which we have learned to look on certain classified cases of abnormality. And our question reduces to this: could, or should, the acceptance of the determinist thesis lead us always to look on everyone exclusively in this way? For this is the only condition worth considering under which the acceptance of determinism could lead to the decay or repudiation of participant reactive attitudes.

It does not seem to be self-contradictory to suppose that this might happen. So I suppose we must say that it is not absolutely inconceivable that it should happen. But I am strongly inclined to think that it is, for us as we are, practically inconceivable. The human commitment to participation in ordinary inter-personal relationships is, I think, too thoroughgoing and deeply rooted for us to take seriously the thought that a general theoretical conviction might so change our world that, in it, there were no longer any such things as inter-personal relationships as we normally understand them; and being involved in inter-personal relationships as we normally understand them precisely is being exposed to the range of reactive attitudes and feelings that is in question.

This, then, is a part of the reply to our question. A sustained objectivity of inter-personal attitude, and the human isolation which that would entail, does not seem to be something of which human beings would be capable, even if some general truth were a theoretical ground for it. But this is not all. There is a further point, implicit in the foregoing, which must be made explicit.

Exceptionally, I have said, we can have direct dealings with human beings without any degree of personal involvement, treating them simply as creatures to be handled in our own interests, or our side's or society's – or even theirs. In the extreme case of the mentally deranged, it is easy to see the connection between the possibility of a wholly objective attitude and the impossibility of what we understand by ordinary inter-personal relationships. Given this latter impossibility, no other civilized attitude is available than that of viewing the deranged person simply as something to be understood and controlled in the most desirable fashion. To view him as outside the reach of personal relationships is already, for the civilized, to view him in this way. For reasons of policy or self-protection we may have occasion, perhaps temporary, to adopt a fundamentally similar attitude to a 'normal' human being; to concentrate, that is, on understanding 'how he works', with a view to determining our policy accordingly or to finding in that very understanding a relief from the strains of involvement. Now it is certainly true that in the case of the abnormal, though not in the case of the normal, our adoption of the objective attitude is a consequence of our viewing the agent as *incapacitated* in some or all respects for ordinary inter-personal relationships. He is thus incapacitated, perhaps, by the fact that his picture of reality is pure fantasy, that he does not, in a sense, live in the real world at all; or by the fact that his behaviour is, in part, an unrealistic acting out of unconscious purposes; or by the fact that he is an idiot, or a moral idiot. But there is something else which, *because* this is true, is equally certainly *not* true. And that is that there is a sense of 'determined' such that (1) if determinism is true, all behaviour is determined in this sense, and (2) determinism might be true, i.e. it is not inconsistent with the facts as we know them to suppose that all behaviour might be determined in this sense, and (3) our adoption of the objective attitude towards the abnormal is the result of a prior embracing of the belief that the behaviour, or the relevant stretch of behaviour, of the human being in question *is* determined in this sense. Neither in the case of the normal, then, nor in the case of the abnormal is it true that, when we adopt an objective attitude, we do so *because* we hold such a belief. So my answer has two parts. The first is that we cannot, as we are, seriously envisage ourselves adopting a thoroughgoing objectivity of attitude to others as a result of theoretical conviction of the truth of determinism; and the second is that when we do in fact adopt such an attitude in a particular case, our doing so is not the consequence of a theoretical conviction which might be expressed as 'Determinism in this case', but is a consequence of our abandoning, for different reasons in different cases, the ordinary inter-personal attitudes.

It might be said that all this leaves the real question unanswered, and that we cannot hope to answer it without knowing exactly what the thesis of determinism is. For the real question is not a question about what we actually do, or why we do it. It is not even a question about what we would *in fact* do if a certain theoretical conviction gained general acceptance. It is a question about what it would be *rational* to do if determinism were true, a question about the rational justification of ordinary inter-personal attitudes in general. To this I shall reply, first, that such a question could seem real only to one who had utterly failed to grasp the purport of the preceding answer, the fact of our natural human commitment to ordinary inter-personal attitudes. This commitment is part of the general framework of human life, not something that can come up for review as particular cases can come up for review within this general framework. And I shall reply, second, that if we could imagine what we cannot have, viz. a choice in this matter, then we could choose rationally only in the light of an assessment of the gains and losses to human life, its enrichment or impoverishment; and the truth or falsity of a general thesis of determinism would not bear on the rationality of *this* choice.[4]

5

The point of this discussion of the reactive attitudes in their rela- tion – or lack of it – to the thesis of determinism was to bring us, if possible, nearer to a position of compromise in a more usual area of debate. We are not now to discuss reactive attitudes which are essentially those of offended parties or beneficiaries. We are to discuss reactive attitudes which are essentially not those, or only incidentally are those, of offended parties or beneficiaries, but are nevertheless, I shall claim, kindred attitudes to those I have discussed. I put resentment in the centre of the previous discussion. I shall put moral indignation – or, more weakly, moral disapprobation – in the centre of this one.

The reactive attitudes I have so far discussed are essentially reactions to the quality of others' wills towards us, as manifested in their behaviour: to their good or ill will or indifference or lack of concern. Thus resentment, or what I have called resentment, is a reaction to injury or indifference. The reactive attitudes I have now to discuss might be described as the sympathetic or vicarious or impersonal or disinterested or generalized analogues of the reactive attitudes I have already discussed. They are reactions to the qualities of others' wills, not towards ourselves, but towards others. Because of this impersonal or vicarious character, we give them different names. Thus one who experiences the vicarious analogue of resentment is said to be indignant or disapproving, or morally indignant or disapproving. What we have here is, as it were, resentment on behalf of another, where one's own interest and dignity are not involved; and it is this impersonal or vicarious character of the attitude, added to its others, which entitle it to the qualification 'moral'. Both my description of, and my name for, these attitudes are, in one important respect, a little misleading. It is not that these attitudes are essentially vicarious – one can feel indignation on one's own account – but that they are essentially capable of being vicarious. But I shall retain the name for the sake of its suggestiveness; and I hope that what is misleading about it will be corrected in what follows.

The personal reactive attitudes rest on, and reflect, an expectation of, and demand for, the manifestation of a certain degree of goodwill or regard on the part of other human beings towards ourselves; or at least on the expectation of, and demand for, an absence of the manifestation of active ill will or indifferent disregard. (What will, in particular cases, *count* as manifestations of good or ill will or disregard will vary in accordance with the particular relationship in which we stand to another human being.) The generalized or vicarious analogues of the personal reactive attitudes rest on, and reflect, exactly the same expectation or demand in a generalized

form; they rest on, or reflect, that is, the demand for the manifestation of a reasonable degree of goodwill or regard, on the part of
others, not simply towards oneself, but towards all those on whose
behalf moral indignation may be felt, i.e., as we now think, towards
all men. The generalized and non-generalized forms of demand,
and the vicarious and personal reactive attitudes which rest upon,
and reflect, them are connected not merely logically. They are
connected humanly; and not merely with each other. They are connected also with yet another set of attitudes which I must mention
now in order to complete the picture. I have considered from two
points of view the demands we make on others and our reactions to
their possibly injurious actions. These were the points of view of one
whose interest was directly involved (who suffers, say, the injury)
and of others whose interest was not directly involved (who do not
themselves suffer the injury). Thus I have spoken of personal reactive attitudes in the first connection and of their vicarious analogues
in the second. But the picture is not complete unless we consider
also the correlates of these attitudes on the part of those on whom
the demands are made, on the part of the agents. Just as there are
personal and vicarious reactive attitudes associated with demands
on others for oneself and demands on others for others, so there
are self-reactive attitudes associated with demands on oneself for
others. And here we have to mention such phenomena as feeling
bound or obliged (the 'sense of obligation'); feeling compunction;
feeling guilty or remorseful or at least responsible; and the more
complicated phenomenon of shame.

All these three types of attitude are humanly connected. One
who manifested the personal reactive attitudes in a high degree but
showed no inclination at all to their vicarious analogues would
appear as an abnormal case of moral egocentricity, as a kind of moral
solipsist. Let him be supposed fully to acknowledge the claims to
regard that others had on him, to be susceptible of the whole range
of self-reactive attitudes. He would then see himself as unique both
as one (*the* one) who had a general claim on human regard and as
one (*the* one) on whom human beings in general had such a claim.
This would be a kind of moral solipsism. But it is barely more
than a conceptual possibility; if it is that. In general, though within

varying limits, we demand of others for others, as well as of ourselves for others, something of the regard which we demand of others for ourselves. Can we imagine, besides that of the moral solipsist, any other case of one or two of these three types of attitude being fully developed, but quite unaccompanied by any trace, however slight, of the remaining two or one? If we can, then we imagine something far below or far above the level of our common humanity – a moral idiot or a saint. For all these types of attitude alike have common roots in our human nature and our membership of human communities.

Now, as of the personal reactive attitudes, so of their vicarious analogues, we must ask in what ways, and by what considerations, they tend to be inhibited. Both types of attitude involve, or express, a certain sort of demand for inter-personal regard. The fact of injury constitutes a prima facie appearance of this demand's being flouted or unfulfilled. We saw, in the case of resentment, how one class of considerations may show this appearance to be mere appearance, and hence inhibit resentment, *without* inhibiting, or displacing, the sort of demand of which resentment can be an expression, without in any way tending to make us suspend our ordinary inter-personal attitudes to the agent. Considerations of this class operate in just the same way, for just the same reasons, in connection with moral disapprobation or indignation; they inhibit indignation without in any way inhibiting the sort of demand on the agent of which indignation can be an expression, the range of attitudes towards him to which it belongs. But in this connection we may express the facts with a new emphasis. We may say, stressing the moral, the generalized aspect of the demand, considerations of this group have no tendency to make us see the agent as other than a morally responsible agent; they simply make us see the injury as one for which he was not morally responsible. The offering and acceptance of such exculpatory pleas as are here in question in no way detracts in our eyes from the agent's status as a term of moral relationships. On the contrary, since things go wrong and situations are complicated, it is an essential part of the life of such relationships.

But suppose we see the agent in a different light: as one whose picture of the world is an insane delusion; or as one whose

behaviour, or a part of whose behaviour, is unintelligible to us, perhaps even to him, in terms of conscious purposes, and intelligible
only in terms of unconscious purposes; or even, perhaps, as one
wholly impervious to the self-reactive attitudes I spoke of, wholly
lacking, as we say, in moral sense. Seeing an agent in such a light as
this tends, I said, to inhibit resentment in a wholly different way.
It tends to inhibit resentment because it tends to inhibit ordinary
inter-personal attitudes in general, and the kind of demand and
expectation which those attitudes involve; and tends to promote
instead the purely objective view of the agent as one posing problems simply of intellectual understanding, management, treatment,
and control. Again the parallel holds for those generalized or moral
attitudes towards the agent which we are now concerned with. The
same abnormal light which shows the agent to us as one in respect
of whom the personal attitudes, the personal demand, are to be
suspended, shows him to us also as one in respect of whom the
impersonal attitudes, the generalized demand, are to be suspended.
Only, abstracting now from direct personal interest, we may express
the facts with a new emphasis. We may say: to the extent to which
the agent is seen in this light, he is not seen as one on whom
demands and expectations lie in that particular way in which we
think of them as lying when we speak of moral obligation; he is not,
to that extent, seen as a morally responsible agent, as a term of moral
relationships, as a member of the moral community.

I remarked also that the suspension of ordinary inter-personal
attitudes and the cultivation of a purely objective view is sometimes possible even when we have no such reasons for it as I have
just mentioned. Is this possible also in the case of the moral reactive
attitudes? I think so; and perhaps it is easier. But the motives for a
total suspension of moral reactive attitudes are fewer, and perhaps
weaker: fewer, because only where there is antecedent personal
involvement can there be the motive of seeking refuge from the
strains of such involvement; perhaps weaker, because the tension
between objectivity of view and the moral reactive attitudes is
perhaps less than the tension between objectivity of view and the
personal reactive attitudes, so that we can in the case of the moral
reactive attitudes more easily secure the speculative or political

gains of objectivity of view by a kind of setting on one side, rather than a total suspension, of those attitudes.

These last remarks are uncertain; but also, for the present purpose, unimportant. What concerns us now is to inquire, as previously in connection with the personal reactive attitudes, what relevance any general thesis of determinism might have to their vicarious analogues. The answers once more are parallel; though I shall take them in a slightly different order. First, we must note, as before, that when the suspension of such an attitude or such attitudes occurs in a particular case, it is *never* the consequence of the belief that the piece of behaviour in question was determined in a sense such that all behaviour *might be*, and, if determinism is true, all behaviour *is*, determined in that sense. For it is not a consequence of any general thesis of determinism which might be true that nobody knows what he's doing or that everybody's behaviour is unintelligible in terms of conscious purposes or that everybody lives in a world of delusion or that nobody has a moral sense, i.e. is susceptible of self-reactive attitudes, etc. In fact no such sense of 'determined' as would be required for a general thesis of determinism is ever relevant to our actual suspensions of moral reactive attitudes. Second, suppose it granted, as I have already argued, that we cannot take seriously the thought that theoretical conviction of such a general thesis would lead to the total decay of the personal reactive attitudes. Can we then take seriously the thought that such a conviction – a conviction, after all, that many have held or said they held – would nevertheless lead to the total decay or repudiation of the vicarious analogues of these attitudes? I think that the change in our social world which would leave us exposed to the personal reactive attitudes but not at all to their vicarious analogues, the generalization of abnormal egocentricity which this would entail, is perhaps even harder for us to envisage as a real possibility than the decay of both kinds of attitude together. Though there are some necessary and some contingent differences between the ways and cases in which these two kinds of attitudes operate or are inhibited in their operation, yet, as general human capacities or pronenesses, they stand or lapse together. Finally, to the further question whether it would not be *rational*, given a general theoretical conviction of the truth of determinism, so to change our world that in it all these attitudes were wholly suspended, I must answer, as before, that one who presses this question has wholly failed to grasp the import of the preceding answer, the nature of the human commitment that is here involved: it is *useless* to ask whether it would not be rational for us to do what it is not in our nature to (be able to) do. To this I must add, as before, that if there were, say, for a moment open to us the possibility of such a godlike choice, the rationality of making or refusing it would be determined by quite other considerations than the truth or falsity of the general theoretical doctrine in question. The latter would be simply irrelevant; and this becomes ironically clear when we remember that for those convinced that the truth of determinism nevertheless really would make the one choice rational, there has always been the insuperable difficulty of explaining in intelligible terms how its falsity would make the opposite choice rational.

I am aware that in presenting the argument as I have done, neglecting the ever-interesting varieties of case, I have presented nothing more than a schema, using sometimes a crude opposition of phrase where we have a great intricacy of phenomena. In particular the simple opposition of objective attitudes on the one hand and the various contrasted attitudes which I have opposed to them must seem as grossly crude as it is central. Let me pause to mitigate this crudity a little, and also to strengthen one of my central contentions, by mentioning some things which straddle these contrasted kinds of attitude. Thus parents and others concerned with the care and upbringing of young children cannot have to their charges either kind of attitude in a pure or unqualified form. They are dealing with creatures who are potentially and increasingly capable both of holding, and being objects of, the full range of human and moral attitudes, but are not yet truly capable of either. The treatment of such creatures must therefore represent a kind of compromise, constantly shifting in one direction, between objectivity of attitude and developed human attitudes. Rehearsals insensibly modulate towards true performances. The punishment of a child is both like and unlike the punishment of an adult. Suppose we try to relate this progressive emergence of the child as a responsible being, as an object of non-objective attitudes, to that sense of 'determined' in which, if determinism is a possibly true thesis, all behaviour *may* be determined, and in which, if it is a true thesis, all behaviour *is* determined. What bearing *could* such a sense of 'determined' have upon the progressive modification of attitudes towards the child? Would it not be grotesque to think of the development of the child as a progressive or patchy emergence from an area in which its behaviour is in this sense determined into an area in which it isn't? Whatever sense of 'determined' is required for stating the thesis of determinism, it can scarcely be such as to allow of compromise, borderline-style answers to the question, 'Is this bit of behaviour determined or isn't it?' But in this matter of young children, it is essentially a borderline, penumbral area that we move in. Again, consider – a very different matter – the strain in the attitude of a psychoanalyst to his patient. *His* objectivity of attitude, *his* suspension of ordinary moral reactive attitudes, is profoundly modified by the fact that the aim of the enterprise is to make such suspension unnecessary or less necessary. Here we may and do naturally speak of restoring the agent's freedom. But here the restoring of freedom means bringing it about that the agent's behaviour shall be intelligible in terms of conscious purposes rather than in terms only of unconscious purposes. *This* is the object of the enterprise; and it is in so far as *this* object is attained that the suspension, or half-suspension, of ordinary moral attitudes is deemed no longer necessary or appropriate. And in this we see once again the *irrelevance* of that concept of 'being determined' which must be the central concept of determinism. For we cannot both agree that this object is attainable and that its attainment has this consequence and yet hold (1) that neurotic behaviour is determined in a sense in which, it may be, all behaviour is determined, and (2) that it is because neurotic behaviour is determined in this sense that objective attitudes are deemed appropriate to neurotic behaviour. Not, at least, without accusing ourselves of incoherence in our attitude to psychoanalytic treatment.

6

And now we can try to fill in the lacuna which the pessimist finds in the optimist's account of the concept of moral responsibility, and of the bases of moral condemnation and punishment; and to fill it in from the facts as we know them. For, as I have already remarked, when the pessimist himself seeks to fill it in, he rushes beyond the facts as we know them and proclaims that it cannot be filled in at all unless determinism is false.

Yet a partial sense of the facts as we know them is certainly present to the pessimist's mind. When his opponent, the optimist, undertakes to show that the truth of determinism would not shake the foundations of the concept of moral responsibility and of the practices of moral condemnation and punishment, he typically refers, in a more or less elaborated way, to the efficacy of these practices in regulating behaviour in socially desirable ways. These practices are represented solely as instruments of policy, as methods of individual treatment and social control. The pessimist recoils from this picture; and in his recoil there is, typically, an element of emotional shock. He is apt to say, among much else, that the humanity of the offender himself is offended by *this* picture of his condemnation and punishment.

The reasons for this recoil – the explanation of the sense of an emotional, as well as a conceptual, shock – we have already before us. The picture painted by the optimists is painted in a style appropriate to a situation envisaged as wholly dominated by objectivity of attitude. The only operative notions invoked in this picture are such as those of policy, treatment, control. But a thoroughgoing objectivity of attitude, excluding as it does the moral reactive attitudes, excludes at the same time essential elements in the concepts of *moral* condemnation and *moral* responsibility. This is the reason for the conceptual shock. The deeper emotional shock is a reaction, not simply to an inadequate conceptual analysis, but to the suggestion of a change in our world. I have remarked that it is possible to cultivate an exclusive objectivity of attitude in some cases, and for some reasons, where the object of the attitude is not set aside from developed inter-personal and moral attitudes by immaturity or abnormality. And the suggestion which seems to be contained in the optimist's account is that such an attitude should be universally adopted to all offenders. This is shocking enough in the pessimist's eyes. But, sharpened by shock, his eyes see further. It would be hard to make *this* division in our natures. If to all offenders, then to all mankind. Moreover, to whom could this recommendation be, in any real sense, addressed? Only to the powerful, the authorities. So abysses seem to open.[5]

But we will confine our attention to the case of the offenders. The concepts we are concerned with are those of responsibility and guilt, qualified as 'moral', on the one hand – together with that of membership of a moral community; of demand, indignation, disapprobation and condemnation, qualified as 'moral', on the other hand – together with that of punishment. Indignation, disapprobation, like resentment, tend to inhibit or at least to limit our good-will towards the object of these attitudes, tend to promote an at least partial and temporary withdrawal of goodwill; they do so in proportion as they are strong; and their strength is in general proportioned to what is felt to be the magnitude of the injury and to the degree to which the agent's will is identified with, or indifferent to, it. (These, of course, are not contingent connections.) But these attitudes of disapprobation and indignation are precisely the correlates of the moral demand in the case where the demand is felt to be disregarded. The making of the demand *is* the proneness to such attitudes. The holding of them does not, as the holding of objective attitudes does, involve as a part of itself viewing their object other than as a member of the moral community. The partial withdrawal of goodwill which *these* attitudes entail, the modification *they* entail of the general demand that another should, if possible, be spared suffering, is, rather, the consequence of *continuing* to view him as a member of the moral community; only as one who has offended against its demands. So the preparedness to acquiesce in that infliction of suffering on the offender which is an essential part of punishment is all of a piece with this whole range of attitudes of which I have been speaking. It is not only moral reactive attitudes towards the offender which are in question here. We must mention also the self-reactive attitudes of offenders themselves. Just as the other-reactive attitudes are associated with a readiness to acquiesce in the infliction of suffering on an offender, within the 'institution' of punishment, so the self-reactive attitudes are associated with a readiness on the part of the offender to acquiesce in such infliction *without* developing the reactions (e.g. of resentment) which he would normally develop to the infliction of injury upon him; i.e. with a readiness, as we say, to accept punishment[6] as 'his due' or as 'just'.

I am not in the least suggesting that these readinesses to acquiesce, either on the part of the offender himself or on the part of others, are always or commonly accompanied or preceded by indignant boilings or remorseful pangs; only that we have here a continuum of attitudes and feelings to which these readinesses to acquiesce themselves belong. Nor am I in the least suggesting that it belongs to this continuum of attitudes that we should be ready to acquiesce in the infliction of injury on offenders in a fashion which we saw to be quite indiscriminate or in accordance with procedures which we knew to be wholly useless. On the contrary, savage or civilized, we have some belief in the utility of practices of condemnation and punishment. But the social utility of these practices, on which the optimist lays such exclusive stress, is not what is now in question. What is in question is the pessimist's justified sense that to speak in terms of social utility alone is to leave out something vital in our conception of these practices. The vital thing can be restored by attending to that complicated web of attitudes and feelings which form an essential part of the moral life as we know it, and which are quite opposed to objectivity of attitude. Only by attending to this range of attitudes can we recover from the facts as we know them a sense of what we mean, i.e. of *all* we mean, when, speaking the language of morals, we speak of desert, responsibility, guilt, condemnation, and justice. But we *do* recover it from the facts as we know them. We do not have to go beyond them. Because the optimist neglects or misconstrues these attitudes, the pessimist rightly claims to find a lacuna in his account. We can fill the lacuna for him. But in return we must demand of the pessimist a surrender of his metaphysics.

Optimist and pessimist misconstrue the facts in very different styles. But in a profound sense there is something in common to their misunderstandings. Both seek, in different ways, to over-intellectualize the facts. Inside the general structure or web of human attitudes and feelings of which I have been speaking, there is endless room for modification, redirection, criticism, and justification. But questions of justification are internal to the structure or relate to modifications internal to it. The existence of the general framework of attitudes itself is something we are given with the fact of human society. As a whole, it neither calls for, nor permits, an external 'rational' justification. Pessimist and optimist alike show themselves, in different ways, unable to accept this.[7] The optimist's style of over-intellectualizing the facts is that of a characteristically incomplete empiricism, a one-eyed utilitarianism. He seeks to find an adequate basis for certain social practices in calculated consequences, and loses sight (perhaps wishes to lose sight) of the human attitudes of which these practices are, in part, the expression. The pessimist does not lose sight of these attitudes, but is unable to accept the fact that it is just these attitudes themselves which fill the gap in the optimist's account. Because of this, he thinks the gap can be filled only if some general metaphysical proposition is repeatedly verified, verified in all cases where it is appropriate to attribute moral responsibility. This proposition he finds it as difficult to state coherently and with intelligible relevance as its determinist contradictory. Even when a formula has been found ('contra-causal freedom' or something of the kind) there still seems to remain a gap between its applicability in particular cases and its supposed moral consequences. Sometimes he plugs this gap with an intuition of fittingness – a pitiful intellectualist trinket for a philosopher to wear as a charm against the recognition of his own humanity.

Even the moral sceptic is not immune from his own form of the wish to over-intellectualize such notions as those of moral responsibility, guilt, and blame. He sees that the optimist's account is inadequate and the pessimist's libertarian alternative inane; and finds no resource except to declare that the notions in question are inherently confused, that 'blame is metaphysical'. But the metaphysics was in the eye of the metaphysician. It is a pity that talk of the moral sentiments has fallen out of favour. The phrase would be quite a good name for that network of human attitudes in acknowledging the character and place of which we find, I suggest, the only possibility of reconciling these disputants to each other and the facts.

There are, at present, factors which add, in a slightly paradoxical way, to the difficulty of making this acknowledgement. These human attitudes themselves, in their development and in the variety of their manifestations, have to an increasing extent become objects of study in the social and psychological sciences; and this growth of human self-consciousness, which we might expect to reduce the difficulty of acceptance, in fact increases it in several ways. One factor of comparatively minor importance is an increased historical and anthropological awareness of the great variety of forms which these human attitudes may take at different times and in different cultures. This makes one rightly chary of claiming as essential features of the concept of morality in general, forms of these attitudes which may have a local and temporary prominence. No doubt to some extent my own descriptions of human attitudes have reflected local and temporary features of our own culture. But an awareness of variety of forms should not prevent us from acknowledging also that in the absence of *any* forms of these attitudes it is doubtful whether we should have anything that *we* could find intelligible as a system of human relationships, as human society. A quite different factor of greater importance is that psychological studies have made us rightly mistrustful of many particular manifestations of the attitudes I have spoken of. They are a prime realm of self-deception, of the ambiguous and the shady, of guilt-transference, unconscious sadism and the rest. But it is an exaggerated horror, itself suspect, which would make us unable to acknowledge the facts because of the seamy side of the facts. Finally, perhaps the most important factor of all is the prestige of these theoretical studies themselves. That prestige is great, and is apt to make us forget that in philosophy, though it also is a theoretical study, we have to take account of the facts in *all* their bearings; we are not to suppose that we are required, or permitted, as philosophers, to regard ourselves, as human beings, as detached from the attitudes which, as scientists, we study with detachment. This is in no way to deny the possibility and desirability of redirection and modification of our human attitudes in the light of these studies. But we may reasonably think it unlikely that our progressively greater understanding of certain aspects of ourselves will lead to the total disappearance of those aspects. Perhaps it is not inconceivable that it should; and perhaps, then, the dreams of some philosophers will be realized.

If we sufficiently, that is *radically*, modify the view of the optimist, his view is the right one. It is far from wrong to emphasize the efficacy of all those practices which express or manifest our moral attitudes, in regulating behaviour in ways considered desirable; or to add that when certain of our beliefs about the efficacy of some of these practices turn out to be false, then we may have good reason for dropping or modifying those practices. What *is* wrong is to forget that these practices, and their reception, the reactions to them, really *are* expressions of our moral attitudes and not merely devices we calculatingly employ for regulative purposes. Our practices do not merely exploit our natures, they express them. Indeed the very understanding of the kind of efficacy these expressions of our attitudes have turns on our remembering this. When we do remember this, and modify the optimist's position accordingly, we simultaneously correct its conceptual deficiencies and ward off the dangers it seems to entail, without recourse to the obscure and panicky metaphysics of libertarianism.

NOTES

1   Cf. P. H. Nowell-Smith, 'Freewill and Moral Responsibility', *Mind*, vol. LVII, 1948.

2   As Nowell-Smith pointed out in a later article: 'Determinists and Libertarians', *Mind*, vol. LXIII, 1954.

3   Perhaps not in every case *just* what we demand they should be, but in any case *not* just what we demand they should not be. For my present purpose these differences do not matter.

4   The question, then, of the connection between rationality and the adoption of the objective attitude to others is misposed when it is made to seem dependent on the issue of determinism. But there is

another question which should be raised, if only to distinguish it from the misposed question. Quite apart from the issue of determinism might it not be said that we should be nearer to being purely rational creatures in proportion as our relation to others was in fact dominated by the objective attitude? I think this might be said; only it would have to be added, once more, that if such a choice were possible, it would not necessarily be rational to choose to be more purely rational than we are.

5   See J. D. Mabbott's 'Freewill and Punishment', published in *Contemporary British Philosophy*, 3rd ser., London, Allen & Unwin, 1956.

6   Of course not *any* punishment for *anything* deemed an offence.

7   Compare the question of the justification of induction. The human commitment to inductive belief-formation is original, natural, non-rational (not *ir*rational), in no way something we choose or could give up. Yet rational criticism and reflection can refine standards and their application, supply 'rules for judging of cause and effect'. Ever since the facts were made clear by Hume, people have been resisting acceptance of them.

2

SOCIAL MORALITY AND INDIVIDUAL IDEAL

Men make for themselves pictures of ideal forms of life. Such pictures are various and may be in sharp opposition to each other; and one and the same individual may be captivated by different and sharply conflicting pictures at different times. At one time it may seem to him that he should live – even that *a man* should live – in such-and-such a way; at another that the only truly satisfactory form of life is something totally different, incompatible with the first. In this way, his outlook may vary radically, not only at different periods of his life, but from day to day, even from one hour to the next. It is a function of so many variables: age, experiences, present environment, current reading, current physical state are some of them. As for the ways of life that may thus present themselves at different times as each uniquely satisfactory, there can be no doubt about their variety and opposition. The ideas of self-obliterating devotion to duty or to the service of others; of personal honour and magnanimity; of asceticism, contemplation, retreat; of action, dominance and power; of the cultivation of 'an exquisite sense of the luxurious'; of simple human solidarity and coopera-tive endeavour; of a refined complexity of social existence; of a constantly maintained and renewed sense of affinity with natural things – any of these ideas, and a great many others too, may form the core and substance of a personal ideal. At some times such a picture may present itself as merely appealing or attractive; at others it may offer itself in a stronger light, as, perhaps, an image of the only sane or non-ignoble human reaction to the situation in which we find ourselves. 'The nobleness of life is to do thus' or, sometimes, 'The sanity of life is to do thus': such may be the devices with which these images present themselves.

Two quite different things may be urged against, or in mitigation of, this picture of a multiplicity of pictures. First, it might be said that the many, apparently conflicting pictures are really different parts or aspects, coming momentarily into misleading prominence, of a single picture; this latter being the composite ideal image of our coolest hours, in which every god is given his due and conflict is avoided by careful arrangement and proper subordination of part to part. And it may be true of some exceptional individuals that they entertain ideal images which exhibit just such a harmonious complexity. I believe this to be rarer than we sometimes pretend; but in any case to describe this situation is not to redescribe the situation I have spoken of, but to describe a different situation. The other mitigating point has more weight. It is that, however great the variety of images which dominate, at one time or another, our ethical imaginations, our individual lives do not, as a matter of fact, exhibit a comparable internal variety. Indeed they scarcely could. Something approaching consistency, some more or less unsteady balance, is usually detectable in the pattern of an individual person's decisions and actions. There are, so to speak, empirical grounds for ordering his ideal images in respect of practical efficacy, even, perhaps, for declaring one of them to be practically dominant. This point I shall grant. I think it is easy to exaggerate it; easy to exaggerate the unity of the personalities of those we say we know, when we really know them only in one or two particular connections; easy to dismiss as phases or moods whatever lacks conformity with our only partly empirical pictures of each other. But I shall not dwell on this. What I shall dwell on is precisely this readiness, which a great many people have, to identify themselves imaginatively at different times with different and conflicting visions of the ends of life, even though these visions may receive the scantiest expression in their actual behaviour and would call for the most upsetting personal revolutions if they received more.

This fact about many people – a fact which partly explains, among other things, the enormous charm of reading novels, bio-graphies, histories – this fact, I say, has important consequences. One consequence is that when some ideal image of a form of life is given striking expression in the words or actions of some person, its expression may evoke a response of the liveliest sympathy from those whose own patterns of life are as remote as possible from conformity to the image expressed. It is indeed impossible that one life should realize all the ideal pictures which may at one time or another attract or captivate the individual imagination. But the owner of one life may with perfect practical consistency wish that his conflicting images should all be realized in different lives. The steadiest adherence to one image may coexist with the strongest desire that other and incompatible images should have their steady adherents too. To one who has such a desire, any doctrine that the pattern of the ideal life should be the same for all is intolerable; as it is to me. The way in which I have just expressed the position makes its practical consistency look more simple than it is. One cannot simply escape the conflict between different ideal images by diffusing their realization over different lives. For different lives interact and one's own is one of them; and there may be conflict in the areas of interaction. One is not forced to welcome this, though one may; it is simply something that in fact goes with the fulfil-ment of the wish for this kind of diversity in the pursuit of ends. Equally one is not precluded from taking one side in a conflict because one has wished that both sides should exist and has some sympathy with both.

I think there can be no doubt that what I have been talking about falls within the region of the ethical. I have been talking about evaluations such as *can* govern choices and decisions which are of the greatest importance to men. Whether it falls within the region of the moral, however, is something that may be doubted. Perhaps the region of the moral falls within it. Or perhaps there are no such simple inclusion-relations between them. The question is one I shall come back to later. I should like first to say something more about this region of the ethical. It could also be characterized as a region in which there are truths which are incompatible with each other. There exist, that is to say, many profound general statements which are capable of capturing the ethical imagination in the same way as it may be captured by those ideal images of which I spoke. They often take the form of general descriptive statements about man and the world. They can be incorporated into a metaphysical system, or dramatized in a religious or historical myth. Or they can exist – their most persuasive form for many – as isolated statements such as, in France, there is a whole literature of, the literature of the maxim. I will not give examples, but I will mention names. One cannot read Pascal or Flaubert, Nietzsche or Goethe, Shakespeare or Tolstoy, without encountering these profound truths. It is certainly possible, in a coolly analytical frame of mind, to mock at the whole notion of the profound truth; but we are guilty of mildly bad faith if we do. For in most of us the ethical imagination succumbs again and again to *these* pictures of man, and it is precisely as truths that we wish to characterize them while they hold us captive. But these truths have the same kind of relation to each other as those ideal images of which I have already spoken. For pictures of the one kind reflect and are reflected by pictures of the other. They capture our imagination in the same way. Hence it is as wholly futile to think that we could, without destroying their character, systematize these truths into one coherent body of truth as it is to suppose that we could, without destroying their character, form a coherent composite image from these images. This may be expressed by saying that the region of the ethical is the region where there are truths but no truth; or, in other words, that the injunction to see life steadily *and* see it whole is absurd, for one cannot do both. I said I would give no examples, but I will allude to one near-contemporary one. Many will remember the recorded encounter between Russell and Lawrence, the attempt at sympathy and the failure to find it. That failure is recorded in such words as: 'I thought there might be something in what he said, but in the end I saw there was nothing' on the one hand; and 'Get back to mathematics where you can do some good; leave talk about human beings alone' on the other. The clash was a clash of two irreconcilable views of man, two irreconcilable attitudes. The spectator familiar with both may say: Russell is right; he tells the truth; he speaks for civilization. He may also say: Lawrence is right; he tells the truth; he speaks for life. The point is that he may say both things. It would be absurd to hope for a reconciliation of the two conflicting attitudes. It is not absurd to desire that both should exist, in conflict.

The region of the ethical, then, is a region of diverse, certainly incompatible and possibly practically conflicting ideal images or pictures of a human life, or of human life; and it is a region in which many such incompatible pictures may secure at least the imaginative, though doubtless not often the practical, allegiance of a single person. Moreover this statement itself may be seen not merely as a description of what is the case, but as a positive evaluation of evaluative diversity. Any diminution in this variety would impoverish the human scene. The multiplicity of conflicting pictures is itself the essential element in one of one's pictures of man.

Now what are the relations between the region of the ethical and the sphere of morality? One widely accepted account of the latter is in terms of the idea of rules or principles governing human behaviour which apply universally within a community or class. The class may be variously thought of as a definite social group or the human species as a whole or even the entire class of rational beings. It is not obvious how these contrasting conceptions, of diversity of ideal and of community of rule, are related to each other; and in fact, I think, the relationship is complicated. One way of trying to harmonize the ideas would be as follows. This way is extremely crude and inadequate, but it may serve as a starting point. It is obvious that many, if not all, of the ideal images of which I spoke demand for their realization the existence of some form of social organization. The demand is in varying degrees logical or empirical. Some ideals only make sense in a complex social context, and even in a particular kind of complex social context. For others, some complexity of social organization seems, rather, a practically necessary condition of the ideal's being realized in any very full or satisfactory way. Now it is a condition of the existence of any form of social organization, of any human community, that certain expectations of behaviour on the part of its members should be pretty regularly fulfilled: that some duties, one might say, should be performed, some obligations acknowledged, some rules observed. We might begin by locating the sphere of morality here. It is the sphere of the observance of rules, such that the existence of some such set of rules is a condition of the existence of a society. This is a minimal interpretation of morality. It represents it as what might literally be called a kind of public convenience: of the first importance as a condition of everything that matters, but only as a condition of everything that matters, not as something that matters in itself.

I am disposed to see considerable merit in this minimal conception of morality. By this I mean not that it is really, or nearly, an adequate conception – only that it is a useful analytical idea. There would be objections to claiming that it was an adequate conception. One objection might be simply expressed by saying that, after all, being moral is something that does matter in itself, that it is not simply an affair of complying with rules in a situation where the observance of some such rules is an indirect condition of approximating to ideal forms of life. There is a lot in this objection. But it is not an objection to *using* the minimal idea of morality. We might for example argue that there was an intricate interplay between ideal pictures of man on the one hand and the rule-requirements of social organization on the other; and that one's ordinary and vague conception of morality was the product of this interplay. This would be one way – I do not say the right way – of using the minimal idea of morality to try to get clearer about the ordinary idea. I shall come back later to this question too.

Meanwhile there is another objection to be considered. I think there is something in it as well, but that what there is in it is not at all straightforward. It turns on the idea of the universal applicability of moral rules. The idea is that it is a necessary requirement of a *moral* rule that it should at least be regarded as applying to all human beings whatever. Moral behaviour is what is demanded of men as such. But we can easily imagine, and even find, different societies held together by the observance of sets of rules which are very different from each other. Moreover we can find or imagine a single society held together by a set of rules which by no means make the same demands on all its members, but make very different demands on different classes or groups within the society. In so far as the rules which give cohesiveness to a society are acknowledged to have this limited and sectional character, they cannot, in the sense of this objection, be seen as moral rules. But the rules which do give cohesiveness to a society may well have this character, whether acknowledged or not. So the prospect of explaining true morality in terms of what I called the minimal conception of morality is a poor one. Now it is possible to admit the principle of this objection, and then meet it with a formal manœuvre. Thus a rule which governs the professional behaviour of Samoan witch-doctors can be said to apply to all men under the condition that they are witch-doctor members of a society with the general characteristics of Samoan society. Or again, a rule which might be held to apply to ten-year-old children, namely that they should obey their parents in domestic matters, could be represented as applying to all men without exception, under the condition that they were ten-year-old children. Obviously there is a certain futility about this manœuvre, and equally obviously there is no compulsion to execute it. We might simply drop the idea of moral rules as universally binding on men as men. Or we might say that though there was something in this idea, it was absurd to try to apply it directly and in detail to the question of what people were required to do in particular situations in particular societies. And here we might be tempted by another manœuvre, which we should note as a possible one even if we do not think that it, either, is altogether satisfactory. We might be tempted to say that the relevant universally applicable, and hence moral, rule was that a human being should conform to the rules which apply to him in a particular situation in a particular society. Here universality is achieved by stepping up an order. A man should perform the duties of his station in his society. This allows for an indefinite variety of societies and of stations within them; and would also seem to allow us, in so far as we regarded the universal rule as a truly moral one, to see at least part of true morality as resting upon and presupposing what I called the minimal social interpretation of morality.

Enough, for the moment, of objections to this minimal idea. Let me set out some of its merits. First we must be clearer about what this minimal interpretation is. The fundamental idea is that of a socially sanctioned demand made on an individual in virtue merely of his membership of the society in question, or in virtue of a particular position which he occupies within it or a particular relation in which he stands to other members of it. I spoke of rules in this connection; and the rules I meant would simply be the generalized statements of demands of this type. The formula I employ for the fundamental idea is deliberately flexible, the notions of a society and of social sanctioning deliberately vague. This flexibility is necessary to do justice to the complexities of social organization and social relationships. For instance, we can regard ourselves as members of many different social groups or communities, some of which fall within others; or again, when I speak of the social sanctioning of a demand which is made on an individual member of a group in virtue of his position in the group, we may think of the social sanction of that demand sometimes as arising only within the limited group in question, sometimes as arising also within a wider group which includes that limited group. A position in a society may or may not also be, so to speak, a position in society. Thus a position in a family generally gives rise to certain demands upon the holder of that position which are recognized both within the family and within some wider group or groups within which the family falls. The same may be true of membership of a profession or even of a professional association. On the other hand, some of the demands of certain class or caste moralities receive little or no extraneous reinforcement from the wider social groupings to which the members of the limited class also belong. Or again what one might call the internal morality of an intimate personal relationship may be as private as the relationship itself. One of the merits I should claim for this approach to morality is precisely that it so easily makes room for many concepts which we habitually employ, but which tend to be neglected in moral philosophy. Thus we talk of medical ethics, of the code of honour of a military caste, of bourgeois morality and of working-class morality. Such ideas fit more easily into an account of morality which sees it as essentially, or at any rate fundamentally, a function of social groupings than they do into the more apparently individualistic approaches which are generally current.

Another merit which I shall claim for the present approach is that it makes it relatively easy to understand such notions as those of conscientiousness, duty and obligation in a concrete and realistic way. These notions have been treated almost entirely abstractly in moral philosophy in the recent past, with the result that they have come to some of our contemporaries[1] to seem to be meaningless survivals of discarded ideas about the government of the universe. But as most ordinarily employed I do not think they are that at all. There is nothing in the least mysterious or metaphysical in the fact that duties and obligations go with offices, positions and relationships to others. The demands to be made on somebody in virtue of his occupation of a certain position may indeed be, and often are, quite explicitly listed in considerable detail. And when we call someone conscientious or say that he has a strong sense of his obligations or of duty, we do not ordinarily mean that he is haunted by the ghost of the idea of supernatural ordinances; we mean rather such things as this, that he can be counted on for sustained effort to do what is required of him in definite capacities, to fulfil the demand made on him as student or teacher or parent or soldier or whatever he may be. A certain professor once said: 'For me to be moral is to behave like a professor'.

Suppose we now raise that old philosophical question: What interest has the individual in morality? The question may force us to a more adequate conception of morality than the minimal interpretation offers by itself. It certainly forces us to strike, or to try to strike, some delicate balances. The only answer to the question so far suggested is this: that the individual's ethical imagination may be captured or fired by one or more ideal pictures of life which require for their realization the existence of social groupings and social organizations such as could not exist in the absence of a system of social demands made on individual members of these groups or organizations. I have already hinted that this answer is

too crude, that the interplay between ethical ideal and social obligation is more intricate than it suggests. The answer is also not crude
enough. The picture of the ideal form of life and the associated
ethical vision of the world tend to be the products of the refined
mind and relatively comfortable circumstances. But when we ask
what the interest of the individual is in morality, we mean to ask
about all those individuals on whom socially sanctioned demands
are made; not just about the imaginatively restless and materially
cosy. We need not, perhaps, insist upon just the same answer for all;
but, if we take the question seriously, we must insist on *some*
answer for all. There may seem to be a broader answer which does
not altogether depart from the form of the over-refined answer. For
who could exist at all, or pursue any aim, except in some form of
society? And there is no form of society without rules, without
some system of socially sanctioned demands on its members. Here
at least is a common interest in morality as minimally conceived,
an interest which can be attributed to all those about whom the
question can be raised. Still we may feel that it is not enough. And
in this feeling is the germ of the reason why the minimal conception of morality is inadequate to the ordinary notion, at least in its
contemporary form; and perhaps, in uncovering the reason for this
inadequacy, we may discover too what there is in the notion of the
universal applicability of moral rules.

   We have arrived at the fact that everyone on whom some form of
socially sanctioned demand is made has an interest in the existence
of some system of socially sanctioned demands. But this fact seems
inadequate to answer the question of what the individual's interest
in morality is. We can begin to understand this inadequacy by
thinking of the different things that might be meant by the social
sanctioning of a demand. 'Sanction' is related to 'permission' and
'approval'; and also to 'power' and to 'penalty'. A socially sanctioned demand is doubtless a demand made with the permission
and approval of a society; and backed, in some form and degree,
with its power. But the idea of a society as the totality of individuals
subject to demands may here come apart from the idea of society as
the source of sanction of those demands. The sanctioning society
may simply be a subgroup of the total society, the dominant

subgroup, the group in which power resides. Mere membership of the total society does not guarantee membership of the sanctioning part of the society. Nor does a mere interest in the existence of some system of socially sanctioned demands guarantee an interest in the particular system of socially sanctioned demands to which one is subjected. But unless at least one, and perhaps both, of these non-guaranteed conditions is satisfied, it does not seem that the fulfilment of a socially sanctioned demand comes anywhere near being what we should regard as the fulfilment of a moral obligation. That is to say, if I have no foothold at all in the sanctioning part of society, and if no interest of mine is safeguarded by the system of demands to which I am subject, then, in fulfilling a demand made upon me, I may indeed, in one sense, be doing what I am obliged to do; but scarcely what I am *morally* obliged to do. No wonder, then, that the question 'What is the individual's interest in morality?' is not answered by mentioning the general interest in the existence of some system of socially sanctioned demands. The answer now scarcely appears to touch the question.

Suppose, then, that we consider the idea of a society such that all its members have *some* interest, not merely in there being a system of socially sanctioned demands, but in the actual system of demands which obtains in that society. It seems that we can ensure such an interest even to the powerless and enslaved by stipulating that the system includes not only demands made on them in the interest of their masters, but also demands made on their masters in their interests. We might be tempted to say that by thus securing to them an interest in the system of demands, we secure to them also some sort of position or foothold in the sanctioning part of society. Certainly, when the master recognizes moral obligations to his slave, we shall be at least one step nearer to allowing that the slave is not merely subject to the demands of his master, but may recognize a moral obligation to fulfil them. Even in this extreme case, then, we can approach the situation which everyone would agree to regard as characteristically moral, the situation in which there is reciprocal acknowledgement of rights and duties.

Still I think we must admit a distinction of two stages in this approach to the characteristically moral situation. Interest in claims on others and acknowledgement of claims on oneself are connected but not identical. It is a tautology, though not an easy one, that everyone subject to moral demands has some interest in morality. For a demand made on an individual is to be regarded as a moral demand only if it belongs to a system of demands which includes demands made on others in his interest. It would be agreeable, as I just now suggested, to be able to argue strictly that this fact carries with it the conclusion that mere self-conscious membership of a moral community implies at least in some degree extending one's sanction to its system of demands, to the extent of genuinely acknowledging as obligations at least some of the claims which others have on one, even if only provisionally and with the strongest desire that the system should be different. But to argue so would be to equivocate with the phrase 'membership of a moral community'. There would be nothing self-contradictory about the idea of one who recognized his interest in the system of moral demands and resolved merely to profit by it as much as he could, fulfilling its demands on himself only in so far as his interest calculably required it. He might get away with it successfully if he were subtle enough in his practice of the hypocrisy which this policy would necessarily involve. But it is an important fact that hypocrisy would be necessary. It is connected with the further fact, a fact of human nature which can probably be explained in a number of ways, that quite thoroughgoing egotism of this kind is rare. But for this fact there could be no such thing as a system of moral demands. We cannot argue that it is a tautology that *anyone* subject to moral demands who recognizes his interest in the system of demands must also genuinely acknowledge some obligations under the system. But we can argue that it is a tautology that the *generality* of those subject to moral demands must genuinely recognize some obligations under the system of demands. For if this were not so, there would be no such thing as a system of moral demands and hence no such thing as being subject to a moral demand.

These steps from a minimal to a more adequate conception of morality (i.e. to a conception which at least begins to square with what we nowadays vaguely understand by the word) may easily encourage abstract exaggerations and distortions in moral

philosophy. For instance, the necessary truth that the members of a
moral community in general acknowledge some moral claims upon
them may be exaggerated into the idea of a self-conscious choice or
adoption of the principle of those claims. So everyone appears,
grandly but unplausibly, as a moral self-legislator. This is an exaggeration which has appealed, in different forms, to more than one
philosopher. Again these steps reveal something genuinely universal in morality: the necessary acceptance of reciprocity of claim.
And *one* way in which a demand made on one individual in the
interest of others can be balanced by a demand made on others in
his interest is through the operation of a general rule or principle
having application to all alike. But it does not follow from this that
all moral claims have, or are seen by those who acknowledge them
as having, the character of applications of universal principles holding for all men. There is no reason why a system of moral demands
characteristic of one community should, or even could, be found in
every other. And even within a single system of reciprocal claims
that moral demand may essentially *not* relate to a situation in
which any member of the system could find himself *vis-à-vis*
any other. Here are two reasons why it is misleading to say that
moral behaviour is what is demanded of men as men. It might,
in some cases, be essentially what is demanded of Spartans by
other Spartans, or of a king by his subjects. What is universally
demanded of the members of a moral community is something like
the abstract virtue of justice: a man should not insist on a particular
claim while refusing to acknowledge any reciprocal claim. But from
this formally universal feature of morality no consequences follow
as to the universality of application of the particular rules in the
observance of which, in particular situations and societies, justice
consists.

One must beware, however, of meeting exaggeration with
counter-exaggeration. It is important to recognize the diversity of
possible systems of moral demands, and the diversity of demands
which may be made within any system. But it is also important to
recognize that certain human interests are so fundamental and so
general that they must be universally acknowledged in some form
and to some degree in any conceivable moral community. Of some

interests, one might say: a system could scarcely command *sufficient* interest in those subject to its demands for these demands to be acknowledged as obligations, unless it secured to them *this* interest. Thus some claim on human succour, some obligation to abstain from the infliction of physical injury, seem to be necessary features of almost any system of moral demands. Here at least we have types of moral behaviour which are demanded *of* men as men because they are demanded *for* and *by* men as men. Another interest which is fundamental to many types of social relation and social grouping is the interest in not being deceived. In most kinds of social grouping for which there obtains any system of moral demand and claim at all, this interest is acknowledged as a claim which any member of the group has on any other; and perhaps most such groupings could scarcely exist without this acknowledgement. When all allowance has been made, then, for the possible diversity of moral systems and the possible diversity of demands within a system, it remains true that the recognition of certain general virtues and obligations will be a logically or humanly necessary feature of almost any conceivable moral system: these will include the abstract virtue of justice, some form of obligation to mutual aid and to mutual abstention from injury and, in some form and in some degree, the virtue of honesty. This guarded recognition of the necessary universal applicability of some relatively vague and abstract moral principles is itself a corrective to the idea of unbounded freedom of choice of such principles on the part of the individual.

I spoke earlier of the need for striking some delicate balances, and I hope that the nature of some of these is now apparent. Constant checks are required if these balances are not to be lost. We have seen in what sense it is true that everyone on whom a moral demand is made must have an interest in morality. But we have also seen that the existence of a system of moral demands (at least as we now understand this concept) requires some degree of general readiness to recognize claims made upon one even when this recognition cannot plausibly be said to be in one's own interest. The existence of some such readiness needs no more to be argued for than the existence of morality in general. But it is necessary to emphasize it in order to correct another exaggeration, the exaggeration which would represent all morality as prudential.[2] To say that this readiness to acknowledge the claims of others does not need to be argued for is not to say that it does not need to be explained. We may discuss its natural sources; and the terms in which we do so will change with the state of our psychological knowledge: the appeal to the concept of sympathy, for example, will scarcely now seem adequate. But, however we explain it, there is no need to sophisticate ourselves into denying altogether the existence or fundamental importance of this recognition of others' claims. Again, we have seen that the fact of acknowledgement of claims may be blown up into the picture of the self-legislating moral agent; and here we should do well to scale down our pretensions to freedom by remembering, if nothing else, the importance of the training we receive and the limited choice we exercise of the moral communities to which we belong. Finally, we have acknowledged some force in the idea of universally applicable principles of moral demand and claim. But to keep within bounds the pretensions of this idea, we must insist again on the flexibility of the concept of a social group, upon the diversity of groups and upon the absurdity of the idea that detailed demands could be shifted indifferently from group to group or apply to all members alike within a group.

There are further important moral phenomena of which the account I have given makes little or no explicit mention. Some of these it might even seem, at first sight, to exclude. Is there not such a thing as moral criticism, from within a society, of the existing moral forms of that society? Cannot different systems of socially sanctioned demand, under which those subject to demands genuinely acknowledge obligations, be the subject of relative moral evaluation? Cannot there be situations in which men may or should recognize moral obligations to each other, although there is no common society of which they are members and there is no concept of a 'social' relationship which can be at all plausibly represented as applying to their situation? Any acceptable account of morality must certainly allow an affirmative answer to these questions; and there are others which will suggest themselves. But they no more yield a reason for mistrusting the approach I have adopted than the inadequacy of what I called the minimal interpretation of morality gave a reason for wholly discarding that idea. By enriching the minimal interpretation with certain applications of the notions of interest, and of acknowledgement of obligation, we obtained what was recognizably a concept of social morality. It is necessary only to draw out the significance of certain elements in *this* conception in order to make room for the ideas of moral criticism, and of a morality which transcends standard forms of social relationship. I have remarked already that, because certain human needs and interests are as fundamental and as general as they are, we shall find correspondingly general types of virtue and obligation acknowledged in some form and in some degree in almost any conceivable moral system. Now it is characteristically by analogy with, and extension of, acknowledged forms of these, that moral development proceeds, and that these ideas themselves assume more refined and generous shapes. And moral criticism at its most self-conscious proceeds characteristically by appeal to, and interpretation of, such general moral ideas as those of justice, integrity and humanity: existing institutions, systems of demand and claim, are criticized as unjust, inhumane or corrupt. We may say that so far from excluding the idea of moral criticism, the concept of social morality, as I have outlined it, makes fully intelligible the nature and possibility of such criticism. For we can perceive how the seeds of criticism lie in the morality itself; and we may even hope, on this basis, to achieve some understanding of the complex interrelationships between social and economic change, the critical insights of individual moralists, and the actual course of moral evolution. (It is, for instance, an easy consequence of our principles that moral *formalism* – i.e. a rigid adherence to the letter, with no appeal to the spirit, of the rules – will tend to be at a maximum in a static and isolated society, and that moral *disorientation* will tend to be at a maximum when such a morality is suddenly exposed to radical change.) Just as a social morality contains the seeds of moral criticism, so the two together contain the seeds of a morality transcending standard social relationships. It is easy to see how the tendency of at least one type of self-conscious and critical morality is generalizing and anti-parochial, as it is anti-formalist. Some moralists would maintain that a true concept of morality emerges only at the limit of this generalizing process. This is a judgement in which, as it seems to me, the sense of reality has become quite subordinated to zeal. But wherever we choose to say that 'true morality' begins, I have no doubt whatever that our understanding of the concept of morality in general is best served by the kind of approach that I have sketched. Where what we are dealing with is a developing human institution, it is no reproach to an explanation that it may be described as at least partially genetic.

But now it is time to return to the question of the relation between social moralities and those ideal pictures of forms of life which I spoke of at the outset. All I have so far explicitly said about this is that the realization of any such ideal requires the existence of forms of social grouping or organization which in turn require the existence of a system of socially sanctioned demands on their members. We have since remarked that a system of socially sanctioned demands would fall short of being a system of moral demands unless those demands were not merely enforced as demands, but also at least in some degree generally acknowledged as claims by those subject to them; and it follows from this that to be a member of a moral community cannot merely be a matter of convenience, except perhaps for those who can practise a sustained hypocrisy of which few are in fact capable. Yet it may still be true in general to say that the possibility of the pursuit of an ideal form of life quite pragmatically requires membership of a moral community or of moral communities; for it is extremely unlikely in fact that the minimal social conditions for the pursuit of any ethical ideal which anyone is likely to entertain could in practice be fulfilled except through membership of such communities. But of course the relations between these two things are much more intricate and various than this formulation by itself suggests. The possibilities of collision, absorption and interplay are many. The way I have just expressed the matter perhaps makes most obvious the possibility of collision; and this possibility is worth stressing. It is worth stressing that what one acknowledges or half-acknowledges as obligation may conflict not only, crudely, with interest and, weakly, with inclination, but also with ideal aspiration, with the vision that captures the ethical imagination. On the other hand, it may be that a picture of the ideal life is precisely one in which the interests of morality are dominant, are given an ideal, overriding value. To one dominated temporarily or permanently by such a picture the 'consciousness of duty faithfully performed' will appear as the supremely satisfactory state, and being moral not merely as something that matters but as the thing that supremely matters. Or again the ideal picture may be not that in which the interests of morality in general are dominant, but rather one in which the dominating idea operates powerfully to reinforce some, but not perhaps others, of a system of moral demands. So it is with that ideal picture in which obedience to the command to love one another appears as the supreme value.

This is still to draw too simple a picture. Let us remember the diversity of communities to which we may be said to belong, and the diversity of systems of moral demand which belong to them. To a certain extent, though to an extent which we must not exaggerate, the systems of moral relationships into which we enter are a matter of choice – or at least a matter in which there are alternative possibilities; and different systems of moral demand are variously well or ill adapted to different ideal pictures of life. The ideal picture, moreover, may call for membership not merely of communities in which certain interests are safeguarded by a system of moral demands, but for membership of a community or of a system of relationships in which the system of demands reflects in a positive way the nature of the ideal. For one crude instance of this, we may think again of the morality of a military caste in connection with the ideal of personal honour. In general, in a society as complex as ours, it is obvious that there are different moral environments, different sub-communities within the community, different systems of moral relationships, interlocking indeed and overlapping with one another, but offering some possibilities of choice, some possibilities of adjustment of moral demand and individual aspiration. But here again, at least in our time and place, it is the limits of the direct relevance of each to the other that must finally be stressed. Inside a single political human society one may indeed find different, and perhaps widely different, moral environments, social groupings in which different systems of moral demand are recognized. But if the one grouping is to form part of the wider society, its members must be subject too to a wider system of reciprocal demand, a wider common morality; and the relative significance of the wider common morality will grow in proportion as the subgroups of the society are closely interlocked, in proportion as each individual is a member of a plurality of subgroups and in proportion as the society is not rigidly stratified, but allows of relatively free access to, and withdrawal from, its subgroups. In a political society which thus combines a wide variety of social groupings with complex interlocking and freedom of movement between them the dissociation of idiosyncratic ideal and common moral demand will doubtless tend to be at its maximum. On the other hand an ideal picture of man *may* tend, in fact or in fancy, to demand the status of a comprehensive common morality. Thus Coleridgean or Tolstoyan dreamers may play with the thought of self-enclosed ideal communities in which the system of moral demands shall answer exactly, or as exactly as possible, to an ideal picture of life held in common by all their members. Such fancies are bound to strike many as weak and futile; for the price of preserving the purity of such communities is that of severance from the world at large. More seriously, there may be some attempt to make the whole moral climate of an existing national state reflect some ideal image of human solidarity or religious devotion or military honour. In view of the natural diversity of human ideals – to mention only that – such a state (or its members) will evidently be subject to at least some stresses from which a liberal society is free.

To conclude. I have spoken of those ideal images of life of which one individual may sympathize with many, and desire to see many realized in some degree. I have spoken also of those systems – though the word is too strong – of recognized reciprocal claim that we have on one another as members of human communities, or as terms of human relationships, many of which could scarcely exist or have the character they have but for the existence of such systems of reciprocal claim. I have said something, though too little, of the complex and various relations which may hold between these two things, viz. our conflicting visions of the ends of life and the systems of moral demand which make social living possible. Finally I have glanced at the relations of both to the political societies in which we necessarily live. The field of phenomena over which I have thus loosely ranged is, I think, very much more complex and many-sided than I have been able to suggest; but I have been concerned to suggest something of its complexity. Some implications for moral philosophy I have hinted at in passing, mainly by way of an attempt to correct some typical exaggerations of contemporary theory. But the main practical implications for moral and political philosophy are, I think, that more attention should be concentrated on types of social structure and social relation, and on those complex inter-relationships which I have mentioned as well as others which I have not. For instance, it is hard not to believe that understanding of our secular morality would be enhanced by considering the historical role that religion has played in relation to morality. Or again, I doubt if the nature of morality can be properly understood without some consideration of its relationship to law. It is not merely that the spheres of morality and law are largely overlapping, or that their demands often coincide. It is also that in the way law functions to give cohesiveness to the most important of all social groupings we may find a coarse model of the way in which systems of moral demand function to give cohesiveness to social groupings in general. Similarly, in the complexity of our attitudes towards existing law we may find a model of the complexity of our attitude towards the systems of moral demand which impinge upon us in our social relations at large – or upon others, in theirs.

Finally, I do not think there is any very definite invitation to moral or political commitment implicit in what I have said. But perhaps one question can be raised, and in part answered. What will be the attitude of one who experiences sympathy with a variety of conflicting ideals of life? It seems that he will be most at home in a liberal society, in a society in which there are variant moral environments but in which no ideal endeavours to engross, and determine the character of, the common morality. He will not argue in favour of such a society that it gives the best chance for the truth about life to prevail, for he will not consistently believe that there is such a thing as the truth about life. Nor will he argue in its favour that it has the best chance of producing a harmonious king-dom of ends, for he will not think of ends as necessarily capable of being harmonized. He will simply welcome the ethical diversity which the society makes possible, and in proportion as he values that diversity he will note that he is the natural, though perhaps the sympathetic, enemy of all those whose single intense vision of the ends of life drives them to try to make the requirements of the ideal coextensive with those of common social morality.

NOTES

1   Cf. G. E. M. Anscombe, 'Modern Moral Philosophy', *Philosophy* vol. XXXIII, January 1958.
2   Cf. P. R. Foot, 'Moral Beliefs', *Proceedings of the Aristotelian Society*, vol. LIX, 1958–9.

3

IMAGINATION AND PERCEPTION

Psychologists have hitherto failed to realize that imagination is a necessary ingredient of perception itself.[1]

1

The uses, and applications, of the terms 'image', 'imagine', 'imagination', 'imaginative', and so forth make up a very diverse and scattered family. Even this image of a family seems too definite. It would be a matter of more than difficulty exactly to identify and list the family's members, let alone establish their relationships of parenthood and cousinhood. But we can at least point to different areas of association in each of which some members of this group of terms ordinarily find employment. Here are three such areas: (1) the area in which imagination is linked with *image* and image is understood as *mental image* – a picture in the mind's eye or (perhaps) a tune running through one's head; (2) the area in which imagination is associated with invention, and also (sometimes) with originality or insight or felicitous or revealing or striking departure from routine; (3) the area in which imagination is linked with false belief, delusion, mistaken memory, or misperception. My primary concern here is not with any of these three areas of association, though I shall refer to them all, and especially to the first. My primary topic is Kant's use of the term 'imagination', in the *Critique of Pure Reason*, in connection with perceptual recognition – a use which may appear something of an outsider, but nevertheless has claims to affinity which are worth considering. I shall refer also to Hume and to Wittgenstein. My paper in general belongs to the species *loosely ruminative* and *comparative-historical* rather than to the species *strictly argumentative* or *systematic-analytical*.

2

Sometimes Kant used the term 'imagination' and its cognates in what is apparently a very ordinary and familiar way; as when, for example, he seems to contrast our imagining something with our having knowledge or experience of what is actually the case. Thus in a note in the 'Refutation of Idealism' he writes: 'It does not follow that every intuitive representation of outer things involves the existence of these things, for their representation can very well be the product *merely of the imagination* (as in dreams and delusions). . . . Whether this or that supposed experience be not *purely imaginary* must be ascertained from its special determinations, and through its congruence with the criteria of all real experience.'[2] Sometimes, however, indeed more frequently, his use of the term seems to differ strikingly from any ordinary and familiar use of it, so that we are inclined to say he must be using it in a technical or specialized way of his own. Suppose, for example, that I notice a strange dog in the garden, and observe its movements for a while; and perhaps also notice, a few minutes later, that it is still there. We should not ordinarily say that this account of a small and uninteresting part of my history included the report of any exercise of the imagination on my part. Yet, in Kant's apparently technical use of the term, any adequate analysis of such a situation would accord a central role to imagination, or to some faculty entitled 'imagination'.

In both these respects there is a resemblance between Kant and

Hume. That is to say, Hume, like Kant, sometimes makes an apparently ordinary use of the term (as when he is discussing the differences between imagination and memory) and sometimes makes an apparently technical use of it; and the latter use is such that he, too, like Kant, would say that imagination enters essentially into the analysis of the very ordinary situation I described a moment ago. It may be instructive to see how far this resemblance goes.

Let us return to our simple situation. Both Hume and Kant would say (a) that my recognizing the strange dog I see as a dog at all owes something to the imagination; and (b) that my taking what I continuously, or interruptedly, observe to be the same object, the same dog, throughout, also owes something to the imagination. By both philosophers imagination is conceived as a connecting or uniting power which operates in two dimensions. In one dimension, (a), it connects perceptions of different objects of the same kind; in the other dimension, (b), it connects different perceptions of the same object of a given kind. It is the instrument of our perceptual appreciation both of kind-identity and of individual-identity, both of concept-identity and of object-identity. The two dimensions or varieties of connecting power are, doubtless, not independent of each other, but they can, to some extent, be handled separately. I begin by referring briefly to (a); then I treat more fully of (b); and then return in section 4, below, to (a).

Kant's doctrine (or part of it) on (a) is sketched in the chapter on schematism, and Hume's in the chapter in the *Treatise* called 'Of abstract ideas'. Kant declares the schema to be a product of, and also a rule for, the imagination, in accordance with which, and by means of which alone, the imagination can connect the particular image or the particular object with the general concept under which it falls. Hume speaks, in his usual way, of the resemblance of particular ideas being the foundation of a customary association both among the resemblant particular ideas themselves and between them and the 'annex'd' general term; so that the imagination is, or may be, ready with an appropriate response whenever it gets a cue, as it were, from anywhere in the associative network. How the mechanism is supposed exactly to work is not very clear either in the case of Hume or in that of Kant. But the obscurity of this very point is something which both authors emphasize themselves, in sentences which show a quite striking parallelism. Thus Kant says of schematism that it is 'an art concealed in the depths of the human soul, whose real modes of activity nature is hardly likely ever to allow us to discover and have open to our gaze'.[3] And Hume, speaking of the imagination's readiness with appropriate particular ideas, describes it as a 'kind of magical faculty in the soul which, though it be always most perfect in the greatest geniuses, and is properly what we call a genius, is, however, inexplicable by the utmost efforts of human understanding'.[4] Imagination, then, in so far as its operations are relevant to the application of the same general concept in a variety of different cases, is a concealed art of the soul, a magical faculty, something we shall never fully understand.

Let us turn now to (b), to the matter of different phases of experience being related to the same particular object of some general type. In both authors this question is absorbed into a larger one, though the larger question is somewhat differently conceived in each of them. The main relevant passages here are, in the *Critique*, the section on 'Transcendental Deduction' and, in the *Treatise*, the chapter 'Scepticism with Regard to the Senses'. Let us begin with Hume.

Hume makes a threefold distinction between sense (or the senses), reason (or understanding), and imagination. His famous question about the causes which induce us to believe in the existence of body resolves itself into the question to which of these faculties, or to what combination of them, we should ascribe this belief, that is, the belief in the *continued* and *distinct* existence of bodies. Certainly, he says, not to the senses alone and unassisted. For 'when the mind looks further than what immediately appears to it, its conclusions can never be put to the account of the senses';[5] and the mind certainly 'looks further' than this, both in respect of the belief in the *continued* existence of objects when we are no longer, as we say, perceiving them, and in respect of the obviously connected belief in the *distinctness* of their existence from that of our perceptions of them. Equally certainly, he says, we cannot attribute these beliefs to Reason, that is to reasoning based on perceptions. For the only kind of reasoning that can be in question here is reasoning based on experience of constant conjunction, or causal reasoning. But whether we conceive of objects as the same in kind as perceptions or as different in kind from perceptions, it remains true that 'no beings are ever present to the mind but perceptions'[6] and all perceptions which are present to the mind are present to the mind;[7] hence it is equally certain that we can never observe a constant conjunction either between perceptions present to the mind and perceptions not present to the mind or between perceptions on the one hand and objects different in kind from perceptions on the other.

The belief in question, then, must be ascribed to the Imagination – or, more exactly, to the 'concurrence' of some of the qualities of our impressions with some of the qualities of the imagination. And here Hume launches into that famous account of the operations of imagination which, on account of its perverse ingenuity, can scarcely fail to command admiration both in the original and the modern senses of the word. It runs roughly as follows: imagination engenders so strong a propensity to confound the similarity of temporally separated and hence non-identical perceptions with strict identity through time that, in defiance of sense and reason combined, we feign, and believe in, a continued existence of perceptions where there is patently no such thing; and so strong is the hold of this belief that, when the discrepancy is pointed out, the imagination can still find an ally in certain philosophers who try, though vainly, to satisfy reason and imagination at the same time by conceiving of objects as different in kind from perceptions and ascribing continued existence to the former and interrupted existence only to the latter.

When we turn from Hume to Kant, it is probably the divergencies rather than the parallels which we find most striking in this case – at least at first. And perhaps we can come at these by considering a *simpliste* criticism of Hume. For Hume's account is full of holes. One of the most obvious relates to his bland assertion that the unreflective, as opposed to the philosophers, take the objects of perception to be of the same species as perceptions of those objects; so that the problem of accounting for the belief, in its *vulgar* form, in the continued existence of objects is the problem of accounting for a belief which reason shows to be ungrounded and ungroundable, namely a belief in the existence of perceptions which nobody has. Of course it is quite false that the vulgar make any such identification and hence quite false that they hold any such belief as Hume presumes to account for. The vulgar *distinguish*, naturally and unreflectively, between their seeings and hearings (perceivings) of objects and the objects they see and hear, and hence have no difficulty in reconciling the interruptedness of the former with the continuance of existence of the latter. Indeed these distinctions and beliefs are built into the very vocabulary of their perception-reports, into the concepts they employ, the meanings of the things they say, in giving (unsophisticated) accounts of their hearings and seeings of things. So Hume's problem does not really exist and his solution to it is otiose.

I think Kant would regard these criticisms as just, but would deny that there was therefore no problem at all for the philosopher. That is, he would agree that the problem was not, as Hume conceived it, that of accounting, on the basis of the character of our perceptual experience, for certain beliefs (beliefs in the continued and distinct existence of bodies). For he would agree that it would be impossible to give accurate, plain reports of our perceptual experience which did not already incorporate those beliefs. The beliefs form an essential part of the conceptual framework which has to be employed to give a candid and veridical description of our perceptual experience. But this does not mean that there is no question to be asked. Hume starts his investigation, as it were, too late; with perceptual experience already established in the character it has, he leaves himself no room for any such question as he wishes to ask. But we ought to ask, not how it can be that on the basis of perceptual experience as it is, we come to have the beliefs in question, but *how it is* that perceptual experience is already such as to embody the beliefs in question; or, perhaps better, *what* it is for perceptual experience to be such as to embody the beliefs in question.

I do not want to invoke more of the complex apparatus of the critical philosophy than is necessary to bring out the parallels with Hume that lie below or behind or beside the divergencies. We know that Kant thought that perceptual experience did not just *happen* to have the general character it has, but *had* to have at least something like this character, if experience (that is the temporally extended experience of a self-conscious being) was to be possible at all. Just now we are not so much concerned with the soundness of this view as with the question of what he thought was *involved* in perceptual experience having this character. One of the things he certainly thought was involved in this: 'A combination of them [perceptions or representations], such as they cannot have in sense itself, is demanded.'[8] And this 'such as they cannot have in sense itself' arouses at least a faint echo of Hume's view that sense itself could never give rise to the *opinion* of the continued and distinct existence of body. The reason Hume gives for this view, it will be recalled, is that in embracing such an *opinion*, 'the mind looks further than what immediately appears to it'. Now could Kant have a *similar* reason for holding that, for the use of concepts of relatively permanent bodies (that is for perceptual experience to have the character it does have), a combination such as perceptions cannot have in sense itself is demanded?

I think he could have. For even when Hume is submitted to the sort of correction I sketched above, there is *something* right about the phrase of his I have just quoted. When I naïvely report what I see at a moment (say, as a tree or a dog), my mind or my report certainly 'looks further' than *something* – not, usually, than 'what immediately appears to me' (tree or dog), but certainly further than the merely subjective side of the event of its immediately appearing to me. Of a fleeting perception, a subjective event, I give a description involving the mention of something not fleeting at all, but lasting, not a subjective event at all, but a distinct object. It is clear, *contra* Hume, not only that I *do* do this, but that I *must* do it in order to give a natural and unforced account of my perceptions. Still, there arises the question of what is necessarily involved in this being the case. The uninformative beginnings of an answer consist in saying that one thing necessarily involved is our possession and application of concepts of a certain kind, namely concepts of distinct and enduring objects. But now, as both Kant and Hume emphasize, the whole course of our experience of the world consists of relatively transient and changing perceptions. (The changes, and hence the transience, may be due to changes in the scene or in our orientation, broadly understood, towards the scene.) It seems reasonable to suppose that there would be no question of applying concepts of the kind in question unless those concepts served in a certain way to *link* or *combine* different perceptions – unless, specifically, they could, and sometimes did, serve to link *different* perceptions as perceptions of the *same* object. Here, then, is one aspect of combination, as Kant uses the word, and just the aspect we are now concerned with. Combination, in this sense, is *demanded*. We could not count any transient perception as a perception of an enduring object of some kind unless we were prepared to count, and did count, some transient perceptions as, though different perceptions, perceptions of the same object of such a kind. The concepts in question could get no grip at all unless different perceptions were sometimes in this way combined by them. And when Kant says that this sort of combination of perceptions is such as they (the perceptions) cannot have in sense itself, we may perhaps take him to be making *at least* the two following unexceptionable, because tautological, points:

(1) that this sort of combination is dependent on the possession and application of this sort of concept, that is, that if we did not *conceptualize* our sensory intake in this sort of way, then our sensory impressions would not be *combined* in this sort of way;

(2) that distinguishable perceptions combined in this way, whether they are temporally continuous (as when we see an object move or change colour) or temporally separated (as when we see an object again after an interval), really are distinguishable, that is different, perceptions.

Of course, in saying that we can find these two unexceptionable points in Kant's Hume-echoing dictum about combination, I am not for a moment suggesting that this account covers all that Kant means by combination; only that it may reasonably be taken to be included in what Kant means.

But now how does imagination come into the picture, that is into Kant's picture? Kant's problem, as we have seen, is not the same as Hume's; so he has no call to invoke imagination to do the job for which Hume invokes it, that is the job of supplementing actual perceptions with strictly imaginary perceptions which nobody has, which there is no reason to believe in the existence of and every reason not to believe in the existence of, but which we nevertheless *do* believe in the existence of as a condition of believing in the existence of body at all. This is not how imagination can come into Kant's picture. But certainly imagination *does* come into his picture; and the question is whether we can give any intelligible account of its place there. I think we can give some sort of account, though doubtless one that leaves out much that is mysterious in Kant and characteristic of him.

To do this we must strengthen our pressure at a point already touched on. We have seen that there would be no question of counting any transient perception as a perception of an enduring and distinct object unless we were prepared or ready to count some different perceptions as perceptions of one and the same enduring and distinct object. The thought of *other* actual or possible perceptions as related in this way to the *present* perception has thus a peculiarly intimate relation to our counting or taking – to our ability to count or take – this present perception as the perception of such an object. This is not of course to say that even when, for example, we perceive and recognize (reidentify as the object it is) a familiar particular object, there need occur anything which we would count as the experience of actually recalling any particular past perception of that object. (It is not in *this* way, either, that imagination comes into the picture.) Indeed the more familiar the object, the less likely any such experience is. Still, in a way, we can say in such a case that the past perceptions are *alive* in the present perception. For it would not be just the perception it is but for them. Nor is this just a matter of an external, causal relation. Compare seeing a face you *think* you know, but cannot associate with any previous encounter, with seeing a face you *know* you know and can very well so associate, even though there does not, as you see it, occur any particular *episode* of recalling any particular previous encounter. The comparison will show why I say that the past perceptions are, in the latter case, not merely causally operative, but alive in the present perception.

Of course when you first see a new, an unfamiliar thing of a familiar kind, there is no question of past perceptions of *that* thing being alive in the present perception. Still, one might say, to take it, to see it, as a thing of that kind is implicitly to have the thought of other possible perceptions related to your actual perception as perceptions of the same object. To see it as a dog, silent and stationary, is to see it as a possible mover and barker, even though you give yourself no actual images of it as moving and barking; though, again, you might do so if, say, you were particularly timid, if, as we say, your imagination was particularly active or particularly stimulated by the sight. Again, as you continue to observe it, it is not just a dog, with such and such characteristics, but *the* dog, the object of your recent observation, that you see, and see it as.

It seems, then, not too much to say that the actual occurrent perception of an enduring object as an object of a certain kind, or as a particular object of that kind, is, as it were, soaked with or animated by, or infused with – the metaphors are *à choix* – the thought of other past or possible perceptions of the same object. Let us speak of past and merely possible perceptions alike as 'non-actual' perceptions. Now the imagination, in one of its aspects – the first I mentioned in this paper – is the image-producing faculty, the faculty, we may say, of producing actual representatives (in the shape of images) of non-actual perceptions. I have argued that an actual perception of the kind we are concerned with owes its character essentially to that internal link, of which we find it so difficult to give any but a metaphorical description, with other past or possible, but in any case non-actual, perceptions. Non-actual perceptions are in a sense represented in, alive in, the present perception; just as they are represented, by images, in the image-producing activity of the imagination. May we not, then, find a kinship between the capacity for this latter kind of exercise of the imagination and the capacity which is exercised in actual perception of the kind we are concerned with? Kant, at least, is prepared to register his sense of such a kinship by extending the title of 'imagination' to cover both capacities; by speaking of imagination as 'a necessary ingredient of perception itself'.

3

Suppose we so understand – or understand as including at least so much – the Kantian idea of the synthesis of imagination. The connection of the idea, so understood, with the application of concepts of objects is already clear. Can we also explain the introduction of the qualification 'transcendental'? If we bear in mind the opposition between 'transcendental' and 'empirical', I think we can put two glosses on 'transcendental' here, both with a common root. First, then, we must remember the distinction between what Kant thought necessary to the possibility of any experience and what he thought merely contingently true of experience as we actually enjoy it. There is, in this sense, no necessity about our employment of the particular sets of empirical concepts we do employ, for example the concepts of elephant or ink bottle. All that is necessary is that we should employ some empirical concepts or other which exemplify, or give a footing to, those very abstractly conceived items, the categories, or concepts of an object in general. Synthesis, then, or the kind of exercise of the imagination (in Kant's extended sense) which is involved in perception of objects *as* objects, is empirical in one aspect and transcendental in another: it is empirical (that is non-necessary) in so far as it happens to consist in the application of this or that particular empirical concept (elephant or ink bottle); transcendental (that is necessary) in so far as the application of such concepts represents, though in a form which is quite contingent, the utterly general requirements of a possible experience.

The second, connected, gloss we can put upon 'transcendental' can be brought out by comparison, once more, with Hume. Hume seems to think of the operations of imagination as something superadded to actual occurrent perceptions, the latter having a quite determinate character independent of and unaffected by the imagination's operations (though, of course, our *beliefs* are not unaffected by those operations). The Kantian synthesis, on the other hand, however conceived, is something necessarily involved in, a necessary condition of, actual occurrent reportable perceptions having the character they do have. So it may be called 'transcendental' in contrast with any process, for example any ordinary associative process, which presupposes a basis of actual, occurrent, reportable perceptions.

4

In so far as we have supplied anything like an explanation or justification of Kant's apparently technical use of 'imagination', we have done so by suggesting that the recognition of an enduring object of a certain kind *as* an object of that kind, or as a certain particular object of that kind, involves a certain sort of connection with other non-actual perceptions. It involves other past (and hence non-actual) perceptions, or the thought of other possible (and hence non-actual) perceptions, of the *same* object being somehow alive in the present perception. The question arises whether we can stretch things a little further still to explain or justify the apparently technical use of 'imagination' in connection with our power to recognize *different* (and sometimes very different) particular objects as falling under the same general concept.

We can begin by making the platitudinous point that the possession of at least a fair measure of this ability, in the case, say, of the concept of a tree, is at least a test of our knowing what a tree is, of our possessing the concept of a tree. And we can progress from this to another point, both less platitudinous and more secure: namely, that it would be unintelligible to say of someone that whereas he could recognize *this* particular object as a tree, he could not recognize any other trees as trees.[9] So it would not make sense to say, in the case of a particular momentary perception, that he who had it recognized what he saw as a tree unless we were prepared also to ascribe to him the power of recognizing other things as well as trees. Now, how are we to regard this power or potentiality as related to his momentary perception? Is it just something external to it, or superadded to it, just an extra qualification he must possess, as it were, if his momentary perception is to count as a case of tree-recognition? This picture of the relation seems wrong. But if we say it *is* wrong, if we say that the character of the momentary perception itself depends on the connection with this general power, then have we not in this case too the same sort of link between actual and non-actual perceptions (now of *other* things) as we had in the previously discussed case between actual and non-actual perceptions (then of the *same* thing)? But if so then we have another reason, similar to the first reason though not the same as it, for saying that imagination, in an extended sense of the word, is involved in the recognition of such a thing as the sort of thing it is. Once more, this is not a matter of supposing that we give ourselves actual images, either of other trees perceived in the past or of wholly imaginary trees not perceived at all, whenever, in an actual momentary perception, we recognize something as a tree. It is not in this way, that is, by being represented by actual images, that non-actual (past or possible) perceptions enter into actual perception. They enter, rather, in that elusive way of which we have tried to give an account. But may we not here again, for this very reason, find a kinship between perceptual recognition (of an object as of a certain kind) and the more narrowly conceived exercise of the imagination – enough of a kinship, perhaps, to give some basis for Kant's extended use of the term 'imagination' in this connection too, and perhaps, this time, for Hume's as well?

5

It does not, of course, matter very much whether we come down in favour of, or against, this extended or technical application of the term 'imagination'. What matters is whether, in looking into possible reasons or justifications for it, we find that any light is shed on the notion of perceptual recognition. And here I want to summon a third witness. The third witness is Wittgenstein. I consider his evidence, first, in this section, without any reference to any explicit use, by him, of the term 'imagination'; then, in the next, I refer to some of his own uses of terms of this family.

On page 212 of the *Investigations* Wittgenstein says: 'We find certain things about seeing puzzling because we do not find the whole business of seeing puzzling enough.' This comes nearly at the end of those twenty pages or so which he devotes to the discussion of *seeing as,* of aspects and changes of aspect. Nearly all the examples he considers, as far as visual experience is concerned, are of pictures, diagrams, or signs, which can present different aspects, can be seen now as one thing, now as another. He is particularly impressed by the case where they undergo a change of aspects under one's very eyes, as it were, the case where one is suddenly struck by a new aspect. What, I think, he finds particularly impressive about this case is the very obviously *momentary* or *instantaneous* character of the being struck by the new aspect. Why does this impress him so much? Well, to see an aspect, in this sense, of a thing is, in part, to *think* of it in a certain way, to be disposed to *treat* it in a certain way, to give certain sorts of explanations or accounts of what you see, in general to *behave* in certain ways. But, then, how, he asks, in the case of seeing an aspect, is this thinking of the thing in a certain way related to the *instantaneous* experience? We could perhaps imagine someone able to *treat* a picture in a certain way, painstakingly to *interpret* it in that way, without *seeing* the relevant aspect, without seeing it *as* what he was treating it as, at all.[10] But this does not help us with the case of the instantaneous experience. It would be quite wrong to speak of this case as if there were merely an external relation, inductively established, between the thought, the interpretation, and the visual experience; to say, for example, that 'I see the x as a y' means 'I have a particular visual experience which I have found that I always have when I interpret the x as a y'.[11] So Wittgenstein casts around for ways of expressing himself which will hit off the relation. Thus we have: 'The flashing of an aspect on us seems half visual experience, half thought';[12] or again, of a different case, 'Is it a case of both seeing *and* thinking? or an amalgam of the two, as I should almost like to say?';[13] or again, of yet another, 'It is almost as if "seeing the sign in this context" [under this aspect] were an echo of a thought. "The echo of a thought in sight" – one would like to say.'[14]

Beside Wittgenstein's metaphor of 'the echo of the thought in sight' we might put others: the visual experience is *irradiated* by, or *infused* with, the concept; or it becomes *soaked* with the concept.

Wittgenstein talks mainly of pictures or diagrams. But we must all have had experiences like the following: I am looking towards a yellow flowering bush against a stone wall, but I see it as yellow chalk marks scrawled on the wall. Then the aspect changes and I see it normally, that is I see it as a yellow flowering bush against the wall. On the next day, however, I see it normally, that is I see it as a yellow flowering bush against the wall, all the time. Some persons, perhaps with better eyesight, might never have seen it as anything else, might always *see it as* this. No doubt it is only against the background of some such experience of change of aspects, or of the thought of its possibility, that it is quite natural and non-misleading to speak, in connection with ordinary perception, of *seeing* objects *as* the objects they are. But this does not make it incorrect or false to do so generally.[15] Wittgenstein was perhaps *over*-impressed by the cases where we are *suddenly* struck by something – be it a classical change of figure-aspects or the sudden recognition of a face or the sudden appearance of an object, as when an ordinary rabbit bursts into view in the landscape and captures our attention.[16] Though there clearly are distinctions between cases, there are also continuities. There is no reason for making a sharp conceptual cleavage between the cases of a sudden irruption – whether of an aspect or an object – and others. We can allow that there are cases where visual experience is suddenly irradiated by a concept and cases where it is more or less steadily soaked with the concept. I quote once more: 'We find certain things about seeing puzzling because we do not find the whole business of seeing puzzling enough.' Perhaps we should fail less in this respect if we see that the striking case of the *change* of aspects merely dramatizes for us a feature (namely seeing as) which is present in perception in general.

Now how do we bring this to bear on Kant? Well, there is a point of analogy and a point of difference. The thought is echoed in the sight, the concept is alive in the perception. But when Wittgenstein speaks of *seeing as* as involving thinking-of-as, as involving the thought or the concept, he has in mind primarily a disposition to behave in certain ways, to treat or describe what you see in certain ways – such a disposition itself presupposing (in a favourite phrase) the mastery of a technique. This is the *criterion* of the visual experience, the means by which someone other than the subject of it must tell what it is. This, taking us on to familiar Wittgensteinian ground, gives us indeed a peculiarly intimate link between the momentary perception and something else; but the 'something else' is behaviour, and so the upshot seems remote from the peculiarly intimate link we laboured to establish in connection with Kant's use of the term 'imagination': the link between the actual present perception of the object and other past or possible perceptions of the same object or of other objects of the same kind. But is it really so remote? Wittgenstein's special preoccupations pull him to the behavioural side of things, to which Kant pays little or no attention. But we can no more think of the behavioural dispositions as merely externally related to *other* perceptions than we can think of them as merely externally related to the present perception. Thus the relevant behaviour in reporting an aspect may be to point to *other* objects of *perception*.[17] Or in the case of seeing a real, as opposed to a picture-object, as a such-and such, the behavioural disposition includes, or entails, a readiness for, or expectancy of, other perceptions, of a certain character, of the same object.

Sometimes this aspect of the matter – the internal link between the present and other past or possible perceptions – comes to the fore in Wittgenstein's own account. Thus, of the case of sudden recognition of a particular object, an old acquaintance, he writes: 'I meet someone whom I have not seen for years; I see him clearly, but fail to know him. Suddenly I know him, *I see the old face in the altered one*.'[18] Again, he says of the dawning of an aspect: 'What I perceive in the dawning of an aspect is ... an internal relation between it [the object] and other objects.'[19]

6

I have mentioned the fact that there are points in these pages at which Wittgenstein himself invokes the notions of imagination and of an image. I shall discuss these points now. He first invokes these notions in connection with the drawing of a triangle, a right-angled triangle with the hypotenuse downmost and the right angle upmost. 'This triangle', he says, 'can be seen as a triangular hole, as a solid, as a geometrical drawing; as standing on its base, as hanging from its apex; as a mountain, as a wedge, as an arrow or pointer, as an overturned object which is meant to stand on the shorter side of the right angle, as a half-parallelogram and as various other things.'[20] Later he reverts to this example and says: 'The aspect of the triangle: it is as if an *image* came into contact, and for a time remained in contact, with the visual impression.'[21] He contrasts some of the triangle-aspects in this respect with the aspects of some other of his examples; and a little later he says: 'It is possible to take the duck-rabbit simply for the picture of a rabbit, the double cross simply for the picture of a black cross, but not to take the bare triangular figure for the picture of an object that has fallen over. To see this aspect of the triangle demands *imagination* (*Vorstellungskraft*).'[22] But later still he says something more general about seeing aspects. 'The concept of an aspect is akin to the concept of an image. In other words: the concept "I am now seeing it as ..." is akin to "I am now having *this* image".'[23] Immediately afterwards he says: 'Doesn't it take imagination (*Phantasie*) to hear something as a variation on a particular theme? And yet one is perceiving something in so hearing it.'[24] Again on this page he says generally that seeing an aspect and imagining are alike subject to the will.

It is clear that in these references to imagination and to images Wittgenstein is doing at least two things. On the one hand he is *contrasting* the seeing of certain aspects with the seeing of others, and saying *of some only* that they require imagination; and, further, that some of these are cases in which an image is, as it were, in contact with the visual impression. On the other hand he is saying that there is a *general* kinship between the seeing of aspects and the having of images; though the only respect of kinship he mentions is that both are subject to the will. Perhaps we can make something of both of these.

As regards the first thing he is doing, the contrast he is making, cannot we find an analogy here with a whole host of situations in which there is some sort of departure from the immediately obvious or familiar or mundane or established or superficial or literal way of taking things; situations in which there is some sort of innovation or extravagance or figure or trope or stretch of the mind or new illumination or invention? Thus, beginning from such simplicities as seeing a cloud as a camel or a formation of stalagmites as a dragon, or a small child at a picnic seeing a tree stump as a table, we may move on to very diverse things: to the first application of the word 'astringent' to a remark or to someone's personality; to Wellington at Salamanca saying 'Now we have them' and seeing the future course of the battle in an injudicious movement of the enemy; to the sensitive observer of a personal situation seeing that situation as one of humiliation for one party and triumph for another; to a natural (or even a social) scientist seeing a pattern in phenomena which has never been seen before and introducing, as we say, new concepts to express his insight; to anyone seeing Keble College, Oxford, or the University Museum or Balliol Chapel as their architects meant them to be seen; to Blake seeing eternity in a grain of sand and heaven in a wild flower. And so on. In connection with any item in this rather wild list the words 'imaginative' and 'imagination' are appropriate, though only to some of them is the idea of an image coming into contact with an impression appropriate. But we must remember that what is obvious and familiar, and what is not, is, at least to a large extent, a matter of training and experience and cultural background. So it may be, in this sense, imaginative of Eliot to see the river as a strong, brown god, but less so of the members of a tribe who believe in river-gods. It may, in this sense, call for imagination on my part to see or hear something as a variation on a particular theme, but not on the part of a historian of architecture or a trained musician. What is fairly called exercise of imagination for one person or age group or generation or society may be merest routine for another. To say this is not, of course, in any way to question the propriety of using the term 'imagination' to mark a *contrast*, in any particular case, with routine perception in the application of a concept. It is simply to draw attention to the kind, or kinds, of contrast that are in question and in doing so to stress resemblances and *continuities* between contrasted cases. It should not take much effort to see the resemblances and continuities as at least as striking as the differences and so to sympathize with that imaginative employment of the term 'imagination' which leads both Hume and Kant to cast the faculty for the role of chief agent in the exercise of the power of concept-application, in general, over a variety of cases; to see why Hume described it as a 'magical faculty' which is 'most perfect in the greatest geniuses' and is 'properly what we call a genius'.

So we find a continuity between one aspect of Wittgenstein's use of the term and one aspect of Hume's and Kant's. What of the other aspect of Wittgenstein's use, where he finds a kinship, in *all* cases, between seeing an aspect and having an image? Well, let us consider the character of Wittgenstein's examples. Some are examples of what might be called essentially ambiguous figures, like the duck-rabbit or the double cross. Others are, as it were, very thin and schematic, like the cube-picture or the triangle. If we attend to the essentially ambiguous figures, it is clear that imagination in the sense just discussed would not normally be said to be required in order to see either aspect of either. Both aspects of each are entirely natural and routine, only they compete with each other in a way which is not usual in the case of ordinary objects. We can switch more or less easily from one aspect to another as we cannot normally do with ordinary objects of perception. But we might sometimes switch with similar ease in what on the face of it are ordinary cases: thus, standing at the right distance from my yellow flowering bush, I can switch from seeing it as such to seeing it as yellow chalk marks scrawled on the wall. So if the affinity between seeing aspects and having images is simply a matter of subjection to the will, and if subjection to the will is thought of in this way as ease of switching, then the affinity is present in this case as in the case of the visually ambiguous figures.

But is the general affinity between seeing aspects and having images simply a matter of subjection to the will? One may point out that the subjection of *seeing as* to the will is by no means absolute or universal. And it may be replied that the same is true of having images. One may be haunted or tortured by images, whether of recall or foreboding, from which one vainly seeks distraction but cannot dismiss, or escape the return of, if dismissed; or, alternatively, one may fail to picture something in one's mind when one tries.[25] So at least a *parallel* between *seeing as* and having images, in respect of subjection to the will, continues to hold.

But surely one may ask whether there is not a deeper affinity between *seeing as* and having an image, one which goes beyond this matter of subjection to the will, and can be found in general between perception and imaging. And surely there is. It has already been expressed in saying that the thought (or, as Kant might prefer, the concept) is alive in the perception just as it is in the image. The thought of something as an *x* or as a particular *x* is alive in the perception of it as an *x* or as a particular *x* just as the thought of an *x* or a particular *x* is alive in the having of an image of an *x* or a particular *x*. This is what is now sometimes expressed in speaking of the *intentionality* of perception, as of imaging.[26] But the idea is older than *this* application of that terminology, for the idea is in Kant.

Of course it is essential to the affinity that the having of an image, like perceiving, is more than just having a thought; and that the more that it is is what justifies us in speaking of an image as an actual representative of a non-actual perception and justifies Hume (for all the danger of it) in speaking of images as faint copies of impressions. As for the differences between them both in intrinsic character and in external, causal relations, there is perhaps no need to stress them here.

7

I began this paper by mentioning three areas of association in which the term 'imagination' and its cognates find employment: in connection with *images*, in connection with *innovation* or *invention*, and in connection with *mistakes*, including perceptual mistakes. I have referred to the first two areas of use, but not, so far, to the last. But perhaps, it is worth glancing briefly at the quite common use of 'imagine' and 'imagination' in connection with the *seeing as* of perceptual mistakes. Suppose that when I see the yellow flowering bush as yellow chalk marks on the wall, I actually take what I see *to be* yellow chalk marks on the wall – as I may well do once, though probably not when I have the experience again. In such a case, as opposed to that of *seeing as* without *taking as*, it would be natural and correct to say: 'For a moment I imagined what I saw to be yellow chalk marks on the wall; then I looked again and saw it was a yellow flowering bush against the wall.'

Now it would be easy, and reasonable, to explain this 'mistake' use of 'imagine' by taking some other use or uses as primary and representing this use as an extension of it or them in such a way as to allow no role for imagination in ordinary routine perception.[27] But we should consider how it would be possible to give a kind of caricature-explanation on different lines. Of course, the explanation would run, this indispensable faculty of imagination is involved in ordinary routine perception. It is just that it would be highly mis- leading to single it out for mention as responsible for the outcome in the case of ordinary routine perception. For to do so would be to suggest that things are not as they normally are in ordinary routine perception. Thus we single the faculty out for mention when it operates without anything like the normal sensory stimu- lus altogether, as in imaging, delivering mental products unmistak- ably different from those of ordinary perceptions; when, in one or another of many possible ways, it deviates from, or adds to, the response which we have come to consider routine; or when, as in the present case, we actually mistake the character of the source of stimulus. But it is absurd to conclude that because we only *name* the faculty in these cases, the faculty we then name is only opera- tive in these cases. We might as well say that the faculty of verbal- izing or uttering words is not exercised in intelligent conversation on the ground that we generally say things like 'He was verbalizing freely' or 'He uttered a lot of words' only when, for example, we mean that there was no sense or point in what he said.

It is not my purpose to represent such a line of argument as correct.[28] Still less am I concerned – even if I could do so – to elaborate or defend any account of what we really mean, or ought to mean, by 'imagination', such as that line of argument might point to. I am not sure that either the question, what we *really* do *mean* by the word, or the question, what we *ought* to mean by it, are quite the right ones to ask in this particular case. What matters is that we should have a just sense of the very various and subtle connections, continuities and affinities, as well as differences, which exist in this area. The affinities between the image-having power and the power of ordinary perceptual recognition; the continuities between inventive or extended or playful concept-application and ordinary concept-application in perception: these are some things of which we may have a juster sense as a result of reflection on Kant's use of the term 'imagination'; even, in the latter case, as a result of reflection upon Hume's use of the term. A perspicuous and thorough survey of the area is, as far as I know, something that does not exist; though Wittgenstein's pages contain an intentionally unsystematic assemblage of some materials for such a survey.

NOTES

1 Immanuel Kant, *Critique of Pure Reason*, trans. Norman Kemp Smith, London, Macmillan, 1933, A120, fn.a.
2 Kant, op. cit., B278–9 (my italics).
3 Kant, op. cit., B180–1.
4 David Hume, *A Treatise of Human Nature*, ed. L. A. Selby-Bigge, Oxford, Clarendon Press, 1888, p. 24. Spelling and punctuation have been changed.
5 Hume, op. cit., p. 189.
6 Hume, op. cit., p. 212.
7 I modify at least the appearance of Hume's argument here. He seems to suppose that the required premise at this point has an *empirical* character.
8 Kant, op. cit., A120.
9 Perhaps it is necessary to add that I do not mean that we could not conceive of any circumstances at all (for example, of mental disorder) in which this would be an apt thing to say.
10 Ludwig Wittgenstein, *Philosophical Investigations*, trans. G. E. M. Anscombe, Oxford, Blackwell, 1953, pp. 204, 212, 213–14.
11 Wittgenstein, op. cit., pp. 193–4.
12 Wittgenstein, op. cit., p. 197.
13 ibid.
14 Wittgenstein, op. cit., p. 212.
15 Wittgenstein resists the generalization. See p. 197, ' "Seeing as" is not part of perception', and p. 195. But he also gives part of the reason for making it; see pp. 194–5.
16 Wittgenstein, op. cit., p. 197.

17 Cf. p. 194; and p. 207: 'Those two aspects of the double cross might be reported simply by pointing alternately to an isolated white and an isolated black cross.'

18 Wittgenstein, op. cit., p. 197 (my italics).

19 Wittgenstein, op. cit., p. 212.

20 Wittgenstein, op. cit., p. 200.

21 Wittgenstein, op. cit., p. 207.

22 ibid.

23 Wittgenstein, op. cit., p. 213.

24 ibid.

25 See p. 53 of Miss Ishiguro's admirable treatment of the whole subject in 'Imagination', *Proceedings of the Aristotelian Society*, suppl. vol. XLI, 1967.

26 See Miss Anscombe's 'The Intentionality of Sensation: A Grammatical Feature' in *Analytical Philosophy*, 2nd ser., ed. R. J. Butler, Oxford, Blackwell, 1965, pp. 155–80.

27 As, for example, by saying that when what presents itself as a perception (or memory) turns out to be erroneous, we *reclassify* it by assigning it to that faculty of which the essential role is, say, unfettered invention; somewhat as we sometimes refer to falsehood as *fiction*.

28 It would be, it will be seen, an application (or misapplication) of a principle due to H. P. Grice. See 'The Causal Theory of Perception', *Proceedings of the Aristotelian Society*, supp. vol. XXXV, 1961, pp. 121–68.

4

CAUSATION IN PERCEPTION

For any given description or specification of what I shall call a material object array (M-array) we can distinguish between three conditions:

(1) perceiving such an array (e.g. seeing a book on a desk in front of you, or hearing an aeroplane flying overhead);
(2) believing or taking it that you perceive such an array;
(3) its sensibly seeming to you just as if you perceive such an array.

These conditions are logically independent of each other in that, for a given specification of a material object array, any one of the three conditions can be satisfied without either of the other two being satisfied and any two can be satisfied without the third being satisfied. For example, think of a case in which you are looking at what you know very well to be a solid object – say a bush – standing in front of a wall; but for a moment it looks to you just like, you *see it as*, something drawn on the surface of the wall. Then, for one specification of an M-array, we have the first two conditions satisfied without the third; and for another specification we have the third condition satisfied without the other two.

I shall refer to these three conditions by the use of the following abbreviations:

(1) M-perception
(2) M-perception-belief
(3) M-perception-experience (or M-experience).

Here is one familiar entailment. If you are having a certain M-perception, then a corresponding M-array exists or corresponding or appropriate M-facts obtain. (If you see a book on a desk in front of you, then there is a book on a desk in front of you.) I shall write this as:

I   (1) → appropriate M-facts.

Of course no such entailment holds with regard to either of the other two conditions.

A certain relation weaker than entailment holds in one direction, though not in the other, between condition (3) and each of the other two conditions – for any given specification of an M-array. *Normally* or *generally*, when condition (3) is satisfied for a given M-array specification, condition (2) is satisfied as well. To put it colloquially, we normally believe, for example, our own eyes or, in general, what our senses seem to tell us. Again, when condition (3) is satisfied for a given M-array specification, condition (1) is normally satisfied as well. (The point indeed might be held to be implicit in the description of condition (3).) Colloquially, we are normally right in believing, for example, our own eyes. We may call this weaker relation than entailment that of *presumptive implication*; and write it as follows:

II   (3) ○→ (1)
III   (3) ○→ (2)

This relation by no means holds in the other direction. For there are countless true specifications or descriptions of the things we, for example, *see* – and countless such descriptions which we believe to be true – which do not, and perhaps could not, figure in any truthful account of, for example, how those things *look* to us. Examples would be the descriptions 'married five times', as applied to a man, or 'once shaken by the Queen', as applied to a hand. So we do not have: (1) ↬ (3); and we do not have: (2) ↬ (3).

The relations I have mentioned have certain further consequences. Thus from I and II there follows

IV   (3) ↬ appropriate M-facts.

If, for any M-array specification, it is normally the case that if (3) then (1), and if (1) entails appropriate M-facts, then it is normally the case that if (3), then appropriate M-facts.

To this we can add

V   (3) ↬ belief in appropriate M-facts.

V holds as a direct consequence of III alone. For, as I am using the expressions, we should not count anyone as believing that he was having a certain M-perception unless he believed that appropriate M-facts obtained.

There is something else we can add. We can say that the fact that relation II holds makes it *normally reasonable* to hold the belief referred to at III; and correspondingly the fact that relation IV holds makes it *normally reasonable* to hold the belief referred to at V. That is to say, we can read the ring-and-arrow of III and V in two ways: both as, originally, 'presumptively implies' and as 'presumptively makes reasonable'. One might express the point by saying that normally an M-experience carries a *belief-title* with it, a title to be taken to be the M-perception it seems to be; and consequently that it carries with it a title to belief in appropriate or corresponding M-facts. This is not to say, of course, that the title cannot be challenged; only that it *needs* to be; that there has to be some special reason for not taking the M-experience to be the M-perception it seems to be, for not taking it that appropriate M-facts obtain.

Now if one is having an M-experience and if corresponding M-facts obtain, does it follow that one is having the corresponding

M-perception? That is to say, does the following hold (for a given M-array specification):

(3) + appropriate M-facts → (1)?

For example, if it sensibly seems to one just as if one were seeing a book on a desk in front of one and if there is in front of one just such a book on just such a desk as it sensibly seems to one as if one were seeing, does it follow that one is seeing the book on the desk in front of one?

Professor Grice has argued convincingly, indeed conclusively, that it does not follow.[1] He makes, and illustrates, the point that it is logically possible that the M-perception-experience should have been produced by unusual methods – e.g. cortical stimulation, suggestion, an arrangement of mirrors and objects – methods which could have been used to produce the M-experience even if there had been no appropriate M-facts. He concludes that for an M-experience to be the M-perception it seems to be, it is necessary not only that the appropriate M-facts should obtain, but also that the M-experience should be causally dependent on those M-facts.

This is not to report him quite exactly. He draws in fact a more general conclusion of which that just reported is a consequence and to which I shall refer later. But let us for the moment consider the restricted conclusion. It would be generally agreed to be a logically necessary condition of an M-experience being the M-perception it seems to be, that appropriate M-facts should obtain. What we are now confronted with is the thought that it is also a logically necessary condition of the M-experience being the M-perception it seems to be, that the obtaining of the appropriate M-facts should be a causally, or non-logically, necessary condition of the occurrence of the M-experience.

Let us accept this conclusion – indeed I think we *have* to accept it – and inquire into its *rationale*, the way it fits into our general concept of perception.

Let us begin by noting another of those presumptive relations, weaker than entailment, which I have been setting out. There is absolutely no need to appeal to any specialist or scientific considerations in order to make the following point; viz. that our M-experience *normally* or *generally is* non-logically or causally dependent on appropriate M-facts. All we need to do to establish the point is to appeal to such familiar facts as this: that if it sensibly seems to one just as if one were seeing a pencil held before one's eyes, then not only is it normally the case that there is a pencil held before one's eyes, it is also normally the case that if the pencil is, say, taken away and held behind the holder's back, one will no longer seem to see it, i.e. no longer have the M-experience in question. It is beyond dispute that such a fact typifies the general or normal character of our perceptual experience. That I correctly count what subjectively happens as seeing a pencil held before my eyes depends in every case, logically, on there being a pencil held before my eyes; but that there subjectively happens that which I *normally* count (correctly or not) as seeing a pencil held before my eyes *normally* depends, non-logically or causally, on there being a pencil held before my eyes.

I have just said that such a fact typifies the general or normal character of our perceptual experience. Of course the thesis of the general or normal causal dependence of M-experiences on appropriate M-facts must be acknowledged to differ in certain respects from many theses of causal dependence. It is not established by noting correlations between independently observable states of affairs. For one cannot *observe* that M-facts appropriate to certain M-experiences obtain without there occurring just such experiences as are in question. Thereby, no doubt, hangs many a tale. But this difference is not such as to *weaken* the general thesis. It serves, rather, to explain why the general thesis is one of those truths which are so obvious that they are easy to overlook.

In addition, then, to the weak relations already noted, we have the following:

VI   (3) ∘→ the M-experience is causally dependent on appropriate M-facts.

Note that VI entails *a fortiori* the truth we have already numbered IV, i.e. (3) ∘→ appropriate M-facts.

But now what of the relations between proposition VI – the presumptive relation resting on the fact that M-experiences are normally causally dependent on appropriate M-facts – and the proposition we seem bound to accept, viz. that a particular M-experience is the M-perception it seems to be only if, besides appropriate M-facts obtaining, that particular M-experience is causally dependent on those M-facts? This proposition is not entailed by proposition VI, nor by the conjunction of proposition VI and proposition I, nor by any other combination of the already established relations. It has yet to be shown that there is a rational connection between these relations and the proposition we seem bound to accept. It can be shown, perhaps, as follows.

The association between M-experiences and appropriate M-facts, though normal, is not, of course, invariable. An M-experience may occur without appropriate M-facts obtaining. Then we may say that it is, in part or wholly, an *illusory* M-experience. Now if an M-experience occurs without appropriate M-facts obtaining, it follows, of course, at once, that the causes of that M-experience, whatever they may be, do not include the obtaining of appropriate M-facts. So we have to recognize the existence of a class of M-experiences of which the causes, whatever they are, do not include the obtaining of appropriate M-facts. Now if we take any M-experience of this class to be the M-perception it seems to be, we shall *normally* be *mistaken* in our belief in the appropriate M-facts; for since its causes do not include the obtaining of appropriate M-facts, it could be no more than a flukish coincidence or outsize piece of luck if, nevertheless, appropriate M-facts did happen to obtain. Of any M-experience which belongs to this class, we may say that it is an essentially *undependable* M-experience.

If an M-experience belongs to this class, then it belongs to this class even if, as a matter of fact, appropriate M-facts do happen to obtain. And here, surely, is the rationale of the proposition that an M-experience is the M-perception it seems to be only if it is causally dependent on appropriate M-facts. The rationale lies in the conjunction of the two facts: (1) that if an M-experience occurs for which the dependence-condition does not hold, and if the subject of the experience believes in the appropriate M-facts then he will normally be mistaken in that belief; and (2) that if he takes the M-experience to be the M-perception it seems to be, then he necessarily has that belief. So we would say in such a case that he is wrong in taking the M-experience to be the M-perception it seems to be even if, by a fluke, he happens to be right in his belief in the appropriate M-facts. The concept of perception is too closely linked to that of knowledge for us to tolerate the idea of someone's being in this way merely flukishly right in taking his M-experiences to be the M-*perception* that it seems to be. Only those M-experiences which are in a certain sense dependable are to count as the M-perceptions they seem to be; and dependability in this sense entails dependence, causal or non-logical dependence on appropriate M-facts.

It is obvious, however, that the foregoing only takes us, at best, a part of the way to understanding the place, in the notion of perception, of the notion of causal dependence of sensible experience on physical object perceived. For one thing, I have so far been exclusively concerned with cases in which M-experience, M-perception (if any) and relevant M-facts (if any) are all specified in the same or corresponding terms. So the account falls sadly short of generality. For obviously I may perceive an X without its sensibly seeming to me just as if I am perceiving an X.

The way in which Grice stated his original conclusion, unlike the way I stated it, does not suffer from this lack of generality. What I said (and sought to explain) was: it is a necessary condition of an M-experience being the M-perception it seems to be that the experience should be causally dependent on appropriate M-facts. What he said was: it is a necessary condition of one's perceiving a material object that one's sense-impressions should be causally dependent on some state of affairs involving that object. Just because of its lack of generality my statement may seem to offer the promise, within its limits, of a very safe and simple step from necessary to necessary-and-sufficient conditions. Grice's statement, on the other hand, just because of its generality, cries out for supplementary *restrictions* to turn it into a statement of sufficient as well as necessary conditions. For obviously our sense-impressions may be causally dependent on states of affairs involving many material objects which we are not currently perceiving, such as our brains and eyes, electricity-generating plant and so on.

Grice's suggestion is that we should proceed by imposing appropriate restrictions on the *ways* or *modes* in which objects contribute causally to the occurrence of sense-impressions. We should not, he says, derive these restrictions from our specialized knowledge of the causal mechanisms of perception; for 'if we are attempting to characterize the ordinary notion of perceiving, we should not explicitly introduce material of which someone who is perfectly capable of employing the ordinary notion may be ignorant'.[2] Both this self-denying ordinance and the reason given for it are obviously sound in themselves. We may put the point, however, a little differently. The aim is to characterize the place of causation in a naïve or non-specialist concept of perception. Consequently we should not draw on any knowledge of the causal conditions of perception except such as may be implicit in the concept of perception in general or in the non-specialist concepts of the different modes of perception.

Grice suggests that the kind of restriction required could be adequately indicated by the use of examples. Thus we might say that 'for an object to be perceived by X it is sufficient that it should be causally involved in the generation of some sense-impression had by X in the kind of way in which, for example, when I look at my hand in a good light, my hand is causally responsible for its looking to me as if there were a hand before me, or in which . . . (and so on), *whatever that kind of way may be*; and to be enlightened on that question one must have recourse to the specialist.'[3] To the example about the hand we are presumably to add other examples relating to other sensory modes of perception than the visual and, perhaps (though it is not quite clear whether this would be thought necessary), examples of artifically mediated perception as well. Clearly, however, we cannot be satisfied with this procedure unless we can at least state the general principles governing the selection of our examples. An unsympathetic critic might be inclined to say that it is impossible to state the general principle without revealing a circularity in the doctrine. For what qualifies the chosen example for a place in the list is nothing other than the fact that when someone is correctly described as looking at his hand in a good light, and having the impression, in part causally dependent on the presence of his hand, that he is seeing a hand before him, then he undoubtedly *is* seeing his hand. So the generalized statement of the doctrine comes to this: for an object to be perceived by X, it is sufficient that it should be causally involved in the generation of some sense-impression of X's in any one of the ways in which, *when X perceives an object*, that object is causally responsible for (or causally involved in the generation of) X's sense-impression. And this is unacceptably circular.

Perhaps this criticism is too unsympathetic. Reconsideration of Grice's chosen example suggests another way of exploiting the idea of imposing restrictions on modes of causal dependence. For his example is not simply an example of an undoubted M-perception. It is an example of a case in which M-experience, M-perception and M-facts are specified in the same terms. It is an example of an M-experience which is the M-perception it seems to be. Perhaps we can make use of this feature to obtain a characterization both general and non-circular of the required restriction.

We prepare for the attempt by returning to my own limited statement of the causal condition. That statement ran: it is a necessary condition of an M-experience being the M-perception it seems to be that the experience should be causally dependent on corresponding M-facts. We may be tempted for a moment to rewrite this straight away as a statement of necessary and sufficient conditions, i.e. to say: it is a necessary and sufficient condition of an M-experience being the M-perception it seems to be that the experience should be causally dependent on appropriate M-facts.

Before we yield to the temptation, however, we should reflect on the case of the capricious philosophical experimenter who, perhaps with a view to illustrating Grice's original point, deliberately contrives, by unusual means, to produce in his subject an M-experience which accords with the M-facts. Why should this make us pause? Isn't the point that the means he uses are such as would produce the M-experience even if the M-facts did not obtain? Yes; but notice that it is part of the description of the situation that the experimenter would not have produced that M-experience had those M-facts not obtained. So there is, after all, a kind of causal dependence of M-experience on M-facts. So the experimenter has not, after all, illustrated his point. But perhaps he has illustrated another point: viz. that causal dependence of M-experience on corresponding M-facts is not in general *sufficient* for M-perception.

Can we deal with the case by writing a negative provision into our limited statement of necessary and sufficient conditions? Well, we can try. We can rule the case out by declaring that causal dependence which runs through the will of a capricious intervener is not to count. Notice the qualification 'capricious'. It does not seem to be the fact that causal dependence runs through the will which makes it necessary (if it is necessary) to rule the case out; but rather the fact that the will is a capricious will. Suppose we imagine a non-capricious contriver, devoted and reliable, whose aim, perhaps, is to make up for the deficiencies of a percipient's perceptual experience, say his blindness. Let his technique be suggestion or cortical stimulation or what you will, only so long as he regularly produces no M-experiences but such as would normally occur in a percipient in his subject's environment. Do we have to imagine him replaced by a *machine*, as we might, in order to say that the percipient *sees* – with artificial aids? Is not one trusty medium as good as another, if it is equally trusty? In some philosophies, when dualism has got out of control, God is invoked as the trusty contriver of M-experiences in general; though, to be sure, this is a sign that dualism has got out of control.

Well, then, let us write a negative provision regarding the capricious will into our limited statement of necessary and sufficient conditions; and proceed. To do so, of course, is to leave a flank exposed; for if one such negative provision is necessary, might not others be necessary too? But we will worry about that later. For the moment we have a limited formula which, apart from the one negative provision, makes no reference to modes of causal dependence. But we have not achieved generality. Perhaps we can now achieve generality by introducing a reference to modes of causal dependence in the following way: (1) introduce the concept of the entire class of ways, or kinds of way, in which – the excluded case apart – M-experiences are causally dependent on appropriate (or corresponding) M-facts, when they are so dependent; and then

(2) declare that it is a necessary and sufficient condition of any sensible experience being a perception of a material object that it is causally dependent on facts involving that material object in one of these ways or kinds of way.

I think there may well be more than one kind of objection to this suggestion. Remember our aim: it is to determine how the general notion of causal dependence of sensible experience on facts about material objects perceived fits into, or finds a place in, the naïve concept of perception of material objects. The kind of objection I want briefly to develop turns on the thought that even the general and unspecific reference to *modes* of causal dependence contained in the two-part formula is, given this aim, unnecessary; and if it is unnecessary, it is obfuscating. What clearly is necessary is that we should somehow move towards generality, away from the limited case where M-experience and M-array or M-facts are specified in the same or corresponding terms. But what, we may ask, underlies the possibility of specifying them in *different* terms, as we can in so many cases of perception? What are the sources of possible difference or discrepancy, in cases of actual perception, between the specification of what it sensibly seems to one just as if one were perceiving and possible, correct specifications of what one *is* perceiving? There are, it seems, two general cases: I shall call them respectively the case of 'excess description' and the case of 'corrected description'.

The possibility of the first kind of case is obvious from the fact that M-experiences which are indeed the M-perceptions they seem to be are never *merely* the M-perceptions they seem to be. It sensibly seems to me as if I see a man; and I do see a man. He is a postman, perhaps, or a Prime Minister. So I see a postman (or a Prime Minister), even though my M-experience could not, we are to suppose, be truly characterized by saying that it sensibly seems to me just as if I see a postman (or a Prime Minister). It sensibly seems to me just as if I see a white object on the side of a hill. I do see such an object. It is a car. So I see a car on the side of the hill, even though my M-experience could not be characterized in these terms.

Is any reference to modes of causal dependence of sensible experience on states of affairs involving objects necessary to account for this kind of difference between sensible-experience-specification and perception-specification? Obviously none is. What makes the 'excess descriptions' correct statements of what is perceived is simply that they contain fuller identifications or further characterizations of the very objects or arrays referred to in that description of what one perceives which would follow from the fact that one's M-experience is *at least* the M-perception it seems to be.

What of the other general case, the case of the corrected description: the case in which the specification of the M-*experience* would include features or detail which would not figure in any correct specification of the M-*perception*; or, to put it differently, the case in which, if we believed our M-experience was at least the M-perception it seemed to be, we would be (at least in part) mistaken?

Let us think of any corrected description of what we perceive, considered in relation to the uncorrected description, as consisting of two constituents: a constituent which it has in common with the uncorrected description and a constituent which is incompatible with the uncorrected description. If it sensibly seems to me as if I perceive a blue cube before me (the uncorrected description) when I actually perceive a black cube before me (the corrected description), the common constituent of the corrected description is 'cube before me' and the incompatible constituent is the qualification 'black'. If we can take care of the common constituent, the incompatible constituent can be left to take care of itself; or, rather, can be regarded as already taken care of by the previous account of excess descriptions.

But we already have the means of taking care of the common constituent. We can see this as soon as we relate the case to our existing formula. Any relatively full or specific description of an M-experience entails or includes less full or more general descriptions of the same M-experience. If it is true that it sensibly seems to me just as if I perceive a blue cube before me, then it is also true that it sensibly seems to me just as if I see a cube before me. So we arrive at the following quite general statement or formula: any M-experience is *the most specific* M-perception it seems to be for which there obtain appropriate M-facts upon which the M-experience is causally or non-logically dependent. The basic specification of material objects or arrays perceived follows from this specification of those M-facts. A fuller specification of those objects or arrays can be obtained in the way already indicated, by adding excess descriptions *au plaisir*. In all this there is no mention at all of kinds or modes of causal dependence of M-experience on states of affairs involving material objects perceived.

This formula seems to work reasonably well for cases of M-experiences which are in fact M-perceptions of some kind. Where an M-experience description requires *correction* to yield the corresponding M-perception description, the rule for correction works, as it were, automatically, with little risk of admitting inadmissible candidates for the role of object perceived. Still, little risk is not the same as no risk. Moreover, an obvious difficulty seems to arise in the case of M-experiences which are not M-perceptions at all, i.e. in the case of totally hallucinatory M-experiences. For any such experience is, doubtless, causally dependent on some state of the subject's brain. And of any such experience it is necessarily true that a description at the limit of non-specificity can be given, viz. the description: it sensibly seems to the subject just as if he is perceiving some material object. So shall we not, in default of any other candidate for the role of object perceived, be forced by the formula to say that the subject is perceiving his own brain? As we shall see in a moment, the formula as it stands may allow, or seem to allow, for other candidates as well. But, by hypothesis, no candidates at all are admissible; for the M-experiences in question are not M-perceptions of any kind.

It might be hoped that this difficulty could be met by requiring some degree of sensible coincidence between an M-experience description and an M-array description as a condition of counting the M-experience described as a perception of the M-array described or of any object mentioned in describing that array. It might be said: M-experiences are perceptions only of those, among the material bodies upon which they non-logically depend, of which they are sensibly representative; and while 'sensible representativeness' is certainly a matter of degree, the bare mention of 'some material body' in the description of an M-experience on the one hand, and of some objective state of affairs on the other, is insufficient to get us across the threshold of this concept.

The suggested requirement, however, at least on its most natural interpretation, is inadequate to its purpose. We need not pause to wonder where exactly the threshold of the concept of sensible representativeness lies. For if it is low enough to admit the cases we must admit, it is far too low to exclude the cases we must exclude. The hallucinated man, asked to describe his experience, *might* give just such a description as one would give who, in good observational conditions, was actually perceiving a human brain suspended before him by an invisible thread.

The difficulty regarding hallucinatory experience may take another form. Kinglake reports that, travelling in the deserts of the Near East, he 'heard' the church bells of his native English village. His experience was surely causally dependent upon past pealings of those bells.[4] Suppose, for simplicity's sake, that a single such pealing were responsible for such an experience, and let the condition of sensible representativeness be as richly satisfied as you please. The case must still be excluded. So, too, if Hamlet, or such a one, 'sees' – what is invisible to the rest of the world – a solid-looking apparition of his father, dressed as he formerly appeared on a single occasion of his now ended life. The experience may be causally dependent on the earlier fleshly appearance, but does not count as a perception of that appearance.

Must we, to avoid these difficulties, fall back on some form of that suggestion which I considered earlier and rejected? Must we, after all, incorporate in our formulae some general, non-specifying reference to ways (to be revealed by natural science) in which objects are causally responsible for the generation of sense-impressions? One may reasonably jib at the suggestion. To bring in a wholly new type of consideration to deal with a tiny minority of peripheral cases is not only disappointingly inelegant, it is suspiciously so.

Let us return, then, to the formula lately arrived at and reconsider it in relation to the hallucinatory cases. The formula ran: any M-experience is the most specific M-perception it seems to be for which there obtain appropriate M-facts upon which the M-experience is causally or non-logically dependent. The formula seems to work reasonably well for those M-experiences which are in fact M-perceptions, and then to break down completely and obviously for those that are not. Let us expand the sense of the formula a little. The idea is that any M-experience description contains an M-array description and entails a series of less specific M-experience descriptions containing less specific M-array descriptions. We work through this series until we come to the most specific M-array description which fits some actual M-array upon which the M-experience causally depends. We then declare the M-experience to the M-perception of the items mentioned in the description of that M-array.

The expansion suggests that what we need, to deal with our cases of hallucination, is some restriction on what is to count as a 'fit' between M-experience descriptions and M-facts. The restriction will scarcely be felt as such so long as we are dealing only with M-experiences which are indeed M-perceptions of some kind; but it must be mentioned explicitly to deal with those that are not. The mention of sensible representativeness was an attempt to introduce the required kind of restriction, but an unsuccessful attempt. Though some restriction of this kind may be necessary, it is not sufficient; for, as we saw, an hallucination, dependent on some state of the subject's brain, could be as *of* a brain, or an hallucination dependent upon a past pealing of bells could be as *of* a peal of bells of just such a musical quality.

Implicit in the naïve concept of perception, however, are restrictions of a different kind. They relate, roughly speaking, to the temporal and spatial positioning, relative to the putative perceiver, of the items, events or situations mentioned in specifying the candidate M-facts. The naïve concept of perception – unaided perception, that is – includes that of a perspective or 'view', from a certain *point* of view determined by the position and orientation of the appropriate organs of sense, on contemporary or near-contemporary states of the world. From this flow all sorts of tautologies, suitably diversified for different sense-modalities, in which the causal and the logical are inseparably intertwined, and in which there figure essentially the concepts of (1) *range* and (2) *masking* or *obstruction*. Thus, as regards range, we have the tautology that, however large the visible thing, if removed far enough away, it will be *out of sight*; and the smaller it is, the nearer is far enough. However loud the report of the cannon, if it is far enough away, it will be *out of earshot*; and the louder it is, the farther is far enough. One's own arc of vision is (contingently) limited, but (necessarily) one can only see what is within one's arc of vision. As regards masking or obstruction, we have the general truth that the perception of an object by a given sense, even though the object is not out of range of that sense, can be *obstructed* or the object *masked* by another object. One cannot see the skin through the clothes, unless they are see-through clothes; one can feel the muscles beneath the skin and even through the jerkin, but not through the plate-armour; the orders of the commander are audible through the sizzling of the fuse, but not through the explosion of the cannon. A suitable tautology could be drafted for every such case, and for every sense: e.g. given two sounds, each separately such as to be within earshot from a given place at a given time, then if one is loud-and-near enough and the other soft-and-distant enough, the first will drown the second.

It seems clear that it is in the light of such restrictions as these that the unhallucinated and unsophisticated observer decides, and has no difficulty in deciding, that there just are no fact-fitting candidates for membership in the appropriate series of M-array descriptions generated by the experience-report of the hallucinated subject. The hallucinated subject may describe an experience as of seeing a brain, and the experience is doubtless causally dependent on, *inter alia*, a contemporary state of his own brain; but he can't be seeing his brain, for his brain is not within his arc of vision and is masked by his cranium even from those within whose arc of vision it is. Hamlet, as his mother remarks, bends his corporeal eye on vacancy, hence on nothing, hence on no M-array at all. The past pealing of bells is disqualified by remoteness both in time and in space from supplying appropriate M-facts, though it supplies M-facts on which the experience causally depends.

Of course these requirements or restrictions are modified in various ways; but not in such ways as to displace them from the basic position they hold in the concept of sense-perception. Thus we recognize artificial means of reducing the limitations of unaided perception, of increasing, so to say, the range, refinement and pene-tration of our organs of perception. Or again, we allow perception of 'reproductions' to count as perception of originals: I *can* be said to perceive, indirectly, my own brain or the past pealing of remote bells; for I can perceive directly, *under* the mentioned restrictions, such things as X-ray photographs or recordings which are them-selves sensibly representative of those originals and causally deriva-tive from them in just this respect of sensible representativeness. But any notion of perception which is thus *aided* or *indirect* or both is clearly derivative from, or dependent on, the concept of direct or unaided perception.

Do these considerations solve the problem posed for our formula by the case of the totally hallucinatory experience? I think it might be said that while the relevance of these considerations is unchal-lengeable, the mode of presenting them is not. Challenge might come from two opposite directions. First, it might be said that there has been a surreptitious or unacknowledged reintroduction of the notion of the *ways* in which an M-experience may be causally dependent on states of affairs involving any material object of which it can be held to be a perception. The point of this criticism would be not that it was wrong to reintroduce that notion, but that it was wrong to disguise or conceal its reintroduction. Second, it might be said that I have represented the relevant restrictions regarding relation to the putative perceiver etc. as outside the scope of the concept of sensible representativeness; but they really fall within it.

Evidently, if either of these criticisms has weight, it weighs against the other. As regards the second, I shall say simply this: if anyone cares to reinterpret the notion of sensible representa-tiveness in such a way as to include the relational restrictions in question, he has my consent. What of the first and countervailing criticism, which, from the point of view of the present argument, is the only one which constitutes an objection? *Has* the notion of modes of causal dependence been reintroduced?

In our ordinary references to the limitations I have mentioned, we say such things as these: that a certain thing is too far away for us to make it out, or that it is too small to be detected at this distance, or that we are too short-sighted, or that the intervening mist is too thick. Here, certainly, we speak of causal conditions of the possibility or impossibility of perception of such a thing. But it does not seem that there is any concealed, implicit reference, however unspecific, to modes or mechanisms of causal dependence such as natural science may ultimately make us acquainted with. *Perhaps* the point is a fine one, *perhaps* not ultimately settleable; for what, after all, is meant by 'a *way*' in which one thing is causally responsible for another? But, for my own part, I should be inclined to maintain a distinction between two things: (1) a specific concept, intrinsic to the naïve concept of perception from a-point-of-view, of the causal *conditions* under which a thing is accessible to perception, namely, that of being within unobstructed range of the relevant organ; and (2) the general idea of causal *ways or means* whereby a material object is causally responsible for producing the experience of perceiving it. It is clear that we have to refer to the former in discharging the task we set ourselves. It is not clear that we have to refer to the latter; and *if* we do, we refer to it only as a dependant of the previous concept and not as an independent factor.

However, the game is not over yet. Long ago I left a flank exposed. There was the case of the capricious will, the intervener who produced in his subject an M-experience which the informed judge would declare to be no M-perception at all, even though both the general condition of causal dependence was, in a way, satisfied and the conditions of accessibility which I have just been describing were satisfied as well. We noted that it was the capriciousness of the will which bothered the informed judge, who might be willing to speak of a form of artificially mediated perception so long as the arrangements, whatever they were, were dependable. But, capricious wills apart, might there not be other similar cases which the unsophisticated judge would take to be cases of perception but which the informed judge would declare was no such thing, would classify rather with Kinglake's hallucination? Surely this might be so if, owing to some complicated and fortuitous combination of physical circumstances, including perhaps some temporary quirk of neuro-physiological functioning, the causal route from M-fact to M-experience were sufficiently bizarre. I forbear to describe cases: the philosophical imagination will be ready enough to supply them. Their common point will be to demonstrate that reference to kinds of causal mechanism is, after all, necessary; for what will rule out the imagined cases from counting as cases of perception is the fact that the causal route is the wrong kind of route, that the causal dependence is not in an acceptable mode.

But we must distinguish. We must distinguish between the naïve or unsophisticated concept of perception and the modifications and refinements that the concept undergoes as knowledge increases and technology advances. The acquisition and progressive increase of knowledge of the normal natural mechanisms of perception, and of the technical possibilities of supplementing them, may well lead us to set up standards in the light of which we would disqualify some imaginable causal routes as too freakish or irregular, or too little amenable to control or exploitation, to qualify as perceptual routes. I do not deny that the enriched or modified concept which permits us to imagine such routes and to make such discriminations is superior to the naïve concept which is blank on the subject. I only say that they are different, that one concept is a development from the other. The development is natural enough, of course, as soon as we ask the question 'How?' And that question is natural enough once an inquiring mind applies itself to our primitive concept of the causal conditions of perception. But there is room for an adequate working concept of perception and its modes in heads which that question has never even entered; and the existence of such a concept is a precondition of that question entering any head at all.

It might now be said: if the concept of perception we are concerned with has this degree of innocence, is it even right to find implicit in it the general idea that causal dependence of M-experience on facts involving the object perceived is a necessary condition of the experience counting as a perception of the object? I think so: for various reasons. Here is one, which should suffice. It would require little enough calculation for that rugged soldier, Macbeth, who rightly identified his M-experience as a false creation proceeding from the heat-oppressed brain, to appreciate that the additional fact of an actual dagger there which made no difference, would make no difference; or for his wife's nurse to appreciate that she couldn't cure Lady Macbeth's delusion ('Here's the smell of the blood still') simply by spreading some actual blood on her hands.

The position I have defended receives, perhaps, some reinforcement from consideration of another, quite different, minor difficulty. There are cases, it might be said, in which the subject undoubtedly is perceiving a material object, but his sensible experience is not properly described as an M-experience at all. Thus it might be the case that a subject's sensible experience was most aptly described by saying that it sensibly seemed to him just as if he was perceiving a deep black shadow when he was in fact perceiving a piece of black cloth which looked like a shadow. The case is perhaps a little dubious, but let us admit it. Then let us point out that a shadow, though not a material object, is a public phenomenal object; and so belongs, together with perceptible material objects, to the wider class of public perceptual objects. Then cases of this kind, together with their perhaps more frequent converses (in which it sensibly seems to one who is in fact perceiving a phenomenal object as if he were perceiving a material object), can readily be accommodated in a widened formula in which the notion of a material object is replaced by that of public perceptual object, comprehending the material and the merely phenomenal alike. Thus throughout our formulae we may replace 'M-experience', 'M-array', 'M-perception' etc. by 'P-experience', 'P-array', 'P-perception' etc., where 'P' stands for 'public perceptual object' just as 'M' stands for 'material object'. Apart from cases in which the material appears as phenomenal or the phenomenal as material, there is a clear gain in generality here, particularly as regards the sense of hearing; for we often find it more natural to speak of hearing, say, a whistle or a roar rather than of hearing something or somebody whistling or roaring. Indeed I partially anticipated this extension in speaking earlier of the conditions of audibility of sounds.

Our wider formula, like our narrower formula, requires the existence of the object perceived, phenomenal or material, to be a non-logically necessary condition of any experience which can correctly be described as a perception of it. The lately mentioned restrictions regarding range and masking apply, *mutatis mutandis*, to phenomenal as to material candidates for the role of object perceived. For sounds can be drowned by other sounds, shadows masked by the objects which cast them, etc. But there is minimal temptation, in the case of phenomenal objects, to regard mention of these restrictions as containing a covert reference to ways or means whereby such an object is causally responsible for producing the experience of perceiving it. It will be said that this is simply because one cannot sensibly ask the question, by what means sounds, for example, produce the experience of hearing them; for sounds are nothing but *audibilia*; and, in general, this form of question has no application to merely phenomenal, as opposed to material, objects. We may grant the point; but should note that it leaves untouched, if it does not emphasize, another point: the perfectly general point that reference to conditions, relating to range and masking, under which a perceptible object in general is accessible to perception from a certain position need not of itself import a covert reference to means, known or unknown, by which the object produces the experience of perceiving it.

NOTES

1   See 'The Causal Theory of Perception', *Proceedings of the Aristotelian Society*, supp. vol. XXXV, 1961.
2   Grice, op. cit., p. 143.
3   Grice, op. cit., pp. 143–4.
4   Kinglake's own diagnosis is worth quoting: 'I attributed the effect to the great heat of the sun, the perfect dryness of the clear air through which I moved, and the deep stillness of all around me. It seemed to me that these causes, by occasioning a great tension, and consequent susceptibility of the hearing organs, had rendered them liable to tingle under the passing touch of some mere memory.' (*Eothen*, London, 1908, Ch. XVII).

5

PERCEPTION AND
IDENTIFICATION[1]

1

Professor Hampshire recognizes a contrast between 'a non-committal description of something perceived on a particular occasion' and 'an identification of it as a thing of a certain kind'.[2] He calls it a necessary contrast. The non-committal descriptions are not thought of as merely whimsically non-committal. They are non-committal because the speaker cannot, for the moment, commit himself further with confidence. He wonders, but neither knows nor thinks he knows, just what it is that he is perceiving. The 'identifications', on the other hand, represent answers to his wonderings, or askings, about what it is that he is perceiving, what the phenomenon is of which he can for the time being give only a non-committal description. Hampshire mentions various features of non-committal descriptions in respect of which they are generally contrasted with identifications. Such descriptions 'must not imply that the thing referred to is a thing of a specific kind'; they carry no implications about the origin, causal properties, history, possible uses or criteria of identity of the thing referred to; they do not represent it as 'standing in specifiable relations to things of other specific kinds in the external world'; they are descriptions available to one for whom the object is 'so far wholly unidentified'; they are 'purely aesthetic' descriptions.

If I have understood Hampshire rightly, his main point is that we must not be seduced by the existence of situations in which a non-committal or purely aesthetic description is the best that can (for the moment) be done, into thinking that in every ordinary perceptual situation there is a clear and general distinction to be drawn between what, in our recognition of what we perceive, we owe to 'the evidence of our senses alone' and what we derive from other sources or from inference from such 'data of sense' or from both together. Hampshire does not think that any one clear, general and philosophically fundamental distinction which merits such a description can be drawn; and neither do I. So I shall not discuss this question further.

2

Instead, I shall discuss some difficulties I feel about Hampshire's class of non-committal descriptions. (I shall confine my remarks to what Hampshire says about 'perception'. I shall not discuss the paragraph in which he speaks of emotions, feelings and states of mind.) Is the class of non-committal descriptions a clearly defined and important class? What does it comprise? Remarks that Hampshire makes near the beginning of his paper suggest that it at least includes a certain sub-class of descriptive phrases, introduced by a demonstrative adjective, which can properly figure in a question of the form 'What is that so-and-so?', *addressed by one person to another*. The only example that he gives is a phrase of this kind, viz., 'that dark elongated shape over there'. (Later there appears the variant phrase, 'that oblong dark shape'.) So we are to imagine A asking B, 'What is that dark elongated shape over there?'

Now it seems to me that anyone who used this form of words in seriously addressing a question to another person would *ordinarily* be taken to be committed to the belief that the 'dark elongated shape' which he saw was at least something that could be seen also by anyone else with vision no worse than his own, standing near him and looking in the direction he indicated. I do not say that we could not describe a special situation in which the use of this form of words in a serious interrogation addressed to another would carry no such implication; though I think it would have to be a quite special one. It is enough for the moment to point out that one who used this form of words in this way would *normally* be taken as having thereby committed himself to this belief: the belief, roughly, that the phenomenon in question, whatever it might be, was at least a publicly visible phenomenon.

It will not do to say that the phrase 'dark elongated shape' does not *by itself* carry any such implication. When we are inquiring into the commitments that our words carry, we must consider the context and manner of their use. If I say 'I could see, in the harbour, the dark elongated shape of the submarine', I am normally committed to the claim that there was a (certain) submarine in the harbour and that I could see it.

Now I want to raise the following question. Is the kind of commitment which, as I say, would normally attend the addressing to another person of the question 'What is that dark elongated shape over there?' such as to exclude the description, so used, from Hampshire's class of non-committal descriptions or not? I will suppose, to begin with and for most of this paper, that the commitment is not such as to exclude the description from this class, that it does count as a member of the class. Now where do the limits of the class fall? Consider some more questions of the same form containing some fairly non-committal descriptions:

(1) What is that dreadful noise?
(2) What is this curious smell?
(3) What is this lump in the bed?
(4) What is that long, low grey expanse on the horizon?
(5) What is that red mark on your cheek?
(6) What is that gleam in the valley?
(7) What is that large object on the table wrapped up in tissue paper?

These questions resemble the original example in that one who asks them would normally be taken to be committed to the belief that the phenomenon which is the subject of his inquiry is something publicly perceptible. Do the descriptions which they contain possess the characteristics attributed by Hampshire to his special class of descriptions? That is,

(*a*) Do they imply that the thing referred to is of a specific kind?
(*b*) Do they carry implications about the origin or the causal properties or the history or the possible uses of the thing referred to?
(*c*) Do they imply (the possession by the speaker of) any criteria of identity for the thing referred to?
(*d*) Do they represent it as standing in specifiable relations to things of other specific kinds in the external world?
(*e*) Are they descriptions which could properly be used by one for whom the object referred to is so far wholly unidentified?
(*f*) Are they purely aesthetic descriptions?

Only if the answer to questions (*a*) to (*d*) is 'No', and to questions (*e*) and (*f*) is 'Yes' do they qualify as descriptions of the kind concerned. To begin with, I shall refer, mainly, to tests (*a*), (*b*) and (*c*); later, I shall have more to say about (*f*).

If we looked at test (*a*) alone, we might be puzzled as to how to apply it to our examples. In our examples we have, variously qualified, the nouns 'noise', 'smell', 'lump', 'expanse', 'mark', 'gleam' and 'object'. It is implied that the phenomena to which the first six nouns are applied are phenomena publicly perceptible (audible, visible, etc., as the case may be) and that the 'object' of the seventh example is 'material'. Are these nouns themselves, so understood, the names of 'specific kinds' of thing? Or do they, when qualified as they are qualified, become or imply such names? If 'dark elongated shape', understood as intended to designate a publicly perceptible phenomenon, does not imply that what it designates is a thing of any specific kind, then perhaps 'expanse' and 'gleam' and 'noise' and 'smell' do not either. Or is there a difference in this respect between 'noise' and 'smell' on the one hand and the sight-words on the other? Perhaps even a difference between 'gleam' on the one hand and 'expanse' or 'shape' on the other? Without further instructions, it is hard to tell. It is hard to tell, too, about 'mark on your cheek', 'lump in the bed', 'material object of a size to stand on a table'. They seem fairly specific descriptions; yet over 'specific kinds' one might hesitate.

I think that Hampshire might say that the uncertainty expressed in the preceding paragraph could arise only from a misunderstanding of test (*a*) and of his intentions in general. Consider again the original example of a non-committal description and the description contained in question (4). Rightly to apply test (*a*) to these descriptions is to ask whether they imply that *the thing referred to* in each case is a thing of a specific kind. We cannot decide this question simply by considering whether phrases like 'grey expanse' or 'elongated shape' can rightly be said to be names of a specific kind of thing. For the applicability of the description by no means guarantees that *the thing referred to* by means of it *is* an expanse or a shape, though it may *appear* as merely an expanse or a shape. *The thing referred to*, the thing the nature of which the question is designed to elicit, might in fact be a bank of cloud, an island or stretch of coast; or it might again be simply a special visual effect of bad light and atmospheric conditions. These are things of very different kinds, with different causal origins and properties and different criteria of identity. And these are also the sorts of alternatives which the questioner might be prepared for when he poses his question. But the description he uses, the best he can do by way of firm, non-speculative description, is non-committal as between these alternatives and perhaps others which he hasn't even thought of, but would acknowledge, when they are suggested, as not intended to be ruled out by his words. The description, then, does not imply that the thing referred to is a thing of any one of these widely different kinds which it may be of; it does not imply that the thing referred to has any one of these widely different kinds of origin or sets of causal properties or criteria of identity which it may have. So these descriptions pass at least these tests for being non-committal descriptions.

If I am right in thinking that the above remarks are faithful to Hampshire's intentions, then certain further questions arise.

3

It is plausible to say that *the thing referred to* by the descriptive phrase used in the visual example (4) is in fact, say, an island (or, it may be, a bank of cloud or a mere effect of light); that it simply *appears* to the questioner (before, and perhaps after, he knows what it is) *as* a long low grey expanse on the horizon; and that the best description he can give of the thing referred to, as it appears to him, is consistent with its being one of a number of widely different kinds of thing (this last fact being what makes his description of it a non-committal description in the sense intended). But if we now consider examples (1) and (2), the examples of sound and smell, the situation seems quite different. Questions (1) and (2) might elicit such answers as the following (I do not mean that *these* would be alternative possibilities in the same inquiry-situation): (1) 'Pile-driving machines in the next block'; 'The Salvation Army'; 'A freight-train going past'; (2) 'Burnt paint'; 'Size'; 'Cats'; 'The children have been experimenting'. It is obviously quite unplausible to say that *the thing referred to* by the questioner, by means of the descriptive phrase 'that dreadful noise' or 'this curious smell', is any of the things mentioned in such answers as these; that one of *these* things simply *appeared* to the questioner *as* no more than a dreadful noise or a curious smell; and that the best description he could give of whichever of *these* things it was was a description of *it* as a smell or a noise. We seem forced to say, in these cases, that the thing referred to *is* just a noise or a smell. This difference from the visual case is important. In the visual case we are not thus forced to say that the thing referred to is just a (publicly visible) expanse or just a (publicly visible) shape. On the contrary, as we have seen, there are various very widely different alternative possibilities, left open by the description, as to what the thing referred to might be; and there are correspondingly very widely different alternative possibilities, left open by the description, as to the causal origin, properties and criteria of identity of the thing referred to. This is not to say that *no* alternatives as to the kind of thing it is that is referred to, and as to the causal origin of the thing, are left open by the description of the thing referred to as 'a dreadful noise', or by any similar description. It is evidently part of the purpose of such an inquiry as 'What is that dreadful noise?' to elicit some information about the source or causal origin of the sound or noise; and since we classify sounds in various ways and one of the ways we have of classifying them is by reference to their sources, an answer that specifies a source may also thereby specify a kind of sound. But the *range* of alternative accounts of the causal origin of the thing referred to is, one might say, circumscribed by the general theory of the generation of sound; and the *range* of alternative accounts of the kind of thing it is that is referred to is circumscribed, at least, by the requirement that it should, after all, be a sound. And both these limitations are given, or implied, in the original description of the thing referred to.

The situation is not dissimilar, though it is perhaps more complicated, with regard to criteria of identity. The criteria of identity of a cloud, an island, an effect of light, any of which *the thing referred to* in the visual case might plausibly be said to turn out to have been, are at any rate widely discrepant, though scarcely, in the case of clouds or light-effects, very settled or well-defined; and if we are to say that the thing referred to is a thing of one of these kinds, then we must also say that the observer who can give no better description of it than that contained in our question can have no definite idea what the criteria of identity for the thing referred to in fact are. But where the thing referred to is, after all, a sound, we cannot say this. Admittedly our criteria of identity for particular sounds are various and fluctuating. We may choose, or not choose, on the strength of further information about sources of sound, to change our modes of reference to sounds in ways which seem to reflect the adoption of different principles of counting sounds as one or two, of distinguishing or identifying sounds. Thus when I learn that the dreadful noise is made by two pile-drivers on one site, one of which (A) operates in the morning and the other (B) in the afternoon, I may choose to distinguish between *two* noises and say that the noise made by B in the afternoons is not so loud as the noise made by A in the mornings. Or I may choose verbally to treat all pile-driving noise emanating from the site as one and the same non-continuous noise, and say that *it, the* noise, is less loud in the afternoons, when B is in operation, than it is in the mornings, when A is in operation. Or I may say both things. The verbal variation here seems to be merely verbal. In other cases such variations might have more significance, reflecting a certain practical discriminatory interest or the lack of it. But this fact of possible variation in counting and identifying principles for sounds has no force at all to show that one who makes a request for 'identification' in which the thing referred to is, and is referred to as, a sound, is so far unequipped with criteria of identity for the thing referred to. 'The sound has stopped', he says; and 'Now it has started again; now it is louder; now its pitch has changed.' We cannot dispute the implied claim to 'constancy of reference' simply on the ground that if he knew more, he might (or might not) choose to make discriminations (or identifications) that he does not at present make.

For all these reasons I am inclined to suppose that Hampshire would not count such descriptions as those contained in questions (1) and (2) as 'non-committal descriptions' in his sense. And now an hypothesis of some importance suggests itself. This is the hypothesis that, at least in those cases where the questioner is committed to the publicly perceptible status of the phenomenon described, *the only non-committal descriptions there are are those based on the sense of sight (or on 'visual experience'), those expressed in visual terms.* Though Hampshire's only example is of this kind, he does not himself mention any such restriction, but speaks throughout of 'the senses' in the plural and consistently uses the traditionally unrestricted word 'perception'. Yet surely if the class of non-committal descriptions (at least of phenomena taken to be publicly perceptible) is limited in this way, this is a fact of some importance, which should be mentioned.

Before embracing this hypothesis, we should surely refer to the important sense of touch. What sort of situation should we imagine? Perhaps that of somebody groping about in the dark, and asking such questions as, 'What is this rough-textured surface?', 'What is this hard object I've just knocked up against?', 'What is this sticky stuff I've got on my hands?' Obviously these questions permit of a considerable range of replies as to the kind of thing it is which the questioner has tactually encountered. Different replies might imply quite different consequences as to the origin and causal properties of the things referred to. They might even lead to revised applications of the notion of identity ('It isn't one thing, it's two', 'It's just another part of the same thing', 'It's blood on your left hand and paint on your right'). Yet I feel fairly confident that such descriptions as those given in the questions are not candidates for inclusion in Hampshire's class of non-committal descriptions. To refer to another of Hampshire's tests – test (*d*), which I have not so far invoked – it seems clear that anyone who asks such questions as those I listed is thereby committed to the belief that the thing referred to is in a specific relation (viz., spatial adjacency, or contact) with a thing of a specific kind, viz., a human body, viz., his own. And he is almost certainly in a position to specify the relations of the thing referred to to other things (e.g. a floor, different parts of his own body) more fully than this. But quite without reference to this particular test, it seems likely that a sufficient reason why such descriptions are not candidates for inclusion in Hampshire's class is simply that the range of possible identifications left open by such questions will not be wide enough to answer to his intentions. If a man bumps into something hard in the dark, and that is all he knows about it, it might be many different sorts of things he has bumped into – it might even be two things and not one – but the *range* of sorts is restricted in just the kind of way which, I think, Hampshire's tests are designed to rule out. I do not think I am here considering too narrow a range of examples. It seems hard indeed to think of any case in which a man, confident that he has encountered *something* tangible, and able to deploy with confidence *some* elements of the vocabulary of tactual encounter, has yet, for example, no idea at all as to whether the thing encountered is solid or liquid.

Perhaps we have now the general reason why, in cases where the questioner is committed to the public status of the phenomenon perceived, only (at most) those descriptions of the specified form which are expressed in visual terms, which are descriptions (we might say) of 'sights', will count as sufficiently non-committal for Hampshire's purposes. When the thing referred to by the questioner is described in terms which commit him to no more than its being a (publicly) visible object exhibiting (perhaps only temporarily) such-and-such a colour, shape or outline, the alternative possibilities which the description leaves open as to the kind of thing it is are perhaps widely enough different to satisfy the requirements which Hampshire appears to have in mind. Solid three-dimensional material objects; 'geographical' features; the surfaces of fluids; vaporous formations; visual phenomena such as rainbows, shadows, reflections; other visual effects for which we have no standard classificatory names; all these and perhaps other kinds of thing represent possibilities that may be left open by such a description. But when the thing referred to by the questioner is described in terms which commit him to its being a sound or a smell or a tangible object or stuff exhibiting such-and-such tactual qualities, then the range of possibilities left open by the description is not (I judge) wide enough to satisfy Hampshire's requirements. If we're committed to the thing referred to being a smell or a solid object, then we're committed (I judge) to too much. We might say, though this would be merely to name, not to elucidate, the difference – that 'visible object exhibiting such-and-such a shape and colour' has a breadth of *category*-spread, a categorial ambiguity, not possessed by 'sound' or 'smell' or by 'tangible object exhibiting such-and-such tactual properties'.[3]

Of course not all descriptions of the currently perceived which (i) are of the required form, (ii) are contained in, or used to supplement, requests for identification, (iii) leave, or might be said to leave, unspecified, what kind of thing it is that is referred to and (iv) are 'based on sight', will also possess the necessary breadth of category-spread. The descriptions contained in my questions (5) and (7) evidently do not. The range of possible identifications left open is not wide enough. A red mark on the cheek might be a scar or a birthmark or a smear of lipstick or blood or a carefully painted indication of rank. But an 'effect of light' on the cheek is not a red mark on the cheek.

4

Can this difference between sight on the one hand, and hearing, smell and touch on the other, be further elucidated?

Smells are too categorially homogeneous, and sounds are too categorially homogeneous, for descriptions of things of either class to count as non-committal descriptions in Hampshire's sense. Fluid and solid objects of touch exhibit a comparable excess of categorial homogeneity. *But the categorial homogeneities of smells and sounds stand in sharp and important contrast with the categorial homogeneity of the objects of touch.* Smells and sounds are too clearly *distinct* from the bodies which emit or cause them for categorial ambiguity to find a place in the relevant descriptions of smells or sounds; the objects of touch are too clearly *identical* with the fluid or solid bodies which they *are* for (enough) categorial ambiguity to find a place in the relevant descriptions of objects of touch.

Sight differs from touch on the one hand, and from hearing and smell on the other, in ways which secure the objects of sight from either kind of excess of categorial homogeneity. Let us consider first a difference from touch. If we were asked which among the objects of sight and touch were most like smells and sounds, I think we should be inclined to answer, for sight, that such things as rainbows, shadows, gleams, and beams of light were most like. Rainbows and shadows, smells and sounds, have physical causes; but neither rainbows and shadows, nor smells and sounds, are bodies; and rainbows and shadows may be insistent visible presences in their own right, as smells and sounds are insistent smellable and audible presences in their own right. But how should we answer for touch? Do the objects of touch include any which resemble smells and sounds in the way in which, among objects of sight, rainbows and shadows resemble smells and sounds? I think we should have to answer that there are no clear cases of such. The public objects of touch are necessarily fluid or solid bodies.

Rainbows and shadows have shape, colour, outline, pattern, definition. So have (some) physical bodies and their surfaces and parts. And colour, line, light, tone define for us, in sight, other publicly perceptible shapes and outlines which are neither the shapes and outlines of physical bodies or their parts, nor the shapes and outlines of such familiarly classified visual non-bodies as rainbows and shadows. So colour, line, light, tone *may* define for us, in sight, what *may* be the outlines of bodies and may not be; and if they are the outlines of bodies, *may* be the outlines of vaporous formations or solid objects or the containing boundaries of a fluid. With touch, it is different. It is true that on the strength of touch we may make judgments about shape and outline. But we shall do so only if we have done such things (or if it seems to us as if we have done such things) as enclosing an object in our hand, or making a tactual exploration of an outline or a surface or a part of a surface.[4] And if we have done (or seem to ourselves to have done) these things, confident that the object of touch is a public object, we cannot then be in doubt that the shape or outline as to which we are prepared to commit ourselves is in fact the shape or outline of a body or surface or a part of a surface of a body. There is nothing else for the shape or the outline to be.

So the public objects of sight, unlike those of touch, escape one kind of excess of categorial homogeneity; and do so without falling, as smells and sounds do, into the other. For when we have clearly identified what we hear or what we smell as, say, a train or a flower, we still cannot but distinguish the sound or the smell, as an insistent sensible presence in its own right, from the train or the flower that produces it. But when we have clearly made out, as a train or a flower, what we *see*, we do not generally find it natural to distinguish anything at all, except the train or the flower itself, as an insistent *visible* presence in *its* own right. For this contrast there are many reasons; but to discuss them now would draw out much longer a paper already in danger of becoming too long.

5

The preceding section bears on the doctrine of Hampshire's which I want next to discuss, viz., his apparent denial that one who gives a non-committal description has 'picked out' a 'phenomenal object'.

Let us continue for a while with the assumption that a speaker's commitment to the publicly perceptible status of the thing referred to does not exclude his description of it from the class of non-committal descriptions. Later I shall examine the consequences of abandoning this assumption.

I have argued that, where a speaker is so committed, a 'non-committal description' of a thing referred to can only be a description in visual terms; and have agreed that in such a case it would be perfectly correct to say that the speaker 'has not committed himself to any criterion of identity through change of that which he perceives', and indeed has no definite idea as to what the appropriate criterion of identity in fact is. It would be correct to say this because it would be correct to say that while the 'thing referred to' or 'that which he perceived' was, in fact, say, an island, the speaker was quite uncertain as to whether the thing perceived and referred to was an island or a bank of cloud or merely an effect of light. But Hampshire appears to draw certain further conclusions from this, which are not clearly correct. He says, or seems to say, that one who gives a description of this kind is not thereby committed to the existence of an object *of any kind whatever*. And he also seems to deny that one who gives a description of this kind has 'picked out' a 'phenomenal object'. I think the reasons he has for this denial are two: first, that one cannot properly be said to have 'picked out' something unless one has some criterion of identity for what one has picked out, and hence has reason for thinking with regard to what one is attending to at some moment that it is the same, or not the same, thing as what one 'picked out' at some previous moment; and, second, that the only thing, if anything, that one *could* relevantly be said to have 'picked out' in a situation of this kind is the same thing as 'the thing referred to' in one's inquiry as to the nature of that thing. I think his argument is that since, by hypothesis, one has no definite idea as to the criterion of identity for 'the thing referred to', then it follows, given the above two propositions, that there is nothing, and hence no 'peculiar kind of phenomenal object', that one can properly and relevantly be said to have 'picked out' in such a situation. And I think the argument for the view that the speaker is not committed to the existence of an object *of any kind whatever* must be somewhat similar. That is, it is assumed that the only object to the existence of which the speaker *could* be said to be committed is 'the thing referred to' in his inquiry as to the nature of that thing; but, by hypothesis, he is not committed to any views as to which of a number of kinds of thing that thing is; hence there is no kind of thing such that he is committed to the existence of a thing of that kind. Summarily, Hampshire's view seems to be that in this sort of situation the speaker succeeds in making a reference to something perceived, but it is a reference to something he knows not what; so there is no particular kind of thing he can be said either to have discriminated ('picked out') or to be committed to the existence of.

These arguments are surely not compelling. It is reasonable, indeed, to say that one has not sensibly discriminated, or distinguished, or 'picked out' something unless one has some reason for counting what one is attending to at some subsequent moment as the same, or not the same, thing as what one discriminated at an earlier moment. But this requirement is by no means sufficient to rule out the view that in situations of the kind concerned the speaker *does* discriminate or pick out a phenomenal (visual) object, which he can non-capriciously count as identical through change or interrupted appearance. Indeed, if he could not discriminate such an object, it is hard to see how the situation in question could arise, how he could make his inquiries at all. (And suppose he and his interlocutor are equally and finally baffled as to the nature of the thing described by the non-committal description. They might nevertheless perfectly well agree about the history of the *visual phenomenon* they both discriminated: 'The black shape swelled, lost definition, grew lighter in colour and finally vanished.') Moreover, if the speaker is committed (as we are still supposing) to the publicly perceptible status of what he sees, he is also likely to be able to claim *some* knowledge of the causal origin of the visual phenomenon he discriminates; and he certainly specifies, or indicates, something about its relations to other things. He is not likely to be in doubt that its causes involve, say, the action of light on physical things, and he at least specifies, or indicates, a time at which and a place from which it is discriminable, and a direction in which one must look to discriminate it. It is not clear that one who *identifies* a visual phenomenon as, say, a rainbow can necessarily say much more than this about *its* origin or specify much more fully *its* relation to other things.

Where arguments are not compelling, one may look for motives.

It is possible that Hampshire's desire to deny that the perceiver 'picks out' a phenomenal object in the case we are concerned with springs from his anxiety to deny a general thesis about other situations of visual perception, situations in which the observer is in no such doubt about the nature of what it is he sees. The thesis in question is the thesis that it is nevertheless the case in all such situations that the observer does discriminate purely visual phenomenal objects and that his identification of the various ordinary objects which he would claim he sees are based upon these prior discriminations. It seems certain that this general thesis is false. But in order to maintain the falsity of this thesis, it is by no means necessary to maintain that no visual phenomenal object is discriminated by the observer who is quite *un*able to identify 'what he sees' and can give nothing better than a 'non-committal description' of it.

Questions remain, however, tricky, if not profound. Let us elaborate the theory of the visual phenomenal object; notice how it suggests an alternative; and then consider whether or not we have to choose between them. If we reject Hampshire's arguments as non-compelling, it may look as if we are committed to a sharp distinction (in our chosen situations) between the visual object discriminated by the observer and the 'thing referred to' in his question, the object which he perceives and as to the nature of which he is quite uncertain. Suppose the object which he describes as 'a grey ambiguous shape' turns out to be an island. Are we to say that, in his state of uncertainty, he really referred to *two things*, both (knowingly) to a grey ambiguous shape and (unknowingly) to an island? And are we to say that, in his state of uncertainty, he actually saw two things, namely (knowingly) a grey ambiguous shape and (unknowingly) an island? This seems repellent. For his question seems to be about one thing, the thing he refers to and sees, and describes, *faute de mieux*, as a grey ambiguous shape. But we must consider whether it isn't the way of putting it that's repellent rather than the substance of what's said. Perhaps, to concentrate for the moment on 'seeing' and leave 'referring' on one side, we can make things sound better by saying: '*In* (knowingly) seeing a grey ambiguous shape, he was (unknowingly) seeing an island.' When the dimness lifts and the clear dawn breaks, he no longer sees at all the grey ambiguous shape (*it* cannot be seen, i.e. discriminated, unknowingly), but continues to see (knowingly) the island which he saw (unknowingly) before. 'What he saw' (before the breaking of the dawn) has, after all, a double reference; for what he saw after the breaking of the dawn both was, and was not, identical with what he saw before it. He did not see, after the breaking of the dawn, the ambiguous grey shape that he discriminated before the dawn; but he did continue to see, after the breaking of the dawn, the island that he saw (*as* nothing but an ambiguous grey shape) before the dawn. Both points display, or half-display, themselves in things we say. For we say: 'Where a moment ago there *had been* an ambiguous grey shape there now appeared, clear in the sunlight, an attractive-looking island'; and we also say, 'The ambiguous grey shape now *identified itself as* an attractive-looking island.'

What if, without any change in the conditions of vision or *in the way what he sees appears, or looks, to him*, he is *told* that what he sees is an island? In this case, too, he now knowingly sees what he before unknowingly saw, viz., an island; but though he knows, he does not yet see, that it is an island. Does he in this case also continue to see the ambiguous grey shape that he saw before? By hypothesis, yes. But he now knows, what he did not know before, that *in* seeing that, he is seeing an island. And because of this, his attitude towards what he sees is modified. He is ready, or prepared, to see as an island the island he sees. He is ready with a criterion of identity for 'what he sees' different from the provisional criteria he has so far employed.

We must remember that the key to the situation we are concerned with is the observer's desire for an identification of 'what he sees'. Though he gives only a 'purely aesthetic' description of 'what he sees', his *interest* in what he sees is not (or not in the same sense) purely aesthetic at all. His interest in the phenomenal object which he can discriminate is provisional. He is prepared at any moment to drop or extend the criteria of identity for 'what he sees' which he is provisionally working with, and embrace another set which, perhaps, as in our example, preserve the identity of what he sees far beyond the bounds which would be set by the provisional criteria. (But it may be that no change is called for. Suppose the phenomenon is identified as an 'effect of light'. Then it may be that his provisional and his final applications and withholdings of 'the same' are just the same.)

This direction of his interest *might* seem to require us to say that, whatever duplicity attaches to the reference of 'what he sees', none attaches to the reference of 'what he refers to'. Perhaps he discriminates, attends to and calls attention to, a purely visual (though public) phenomenal object; and certainly he uses the refer-ring expression 'that grey ambiguous shape'. But what he uses the expression to refer to is (it seems) simply the something he knows not what (and wants to know what) which is in fact an island. And an island is not a purely visual phenomenal object.

It *might* seem, on the other hand, that since the observer may implicitly claim 'constancy of reference' over a time to what he refers to; and since he does not know that the criterion of identity is for the 'something he knows not what' which he sees; his claims to constancy of reference must be based on his provisional criterion of identity i.e. his criterion of identity for the phenomenal object he discriminates; and therefore the reference of 'what he refers to' has the same duplicity as the reference as 'what he sees'. But this does not follow. For the observer may perfectly reasonably, even if mis-takenly, suppose, so long as he is seeing the same phenomenal object (e.g. what he is disposed to count as the same, perhaps chang-ing, shape), that the object-he-knows-not-what which he is seeing is also the same. He need not know just what the criterion of iden-tity for the object in question is, in order to suppose *this* much about its criterion of identity. And his supposing *this* much may show in a claim to constancy of reference to *that* object. So there is no need to suppose a duplicity of reference in 'what he refers to'.

But now cannot we argue back from this position to challenge the previously adopted position, viz., that he certainly does dis-criminate, see, possess some notion of identity for, a purely visual phenomenal object? Cannot we say: he sees no such object, but only the object, whatever it is, about the nature of which he is ignorant (unless, indeed, *this* object is in fact a purely visual phe-nomenal object, e.g. an effect of light)? The (philosophical) illusion that, whatever the status of the unidentified object, he in any case sees a purely visual phenomenal object arises from the fact that though he does not know what the object he sees is and hence has no complete or definite notion of its criterion of identity, yet he has *some*, incomplete and possibly mistaken, notion; enough of a notion for it to show in his claim of constancy of *reference* through the period of uncertainty, *and enough also* to account, by itself, and without invoking the 'discrimination of a phenomenal object', for his disposition to count 'what he *sees*' as the same even while he can give no better description of it than a 'grey shape'. ('Be it cloud or island or effect of light, what I *see* is surely, so far, the same.') So there is no need to suppose a duplicity of reference either in 'what he sees' or in 'what he refers to'.

If we adopt this position, *and reject the other*, we shall be closer to Hampshire in one respect. For we shall now be agreeing that the observer has not 'picked out' a purely visual phenomenal object (unless, as it happens, the object in question is a purely visual object). Where we spoke of two sets of criteria of identity for what is seen, one provisional (because for the phenomenal object) and the other final (because for the identified object), we shall now speak of one set, first in a highly provisional and incomplete state (for the object seen but as yet unidentified) and then in a complete and final state (for the object when identified). Where we shall still differ from Hampshire is in rejecting the view that the observer, in his state of uncertainty, is, so to speak, operating with no notion of identity at all and cannot be said to have picked out or discriminated anything at all. Instead we shall have to distinguish two possible cases; and say that in one case he has picked out, or discriminated, not a purely visual phenomenon, but a *visible object* which may be one of several kinds of thing (he does not yet know which), but which he is nevertheless prepared, and rightly prepared, to count as the same from moment to moment; and in the other case that he thinks he has done just this, but in fact has either confounded two or more visible objects or is mistaken in thinking there is anything there 'to be seen' at all.

Now it may seem that we should ask which of these two positions is right: the position according to which the perceiver has in any case discriminated a purely visual phenomenal object, or the position according to which his taking the visible object he sees, whatever it is, to be the same from moment to moment, is explained without reference to a purely visual phenomenal object. But it is not clear that the two positions exclude each other. The adoption of the second makes possible, but does not necessitate, the rejection of the first. The adoption of the first permits, but does not require, the addition of the second. We have two explanations of the observer's preparedness to count what he sees, in his state of uncertainty, as one and the same from moment to moment; and one need not suppose that the thought that one is surely seeing the same thing (whatever it is) excludes the thought that one is, in any case, seeing the same grey shape.[5] Nor need one suppose that it is necessary to invoke both accounts in every case; but, given the multifariousness of the ways we think and speak, it would be wise to preserve the right to invoke each where it seems to fit.

6

I have so far considered only that possible sub-class of 'non-committal descriptions' in giving which the speaker is at least confident of the publicly perceptible status of what he perceives. That is to say, I have considered only cases in which the speaker's uncertainty does not extend to the point of his envisaging it as a serious possibility that what he perceives is such that no one but himself *could* perceive that very thing. It is not entirely clear whether Hampshire really intended to include cases of this kind in the scope of his discussion at all. It *is* clear, however, that he did not intend the scope of his discussion to be *limited* to cases of this kind. We must therefore consider situations in which the perceiver is not committed to the publicly perceptible status of what he perceives.

These cases may themselves be divided into two classes. First, there might be cases in which the perceiver, though uncertain quite what account to give of the phenomenon engaging his attention, is at least certain that it has *not* the status of a publicly perceptible phenomenon. One who employs such descriptions as 'spots before my eyes', 'a queer buzzing sound in my head' will generally feel this kind of certainty. It seems to me quite clear that whatever uncertainties as to classification may be felt by someone possessed of *this* kind of certainty, they will not be radical or wide-ranging enough for Hampshire to be willing to count his descriptions of the phenomenon in question as non-committal descriptions.

This leaves us with the cases in which the perceiver is genuinely *uncertain* as to the public or private status of what he perceives. Such a case, it seems, would be one in which the uncertain subject is genuinely uncertain as to whether, when what he sees is finally identified, it will turn out to be, or have been, e.g. a solid object or an effect of light or a shadow *on the one hand* or ... what? ... an 'hallucinatory image', perhaps, *on the other*. I must confess to a very strong suspicion that cases with just the characteristics required by Hampshire are at best exceedingly rare. It must be remembered that we are not discussing cases of perceptual mistake. Nor are we discussing such cases as those in which an hallucinated subject either believes or disbelieves in the reality of his hallucinations. An essential characteristic of the case we are discussing – or looking for – is radical *uncertainty* as to the status of what is perceived, as to whether, for the case of visual experience, there is or is not anything there 'outside one' to be seen. Hampshire, it is true, offers us the example of Macbeth; and one certainly does not want to say that Macbeth's speech is unintelligible, that one can form no coherent notion of what kind of experience such a soliloquy might express. Still, the interpretation of the example is not quite clear; and hence it is not quite clear, as we shall see, that it is really quite the kind of example that Hampshire needs. Let us look for others.

A possible example relating to 'visual experience' might be the following. An anxious sentry, watching for signs of movement in the dark, might say: 'Did (do) you see something moving over there; or is it only my imagination?' The assurance that it is only his imagination will scarcely count as an identification of 'what he perceives'. Nor will the confirming judgment that there is indeed something moving over there. And if he is assured that he saw a cow moving, this will not count as an identification of something *both* perceived *and* described by a description non-committal as to the public or private status of what is described. The sentry's question is the question whether he saw, or only fancied that he saw, something moving. He produces no description of 'something perceived' non-committal as between the two possibilities and equally applicable in either case.

But then there is the following possibility. A man submits to experiments in the course of which (*a*) sometimes he is shown coloured shapes on a screen, or other publicly perceptible objects and (*b*) sometimes the operation of his optic nerve is interrupted, but his brain is independently stimulated in such a way as to produce visual impressions similar to those which he has in case (*a*). He knows that this is the character of the experiment but does not know whether alternative (*a*) or alternative (*b*) is actualized on any given occasion, and is unable to tell from the character of the experience. On each occasion he is asked to describe 'what he sees'. Then, indeed, whatever form his descriptions take, they will be non-committal as between the public and the private status of 'what he sees'.

This last case might serve as a model for others; i.e. for any case in which a man *knows* that he is subject in certain circumstances to the strong impression that he is seeing something of such-and-such a kind when he is not, and has some reason to think that those circumstances currently obtain, but cannot be sure whether they do or not. But I doubt if any such case is of the kind that Hampshire intended.

Let me put the point provisionally as follows. A man may be quite confident[6] that he is seeing something publicly perceptible, but owing to bad light, impaired vision or other factors, may be unable to give a firm, non-speculative description of it except in terms of shape, colour, definition (clarity of outline) and of change in these (i.e. in 'purely aesthetic' terms). So far his description is non-committal in the manner of those visual descriptions previously considered (i.e. such a one as that discussed in the previous section). But this situation is in sharp contrast with the sort of case I have just described. In that sort of case a man might indeed be quite unsure as to whether he sees a publicly perceptible object or not; but his uncertainty on this point has *nothing to do* with inability to produce a description except in 'purely aesthetic' terms. Uncertainty as to whether he saw a publicly perceptible object or not would be quite incompatible with complete assurance that the object (if any) was a tiger; or that the object (if any) was a film of a tiger; or that the object (if any) was a cube of some translucent material; or that the object (if any) was a projected image of such a cube. It might *also* happen, in such a case, that the subject could give descriptions only in terms of shapes and colours; but this limitation would be *irrelevant* to the uncertainty as to 'whether there were coloured shapes there to be seen' or not.

Again, I suppose it might happen that what a man saw or seemed to see was so *extraordinary* that he did not know whether to 'believe his own eyes' or to conclude that he was 'seeing things'. Here, once more, would be radical uncertainty as to the status of what was seen. But it would be far from being a case of inability to produce descriptions in any but purely aesthetic terms.

To restate the point in a more general way. There *are* cases of uncertainty as to the nature of what one sees (including perhaps most or all cases of uncertainty as to whether what one sees is solid body, vaporous formation or effect of light) in which the nature of the uncertainty is *essentially connected* with the fact that one is able to give no firm[7] description of what one sees except in 'purely aesthetic' terms. There are *also,* as I have illustrated, cases of uncertainty as to whether what one sees is 'public' or 'private', 'outside one' or 'inside one'. But I think it is at least very rarely, and perhaps never, the case that uncertainty on *this* point is attributable to, or essentially connected with, the inability to give firm descriptions of what one sees except in 'purely aesthetic' terms. No doubt one could contrive an example in which both kinds of uncertainty were *found together*. But to contrive their coexistence is not to effect their logical linkage. I conclude that the visual field is not a fruitful one in which to search for examples of cases in which there is uncertainty as to the private or public status of what is perceived *and* in which precisely *this* uncertainty is reflected in the fact that the subject can give only 'purely aesthetic' or (in Hampshire's sense) 'non-committal' descriptions of what he perceives.

Does the search for such examples fare better in other fields? A man might suffer intermittently from a buzzing or roaring or ringing in his ears and be sometimes uncertain whether a buzzing or ringing that he heard was, or was not, merely 'in his head'. If, in this state of uncertainty, he asks himself 'What is this buzzing noise?' does the description 'this buzzing noise' count as a non-committal description in Hampshire's sense? Let us remind ourselves first of the sort of case, already considered, in which a speaker confidently addresses to another person the question, 'What is *that* buzzing noise?' Though his description might fairly be said to be 'purely aesthetic', it seemed that the fact that what he was referring to was plainly identified as, at least, a noise, was sufficient to rule this description out from the class of non-committal descriptions. In the case we are now considering, the subject's uncertainty is of a different order, since he is now uncertain whether or not there is any external source at all of the sound he hears. Yet if Hampshire were to agree that '*that* buzzing noise' in the confidently other-addressed question is *not* a non-committal description and also affirm that '*this* buzzing noise' in the self-addressed question *is* a non-committal description, it seems that the classification of descriptions here (i.e. in the case of sounds) would reflect *nothing but* the difference between the case where a man is uncertain whether a sound he hears is, or is not, merely 'in his head', and the case where he does not suffer from this uncertainty. I find it hard to believe that Hampshire intended his classification to mark, in the case of sounds, simply *this* distinction.

Cases of uncertainty as to whether one is in contact with something, or it merely feels as if one is or might be, no doubt also occur. But it seems that either they are of the general kind typified, for the case of sight, by the example of the man who submits to the experiment; or they shade off in the direction of those ambiguous sensations like (some) tickles, which might be caused by something's tickling one's leg or might be merely a tickle in the leg. It seems too obvious for argument that neither sort of case supplies satisfactory candidates for Hampshire's class of non-committal descriptions of something perceived.

7

Near the beginning of his paper Hampshire speaks of the 'necessity' of the contrast between 'non-committal descriptions' and 'identifications' of things perceived. I have argued that the class of cases which possess, to any reasonably satisfactory degree, just the features which Hampshire intends by *his* use of the expression 'non-committal description of something perceived' is a relatively restricted class. Descriptions in visual terms, which mention such things as colour, shape and outline are not, as he implies, just typical members of this class. They are the only members of it. The necessity of recourse to such descriptions is held to arise from a certain kind of uncertainty, a kind of uncertainty essentially connected with the inability to give firm descriptions other than those. But it appears that the sort of uncertainty which is essentially connected with this inability is narrower in its range than Hampshire suggests; for it seems that rarely, if ever, is uncertainty as to the public or private status of 'what is seen' conjoined in any but an accidental way with this limitation on the subject's power of firm description.

Towards the end of his paper Hampshire seems to acknowledge this restrictedness of scope; for he writes that we shall 'exceptionally' need to find a non-committal description of experience. Why at the beginning does he insist so strongly on the 'necessity' of his contrast? He may there have been thinking of a much broader topic. In the context of a *general* discussion of identification of things perceived, the notion of a description which is the best the inquirer can give but which stops short of the identificatory or classificatory needs of the situation (and might so far be said to be non-committal) is, of course, a notion of vastly wider scope. There are very many cases, and types of case, in which we find it necessary to raise questions about the classification and identification of things perceived; and in raising such questions we may find it necessary to give some description of the thing perceived about which we wish to raise the question. What counts as identification, what merely as description here will depend on the special needs of the situation. We have here, between description and identification, a contrast which is necessarily involved in, and assumes different forms in, many situations. But this is another, and a wider, subject.

NOTES

1   © 1961 by The Aristotelian Society.
2   Stuart Hampshire, 'Perception and Identification', *Proceedings of the Aristotelian Society*, supp. vol. XXXV, 1961.
3   It might be suggested that we could, after all, admit 'non-committal descriptions' based on the senses of hearing and smell, by making the *thing explicitly referred to* in the inquiry the *source* of the sound or smell rather than the sound or smell itself; e.g. 'What is it that is *making* that dreadful noise?', 'What is the *source* of this curious smell?' But it seems doubtful whether *these* descriptions would count, in the required sense, as descriptions of phenomena currently perceived; certain that *they* are not descriptions in purely aesthetic terms; and doubtful again whether questions containing *them* would admit a sufficiently wide range of alternatives.
4   I am indebted here to discussion with Mrs Jean Austin.
5   Though, of course, if one turned out wrong on the first point, one might (or might not) revise one's way of talking on the second. The situation with regard to criteria of identity of visual phenomenal objects might in this respect resemble the situation with regard to criteria of identity for sounds.
6   I must stress that I do not mean he must be *right* on this point. We are concerned, not with error, but with uncertainty.
7   Only 'no *firm* (non-speculative) description'. For of course a man in such a state of uncertainty might say: 'It *might be* an island . . . or an effect of light . . . or a cloud' or 'It is something like (faintly suggestive of, etc.) a so-and-so . . . or a such-and-such.' Perhaps such remarks could be counted as 'descriptions' of what he sees, though not as 'descriptions in purely aesthetic terms'.

6

CATEGORIES

RYLE'S INTRODUCTION OF THE TOPIC

The matter is introduced by Ryle in his 1938 article in a sufficiently striking way. It is, he says, a matter of some importance, 'for not only is it the case that category-propositions (namely, assertions that terms belong to certain categories or types) are always philosopher's propositions, but, I believe, the converse is also true. So we are in the dark about the nature of philosophical problems and methods if we are in the dark about types or categories.'[1] In *Philosophical Arguments* (1946) he seems, though less explicitly, committed to the same view. It appears again, robustly enough, in the Introduction to *The Concept of Mind* (1949): 'Philosophy is the replacement of category-habits by category-disciplines.'[2] It is echoed in his declaration, made in the first chapter of that work, that the 'official theory' he is bent on destroying is 'one big mistake . . . namely a category-mistake';[3] or, perhaps, a 'family' or 'batch' of category-mistakes.[4]

A few years later the note has changed. The idiom of sameness and difference of category 'can be helpful as a familiar mnemonic with some beneficial associations'. There is no 'exact professional way of using it'; but there is 'an inexact, amateurish way of using it' in which, though 'it gives the answers to none of our questions', it can nevertheless be made to arouse people to the questions in a properly brusque way.[5]

It looks as though Ryle came later to abandon, if he ever held, the view that there could be such a thing as a theory of categories – a clear and general explanation of the notions of sameness and difference of category and hence of the notions of category-confusion and category-mistake. Did he ever hold it? It is clear that there is one view he never held: the view, namely, that there is some definite short list of nameable categories, comparable with a traditional grammarian's list of word-classes or parts of speech. The following sentence from *Dilemmas*, with the substitution of 'category' for '*métier*', could be introduced without incongruity in any of his earlier treatments of the subject: 'The truth is that there are not just two or just ten different logical *métiers* open to the terms or concepts we employ in ordinary and technical discourse, there are indefinitely many such *métiers* and indefinitely many dimensions of these differences.'[6]

Still, to hold that there are indefinitely many differences of a certain sort is not the same thing as to hold that the general nature of that sort of difference must be indefinitely resistant to explanation. A hard-liner might indeed say that no one who holds the second view has a right to the first. Whatever the reply to this may be, if there is one, and whatever the state of Ryle's views on the question when he came to write *Dilemmas*, it seems reasonable to suppose that at the time of composition of the earlier works cited he did think that some general theoretical account could be given of the notions of category, of category-difference and category-mistake. It was not for the sake of elegant verbal variation that he declared philosophical problems to be category-problems and philosophical error to rest on category-confusion. He held, at least, that the notions of the category group could be connected, in an explanatory way, with certain other notions already available in the professional vocabulary.

The most striking of these connections were those between the logical types or categories of proposition-factors and the logical forms and powers (or 'liaisons') of propositions; where the 'logical

powers' of a proposition were explained as the set of facts about
what other propositions it followed from, was incompatible with,
and implied. The connections were declared to be very close indeed;
to amount, in fact, to identities. In *Categories* we find the following
passages:

> To know all about the logical form of a proposition and to know all about
> the logical types of its factors are to know one and the same thing.
>
> (p. 196)

> Now, any respect in which two propositions differ in form will be
> reflected in differences in their liaisons. So two propositions which are
> formally similar in all respects save that one factor in one is different in
> type from a partially corresponding factor in the other, will have
> liaisons which are correspondingly dissimilar. Indeed the liaisons do
> not merely *reflect* the formal properties of the proposition and, what
> this involves, those of all its factors. In a certain sense, they are the
> same thing. To know all about its liaisons is to know all about the
> formal structure of the proposition, and *vice versa*. . . .
>
> The operation of extracting the type of a factor cannot exclude
> the operation of revealing the liaisons of propositions embodying it. In
> essence they are one operation.
>
> (p. 205)

and in *Philosophical Arguments* the following:

> In fact the distinction between the logical types of ideas is identical with
> the discrimination between the logical forms of the propositions from
> which the ideas are abstractions. If one proposition has factors of dif-
> ferent types from those of another proposition, those propositions are
> of different logical forms and have different sorts of logical powers. The
> rules governing the conjunctions of propositions in valid arguments
> reflect the logical constitutions of their various abstractible factors and
> features. There are as many types of terms as there are forms of
> propositions, just as there are as many uphill as downhill slopes.[7]

It seems clear that Ryle cannot, in these passages, be using the expression 'logical form' as a formal logician uses it. Any two propositions exemplifying the schemata 'p or q' and 'p and q' are classically different in form; as are any two propositions exemplifying the schemata 'All F are G' and 'Some F are G'. But if we exclude the connectives and the quantifying adjectives themselves, there need be no difference between the types of the proposition-factors in one proposition of such a pair and the types of the proposition-factors in the other proposition of that pair; for they may be the very same factors. If we make no such exclusion, we have, certainly, the difference between 'or' and 'and' in the one case and 'all' and 'some' in the other. It may be questioned whether the notion of type or category has any application to such factors as these. But assuming an application for it – such as both texts seem to favour – then one might surely have expected that if any pair of non-synonymous expressions exhibit non-difference of type or category, 'or' and 'and' would be one such pair and 'all' and 'some' another.

There is a complementary reason, equally potent, for holding that 'logical form' must in these passages receive an interpretation enlarged beyond the formal logician's. Just as it appears to be false that differences of form of proposition (in the logician's sense of 'form') carry with them differences of type of proposition-factor, so it appears to be false that differences of type of proposition-factor carry with them differences of form of proposition (in this sense of 'form'). The mathematical proposition 'There exists just one number which is both even and prime' is of the same form as the theological proposition 'There exists just one person who is both human and divine'; but surely some of their factors exhibit category-difference if any factors do.

Ryle cannot mean by 'logical form' what a logician means by this phrase; for a logician, in exhibiting form, is concerned to abstract from *all* differences in subject-matter and hence all differences in type or category of subject-matter.

If we now seek help by invoking the remaining identity – the identity of the logical form of a proposition with the totality of its logical powers – we are in no better case. We are still obliged to say that 'or' and 'and' belong to different categories, if the notion applies to them; and we are now also obliged to say that '29' and '31' are expressions of different types, as are also 'red' and 'green', 'tall' and 'short', 'father' and 'mother', 'round' and 'square' and so on. For it is easy to construct pairs of propositions of which the factors are identical save that one member of one of these pairs of expressions replaces the other and which are also such that each member of a proposition-pair has different powers or liaisons from the other. But then, if their liaisons are different, their forms (in our new sense of 'form') are also different; and if their forms are different, there is a difference in the types of their proposition-factors; and this difference must be located in the only place where there is any difference at all.

It may be said that this is to press unsympathetically hard on the interpretation of the identities which appear to be announced in the quoted passages. It is not a matter of *all* differences in the liaisons of a pair of propositions implying a difference in their form and hence a difference in the types of their factors. Only certain *sorts* of differences in proposition-powers imply these further differences.

Certainly this is a more sympathetic interpretation, and we must adopt it. But in adopting it, we forfeit the expected benefit of the connections. We hoped for light on the relatively ill-understood notions of type or category of proposition-factor, to be cast by the relatively well-understood notions of the logical forms and powers of propositions. But if the explanatory application of these notions is to be understood as subject to certain enlargements and restrictions, our understanding of the problematic notion is no firmer than our grasp of these enlargements and restrictions. Just *what* sorts of differences in propositions' powers, we must ask, imply differences in their logical forms (in the relevant sense) and hence differences in the types of their factors?

Unfortunately no direct answer is offered to this question. And what indirect hints there are seem unconvincing, seem to point, even, in the wrong direction. In *Philosophical Arguments* it is repeatedly suggested that, since to mistake the logical type of a proposition-factor will be implicitly to credit propositions containing it with logical powers they do not possess, the working out of the consequences of the mistaken interpretation will eventually issue in contradiction; for (e.g.) the mistakenly attributed powers will be found to be irreconcilable with the genuinely possessed powers. Hence the instrument *par excellence* of the exposure of type-confusion is the *reductio ad absurdum* argument. But this thesis is not stated in such a way as to be easily assessed. It is not convincingly illustrated. And it leaves one with a strong sense of misdirection; for contradiction, in its clearest cases, seems to be a relation of terms, or of propositions in respect of terms, between which we are the least disposed to find differences of type or category. Finally, even if the thesis could be made out, it would leave us with the same question as before on our hands. For it is not maintained that all *reductio ad absurdum* arguments reveal type-confusions in their premises, that all contradictions emerge from category-mistakes. So we should still have to ask which are the ones that do, and why these and not the others.

However, there are different kinds of absurdity, and, hence, different kinds of reduction to absurdity. When Ryle speaks of the absurdities which result from violating category-restrictions, it is clear that he does not always have in mind that rather stiff and formal kind of absurdity which we find at, or just before, the terminus of a *reductio ad absurdum* argument. When he offers, in the most frequently quoted of all the sentences he has written on the topic, his criterion for difference of type or category of proposition-factors, it is again clear that it is not this kind of absurdity he has in mind. If it were, the criterion would yield immediately unacceptable results.[8] There must be a *distinctive* sort of absurdity which a sentence suffers from, when 'at least one ingredient expression in it is not of the right type to be coupled or to be coupled in that way with the other ingredient expression or expressions in it'.[9] In putting us on the track of this distinctive kind of absurdity – which he does by means of a host of vivid examples scattered throughout his writings – Ryle does more to point the way towards a general theory of the topic than he does by the over-general references to logical forms and powers. He points the way, but does not follow it. Instead, he ends his classical article on the subject with a question: 'What are the tests of absurdity?'

Something of the unresolved character of Ryle's treatment can, I think, be understood. Listening attentively to what he has said on the topic, one can detect, not just one theme, but two or even three. First there is a concern with philosophy in general; a sense that philosophical problems typically arise from limitations or imperfections – which may be recognized as such, or not recognized – in our reflective understanding of our own equipment of ideas or forms of thought; or, what is the same thing, from limitations or imperfections in our reflective understanding of the force, and modes of functioning, and mutual relations, of the items which make up our own equipment of linguistic expressions and constructions. In particular we may be prone to overlook differences, to assume or imagine non-existent parities. So it may be useful to multiply classifications, in the process of forestalling, or correcting, mistaken assimilations. And so we may come to speak of different *types* of expression in a sense of this phrase generous enough to harbour *any* classification which a philosopher finds it useful to employ or worthwhile to invent. When Ryle says, as in the sentence I began by quoting, that type-concerns are the philosopher's whole concern, it must be at least such a capacious sense of the phrase as this that he has in mind; as also when he shows himself prepared to speak of the logical type of connectives or quantifiers or token reflexive words. Even this generous conception of a type, however, seems not wholly adequate to cover the field of a philosopher's activity. The classical procedure of analysis, for instance – as applied to a concept like 'cause' or 'intention' – seems incompletely characterized by reference to such a conception. Here, then, is a motive for extending the notion of a type yet further, so that our knowledge of the type of a problematic concept embraces knowledge of the unobvious liaisons of propositions in which it figures. And this extension Ryle effects, as we have seen, through the mediating notion of form. But by now – indeed before now – the notion of a category or type has become over-extended.

The second theme, included in the first, yet emerges with a certain distinctness in *Dilemmas*, where Ryle is concerned with the apparent conflicts which may arise between different specialist accounts of the same thing or between a specialist and a non-specialist account. Propositions emerging from backgrounds thus diverse, yet concerned with what is in some sense the same subject-matter, may appear to have incompatible consequences regarding the nature of that subject-matter. But when they do, this is often because we have, in our thinking, allowed one or both of the apparently conflicting propositions, and the terms they contain, to become detached from the background of theoretical or practical concern from which they derive their life and their force. Concepts which do not clash during their working hours may generate imaginary conflicts as they idle through the speculative mind; and the discipline reimposed by the critical philosopher – who, indeed, may have to be prepared for certain reforming adjustments – is a species of category-discipline. Evidently this application of the notion of a category has some affinities with Wittgenstein's conception of a 'language-game' or of a 'form of life'. (I do not at all mean to suggest, what would clearly be false, that in *Dilemmas* Ryle is thus intentionally reinterpreting the notion of a category; only that we have here an aspect of his use of the term which comes most prominently to the fore in that work.)

There remains the third theme. It is not something quite separate from the other two, but, rather, something which can be extracted from them and which offers, as they, being so general and indeterminate, do not offer, at least the hope of systematic elucidation. We hear this theme whenever we are confronted with an example of a sentence which is absurd in the sense already alluded to, which resists literal, and sometimes invites figurative, interpretation, and which lends itself to a certain familiar style of elaborated disjunctive negation: as

> People are born and die and sometimes wear boots; *meanings are not born and do not die and they never wear boots – or go barefoot either.*[10]
> *Letters are not easy to spell nor insuperably hard to spell.*[11]

Here, and in all such examples, we have, stimulated in 'a properly brusque way', that sense of conceptual disparateness which is the sense of our topic, if we have a topic. But have we? Is the sense of a distinctive kind of absurdity to be trusted?

DOUBTS AND DIFFICULTIES; CLUES AND ENCOURAGEMENTS

The doubts go more, or less, deep. The deepest-going of all are the doubts – or, rather, the negative certainties – of those who find no irreducible difference properly described as the difference between propositions acceptable or rejectable 'in virtue of meaning alone' and propositions acceptable or rejectable in virtue of the constitution of things.[12] Why bother to distinguish categorial absurdity from, or as a special case of, analytic falsity, if the more general distinction which both notions presuppose is itself an illusion? Why distinguish vaporous illusions within a vaporous illusion?

These doubts I shall disregard. To put it with maximum concessiveness: we miss too much if we refuse to try to draw distinctions at one level of philosophical analysis because of a persuasion that viewed from another, sufficiently lofty, level, those differences will appear simply as differences of degree or will be in some other way, as it used to be said, 'transcended'.

To disregard these doubts is to allow ourselves the distinction between what is rejectable or acceptable 'in virtue of meaning alone' – or, as I shall say, what is *a priori* acceptable or rejectable – and what is not. Then the domestic difficulties begin; and they are difficulties of a familiar kind. The notions we seek to explain form an interconnected group: the notion of category-inappropriateness or category-absurdity, the notion of sameness or difference of type or category, and the notion of a categorial predicate. The difficulty is to explain any one of these without the explanation's resting on one of the others in the way in which Ryle's explanation of type-difference rests on the notion of category-absurdity. Consider, by way of illustration, the problem of distinguishing sentences which are *a priori* rejectable because they involve contradiction but no type-absurdity from those which are *a priori* rejectable because they involve a category-absurdity. Thus we wish to say that the sentence 'She is younger than her own daughter' cannot, taken literally, express a truth because it is, taken literally, self-contradictory; whereas the sentence 'The number 5 is more than twice as tall as the number 2' cannot, taken literally, express a truth, because numbers are not of the right type to have spatial dimensions predicated of them, because such predication is categorially absurd. Pressed for a further account of the difference which does not rest on a free invocation of the problematic notions, we may say that a contradiction is distinguishable from a category-absurdity by the fact that from it we can derive, by linguistically certifiable steps, a *formal* contradiction. But cannot we do the same in the case of the category-absurdity? Cannot we derive from it the consequence that there is something which (as being a number) does not have, and (as being taller than something else) does have, spatial dimensions? To this the reply might be that we can derive the formal contradiction in this case only by making use of a predicate ('having spatial dimensions') which, as being a *categorial* predicate, is not to be permitted in such test-derivations. What, then, is a categorial predicate? A traditional answer here is that it is a predicate which is *a priori* acceptable of some subjects and which is either *a priori* rejectable or *a priori* acceptable of any subject. But now we need some restrictive interpretation of this last phrase. For if I say 'What John is thinking of has spatial dimensions' or 'The first item mentioned on p. 22 of John's book has spatial dimensions', I do not say something *a priori* acceptable or *a priori* rejectable. And the question arises: can we impose the necessary restriction without once more invoking a notion of the problematic group?

If there are doubts and difficulties, there are also clues and encouragements. The grammarians, and linguistic theorists, are willing enough to distinguish classes of linguistically deviant sentences in terms of a technical apparatus worked out (not indeed fully, but at least partially) with quite other purposes in view than the protection of philosophical investments. The distinctions the philosopher wishes to draw between the grammatically irregular, the category-absurd and the merely contradictory are in a fair way to finding their counterparts in distinctions between kinds of rule-violation involved in the generation of sentences so classified.[13] Thus reinforced, the category-minded philosopher may feel in a position to serve the deep-going doubters from their own table. The latter accept a distinction between the true and the false, between sentences which stand up to the pressures of experience and those which do not. They question only whether any clear distinction can be drawn between those which collapse without, as it were, being touched and the other non-survivors (the 'empirically falsified'); and, *a fortiori*, question whether any clear distinctions can be drawn *within* the former class. Yet, if the undifferentiated notion of *falsity* is to be tolerable at all, it would seem that they must accept one further distinction; viz., that between a (declarative) sentence and a non-sentence, between strings of words which qualify for assessment as true or false and those which fail to fulfil some minimal grammatical requirement for such assessment. But then surely mere intuitions of minimum grammaticalness should be regarded with no less suspicion than those other linguistic intuitions which provide the basis for differentiation within the favoured, undifferentiated concept of falsity. It may be said: linguists can construct sets of rules which yield results conformable with intuitions of minimum grammaticalness. But the rejoinder to this we have already before us. It would be rash indeed to maintain that linguists cannot construct sets of rules which yield results conformable with the other intuitions in question.

Discouragement from (some) logicians, then, may be offset by encouragement from (some) linguists. And against the domestic difficulties we may set the strength, and the *form*, of the relevant intuitions. The form, especially; for this gives us a clue we badly need to the direction in which we should look. When category-points are made with that 'proper brusqueness' which Ryle commends, it is the inappropriateness of some range of *predicates* to some class of *subjects* that is normally stressed in the style of the making. 'Xs are not the sort of thing that can be Φ'; '*x*s neither Φ nor fail to Φ'; ' "Φing" (or "being Φ") cannot be significantly predicated of *x*s'. This is the brusque style of making category-points; and there is no such point that cannot be made in this style, even though category-mismatch may manifest itself in other *grammatical* relations, e.g. as between verb and adverb or noun and modifying adjective. If we can give a non-circular account of category-inappropriateness in predication, of category-mismatch as between subject and predicate, we may assume that the explanation of the other notions of the problematic group will present comparatively little difficulty.

A satisfactory philosophical account will have two aspects. First, it will fit our intuitions. It will distinguish the cases we want to distinguish from other cases. That is the technical problem. Second, it will have some explanatory force. It will give us some understanding of the distinctive character which category-points seem to have and of their place in philosophy. I do not think I can produce anything like complete solutions either to the technical or to the explanatory problem. I can at most sketch some lines of approach which may possibly lead in the right direction. This, at any rate, is what I shall try to do.

CATEGORY-MISMATCH AND CATEGORIAL PREDICATES

We attend, then, to singular subject-predicate propositions in which some single item is somehow specified by the subject-expression (a definite singular term) and somehow characterized by the predicate-expression. One favoured way of characterizing category-mismatch for these propositions is as follows. We have such a mismatch when the individual item specified by the subject-expression is of such a sort that both the affirmation and the denial of the predicate in question of that individual are *a priori* rejectable. Such a characterization raises questions. We must be careful that the expression 'of such a sort' does not conceal a reference to another notion of the group of notions to be explicated and hence import the kind of circularity we are to avoid. We must be prepared to take account of scepticism regarding the implied distinction between two styles of *a priori* rejection of an affirmative predication, viz., that in which the rejection is consistent with rejecting the denial as well as the affirmation of the predicate and that in which it amounts to just the same thing as the denial of the predicate.

Perhaps we can ultimately guard ourselves on both these points by attending to a prior question. To predicate having a certain colour of a number or having a certain temperature of an after-image would, one is inclined to say, be a clear case of category-mismatch if anything was. Yet if I say 'The item I have in mind is blue', what I say is not *a priori* rejectable in any style, even if the item I have in mind is a number; and if I say 'The green thing currently engaging my attention is at a temperature of 10°C', what I say is not *a priori* rejectable even though it is in fact a green after-image which is currently engaging my attention.[14] Clearly, then, the proposed characterization of category-mismatch is to be understood as relative to some restricted style of specification of individuals. Let us consider the suggestion that an individual is specified in the required style when it is specified by an 'adequately identifying' designation. I have now to explain this phrase.

A sufficient condition of a designation's being adequately identifying is that it *completely specifies* the individual it designates. Only those individuals of which the identity is completely determined by their *essential* properties (or character) can be 'completely specified', in the sense in which I am using this phrase; and any designation of such an individual completely specifies it when the *essential* properties (or character) of that individual are determinable *a priori* from the meaning of the designation. The following expressions satisfy this condition for being adequately identifying: 'the proposition that snow is white'; 'the number 5'; 'justice'; 'the colour blue'; 'the number which, when multiplied by 12, yields 36'.

There would be objections, both remote and immediate, to making it a necessary condition of a designation's being adequately identifying that it should be completely specifying. An immediate objection is that there can be no completely specifying designations of (empirical, or spatio-temporal) particulars. However, there are many general terms or descriptions under which particulars fall, and many others under which non-particular individuals fall, which embody in their meaning principles for distinguishing or picking out individuals which fall under them from other things, for counting or enumerating such individuals (though perhaps only under favourable circumstances) and for identifying such an individual encountered in one connection or referred to under one description as the same item as one encountered in another connection or referred to under another description. Thus for particulars we have such general terms as animal, person, island, storm, shipwreck, river, day and a host of others, more or less specific. For non-particular individuals we have such general terms as sentence, natural number, flag, sonnet, sonata, disease, game, word, and many others, more or less specific. (It is to be noted that some of these general terms under which non-particular individuals can be individuated are also terms under which particular individuals can be individuated.) Any specification of an individual item, whether a particular or a non-particular, which embodies or implies any such general characterization of that individual I shall say is adequately identifying. Thus the expression 'The natural number I have in mind' is an adequately identifying expression in the stipulated sense, and so is 'That number which is in fact the number of planetary satellites in the Milky Way', even though no one knows what that number is and the expression is not likely to have much use for the ordinary purposes of identifying reference. Of definite singular terms which include no general terms we may count ordinary proper names – e.g. 'Socrates', 'France' – as adequately identifying on the ground that they cannot be commonly understood by different users unless they are taken as implying a term of the kind just described; or, as some would say, their sense in use includes the sense of such a term.

The requirement that an adequately identifying designation, if not completely specifying, should embody or imply a general term of the kind I have just described is still too stringent. Let us call terms which clearly satisfy that description 'clearly individuating terms'. There are other terms which in one way or another fall short of being clearly individuating, yet are such that if a designation of an individual brings that individual under one of these terms, that designation is to count as adequately identifying. One relatively uninteresting case in which a term may fall short of being clearly individuating is the case in which the criteria of identity to be associated with the term are in dispute. Thus philosophers dispute about the criteria of identity for propositions and hence, perhaps, for facts. This does not mean that there are no such criteria; only that the criteria are, so to speak, adjustable, depending on the purposes for which we wish to use the notion or the place we wish to give it in our theories. What we have here is the case where the meaning of the term is unsettled or disputed, but where any settlement of it would yield a clearly individuating term.

More interesting and more extensive is the class of cases in which (a) the meaning of the term is not in dispute, (b) the term does not of itself supply quite definite criteria of distinctness and identity for items falling under it but (c) the term is such as to supply principles for determining such criteria. The last provision is perhaps not very clearly stated, and I must illustrate it. Another way of putting it would be this: the term allows for a certain measure of play in the criteria of distinctness and identity for items falling under it, but determines the dimensions of play. Examples of such terms would be: for non-particular individuals, the terms 'colour' and 'sound' or 'noise'; for particular individuals, the terms 'sound' or 'noise' again and, say, the term 'extent of ground'. Take the term 'colour'. It will not do to say that there are no criteria of distinctness and identity for colours; only that they are more or less elastic and not wholly determined in advance by the term 'colour' itself. Or take the term 'sound' as used to refer to particulars. Here again, and more determinately, there is a variety of possible principles for counting and identifying particular items to which the term applies. When two instruments play together, we may speak of the single sound they jointly make or of the two separate sounds they severally make. Or where one speaker refers to a succession of temporally separated sounds, each lasting for a few seconds, another may speak of a single discontinuous sound, lasting for, say, a minute-and-a-half. The concept of a sound in general is indeterminate in relation to this variety of possible principles; but it determines the range of the possible variation of principle. We know *a priori* what is permissibly but not obligatorily used to count for difference (e.g. difference of source, discriminable timbre, variation of pitch, discontinuity). Consider, finally, the somewhat different case of the concept of *an extent of ground*. This leaves open to us any way we please of tracing out the boundaries of such extents, and thereby determining particular individuals which fall under the term; but it also *requires* that we adopt some boundary-indicating procedure if we are to specify *any* individual under the term. And in contrast with this tolerance of boundary-indicating procedures for initially distinguishing such individuals, the concept is very strict as regards their subsequent identity-conditions. We are free to distinguish individuals of this kind by tracing boundaries as we please; but once created, then, unlike the boundaries of fields, counties or countries, they can never change. (Of course the phrase itself is ambiguous. In 'The extent of ground now occupied by College X was formerly parcelled out in small lots' we have the sense of the phrase we are concerned with; in 'The extent of ground occupied by College X has grown over the years' we have not.)

I am aware that I have only indicated, rather than clearly defined, the character of the class of terms which I have been illustrating. Nevertheless I hope that my indications are clear enough to justify my naming the class. I shall call it the class of variably individuating terms, and I shall define individuating terms in general as the logical sum of clearly individuating and variably individuating terms. A sufficient and necessary condition for the designation of an individual item to be an adequately identifying designation is that it either completely specifies that item or that it embodies or implies an individuating term under which the item is presented as falling.

Next, some remarks about the relevance or appropriateness of this notion. It is, I think, now generally recognized that any adequate theory of categories must provide for a distinction which may be described as the distinction between relative and absolute categories.[15] Two items belong to some one relative category if there is a predicate or set of predicates such that that predicate or every member of that set of predicates can be predicated without category-mismatch of both items. Two items belong to the same absolute category if every predicate which can be predicated without category-mismatch of one can also be predicated without category-mismatch of the other. Evidently two items belong to the same absolute category only if they have all their relative categories in common; and any single item can belong to a number of different relative categories but only to one absolute category.

The items thus assignable to categories are not necessarily expressions or concepts, though they will include both expressions and concepts. They are individuals in the sense in which I have throughout been using this expression. An individual is anything whatever; i.e. anything which can in principle, in any way whatever, be distinguished, as the single thing it is, from all other items and identified as the same item under different presentations or descriptions or in different manifestations. Belonging or not belonging to some relative or absolute category is not a characteristic which an individual can, as it were, put on or shrug off; it is a characteristic which belongs essentially to the individual and covers its whole temporal span, if it has one. Further, it is a feature which adheres essentially to the individual not in virtue of its being the particular individual that it is, but in virtue of its being the *sort* of individual that it is. The word 'sort' is not by itself very helpful; for any sort of sorting constitutes a sort. But one sort of sorting imposes itself here; viz., the sort of sorting to which individuals in general, we may say, owe their very existence (i.e. their discriminability and identifiability) as individuals. And this is just the sort of sorting provided for by individuating terms: terms which embody or imply principles for distinguishing, counting and identifying individuals, as clearly individuating terms do, or terms which supply principles for determining such principles, as variably individuating terms do. It seems prima facie reasonable to suppose that the *a priori* assignment of individuals to categories depends on some knowledge of what sort of individual, in *this* sense of 'sort', we have to deal with.

However, a qualification is necessary here. For it is not quite true that all individuals owe their existence, i.e. their discriminability as individuals, to the sort of sorting provided for by individuating terms. Thus we have the idea of moral qualities or qualities of mind or character. And we can certainly discriminate individual qualities (such as justice, honesty, perseverance, or benevolence) which fall under one or another of the general heads, moral quality, quality of mind or quality of character. But it would not be very plausible to represent the general heads, in these cases, as supplying either clear or variable principles for distinguishing and identifying individuals (e.g. justice or benevolence) which fall under them. For it would be too difficult to state what the principles, or the principles of variation of principle, were. However, it is always possible completely to specify the individual, by naming it or giving a defining description of it, in such a case. And we can be *a priori* certain that such a complete specification of the individual will imply *a priori* all the information about its sort, in a now looser sense of 'sort', which is relevant to its *a priori* assignment to a category. This, then, is why I defined 'adequately identifying designation of an individual' disjunctively: such a designation *either* brings its individual under an individuating term *or* completely specifies it.

Now from the point we have reached, there is more than one path we might follow. We might try to define the category-inappropriateness of a predicate to an individual directly as follows: an individual *i* and a predicate P are category-mismatched if, and only if, P and the denial of P are alike *a priori* rejectable for every adequate identifying designation of *i*. Apart from other possible objections, such a definition would leave us unprotected from scepticism of a kind I have already alluded to, viz., scepticism regarding the distinction, within the general class of *a priori* rejections of an affirmative predication, between those which involve simply the denial of the predicate and those which do not, but are consistent with rejecting that denial. A sceptic on this point will challenge us to show a basis for this distinction of two styles of *a priori* falsity, to explain why the *a priori* rejection of the denial of a predicate is not to be taken as equivalent to the affirmation of that predicate.

Clearly it would be desirable, if possible, to circumvent this demand by freeing the definition of category-mismatch from dependence on such a distinction. (In doing so, one will incidentally go some way to meeting the demand and explaining the distinction.) Prima facie it should be possible to do this. For when one makes a category-point in the brusque, informal way by saying of an individual that it is not the sort of thing which can be or fail to be Φ, then there is surely one predication here that one is rejecting in a quite unproblematic style, viz., the predication (of that individual) of the predicate 'is the sort of thing which can be or fail to be Φ'. It should surely be possible to find a less questionable characterization of that *sort of thing* which would yet yield the same consequences as regards category-mismatch. For example, instead of saying that the predicate 'is in the drawing-room' is mismatched to some individual because both that predicate and its negation, viz., 'is not in the drawing-room', are alike *a priori* reject-able for all adequately identifying designations of that individual, we should seem to miss no essential point if we said that the predi-cate in question is mismatched to that individual because it *implies* a predicate of *a special kind*, viz., 'has some spatial location', and this *implied* predicate is *a priori* rejectable for all adequately identi-fying designations of that individual. The *a priori* rejectability of the implied predicate is not a special style of *a priori* rejectability consistent also with the rejectability of its denial. We do not wish to say that the individual in question neither has nor does not have spatial location. We wish to say, *sans phrase*, that it has no spatial location, and that is why any predicate ascribing a spatial location (such as 'is in the drawing-room') is category-mismatched to it.

As our example illustrates, it is easy enough in some cases to find a predicate of the desired kind – a categorial predicate. Even when we cannot find a very natural-sounding predicate of the desired kind, it should be possible to devise one. For if we really have a topic at all, then – to repeat the point – the predicates the non-mismatching applicability of which define a relative category must form a unified range, and there must be ways of stating the prin-ciple of its unity other than the jejune form of observation that any individual which lies outside its range is neither Φ nor not Φ (for some value or values of Φ). We should not be unduly dismayed if, in framing predicates which incorporate such principles, we find that some of them have a pretty artificial look; nor even if we find that we are *guided* in their selection and construction by that jejune but, after all, intuitively apt form which I have just referred to. Neither fact would mean that we could not *explain*, in a more long-winded way, the principle we were seeking to compress into a predicate.

Of course, this reflection, though it indicates a possible direction of escape from our difficulty, does not actually get us out of it. We need a *general* characterization of the kind of predicate in question and one which does not rest on the distinction held to be questionable. However, if the general line I have hitherto followed is correct, it seems reasonably clear what form that general characterization should take. Let us define a categorial predicate as follows. A categorial predicate is a predicate which satisfies the following two conditions: (1) it is *a priori* acceptable for at least some individuals under all adequately identifying designations of those individuals; (2) it is either *a priori* acceptable or *a priori* rejectable for any individual whatever under all adequately identifying designations of that individual. The definition of category-mismatch follows at once. A predicate is category-mismatched to an individual if and only if it implies a categorial predicate which is *a priori* rejectable for all adequately identifying designations of that individual.[16] Since every predicate implies itself, this means that we shall have to say that the predication of a categorial predicate itself may involve category-mismatch, even though (as already suggested) such a predication does not involve the distinctive style of absurdity we associate with category-mismatch. For example, we shall have to say that 'The number 5 has spatial location' involves category-mismatch no less than 'The number 5 is in the next room', even though the first does not have, and the second does have, that characteristic feature. But this is surely a consequence of no importance, one not worth making special provision to avoid. It is easy enough to explain why the distinctive air of absurdity should attach to one case and not to the other; and I shall not dwell on the point.

Would a theory on the above lines give us what we want? Would it enable us to locate category-mismatch in all the cases in which our intuitions find category-mismatch and in none in which they do not? Well, it is clear that what such a theory *would* give us depends on the notion of an identifying designation, or the class of all identifying designations, of an individual. And this notion in its turn rests on that of principles of identity for individuals. Neither notion, it might be said with some justice, has been adequately clarified, let alone adequately explored. And I shall not explore them now. Instead I shall make some general comments on the acceptability of a theory of categories.

The merit of the sort of theory suggested is that it offers us a way of escape from the circle of problematic notions in which discussions of this topic seem otherwise destined to wander. It is peculiarly important for any theory of categories to find such a way of escape. For if none is found, the very idea of this topic is exposed, not just to that general style of scepticism to which, say, the notion of analyticity and related notions are exposed, but to a specific and argued scepticism. Let me try to sketch the nature of this specific scepticism.

The notion of a question being applicable or not applicable is not one that requires any philosophical justification. Thus if it is said of someone that he is a flute-player, the question with what degree of accuracy of intonation he plays is an applicable question. So, also, if he is said to play any other wind or string instrument. But if someone is known not to play any musical instrument at all, then *eo ipso* that question is not applicable in respect of that person. Similarly if something is acquired by purchase, the question of how high a price was paid is applicable in respect of the transaction; if it is given, the question is not applicable. All propositions purporting to specify the kind of information sought by such a question suffer, if that question is not applicable, from a peculiar kind of inappropriateness defined by this very description of them. Now, given any general classification or description, we can in general correlate with it sets of questions which are at least prima facie applicable and sets of questions which are at least prima facie inapplicable to anything to which that general classification or description applies. And correspondingly we can correlate with that general description sets of sets of predications which will prima facie suffer, or prima facie be free, from the special kind of inappropriateness just referred to.

These notions of applicability and inapplicability of questions and the associated notions of appropriateness or inappropriateness of predications or propositions require, as I have said, no special philosophical justification. Neither does the notion of such correlations as I have mentioned. (Some may indeed say of the correlations that they depend only on the meanings of the expressions involved on either side, while others may be unwilling to say this. But both parties to *this* dispute may admit the existence of such correlations.) Now the sceptic notes that *some* of these correlations between general classification or description on the one hand and applicability or inapplicability, appropriateness or inappropriateness, of question or predication on the other excite a particular interest in some philosophers; and this interest they mark by willingness to employ the terminology of categories, and of category-match or mismatch. But this kind of interest is excited only in some cases, not in others. We can take the points that an individual who is dead neither cares about, nor is indifferent to, some issue; that someone blind neither spots nor overlooks the fly in the ointment; that a gift costs its recipient neither a large nor a small sum; that not being a player of any instrument is not being the sort of thing which has perfect or poor intonation. But philosophers show no disposition to treat these as category-points. In yet other cases a philosopher might feel, or be induced to feel, hesitation. Thus, as an earlier quotation suggests, Ryle might be disposed to treat 'having a spelling' as defining a category; but if we say of a word that, being written, if at all, only in ideograms, it is neither hard nor easy to spell, then will it seem clear that we are making a category-point – or rather one of those points which one is not disposed to treat as category-points?

The sceptic suggests, then, that the particular interest excited by some cases of these correlations and not by others reflects nothing but a sense of *depth* or *strikingness* or, sometimes, of philosophical *importance*, as attaching to some cases and not to others; and that this is why theories of categories tend to move in circles. For this is the result that inevitably ensues when an attempt is made to present as resting on a clear and general distinction a habit of classification which in fact rests on nothing but differences in degree of impressiveness.

If we are to resist such scepticism, a way of escape from the circle must be found; and if one can be found on the lines indicated, then perhaps we should be willing, if necessary, to pay a certain price for it: the price, namely, of readiness to correct *some* intuitions in the light of theory.

In the foregoing I have said nothing about the equivocal or non-equivocal use of terms. It seems to be unnecessary to do so.

For where a term is unequivocally predicable, without category-mismatch, of items which do not have all their relative categories in common, we should be able to *give an account* of its common sense; whereas when a term is only equivocally so predicable, we cannot do this, but can only give accounts of its disparate senses, supplemented, perhaps, by an explanation of its having these disparate uses.

CATEGORIES, GRAMMAR, AND PHILOSOPHICAL CRITICISM

Under this head I have not even the sketch of a theory to offer. But I wish to bring together two kinds of consideration in the hope that they may suggest a way of approach to a part of the explanatory problem.

Theorists of categories have normally differentiated category-absurd sentences from ungrammatical sentences. They have even, surely with some exaggeration, suggested that only grammatically correct sentences are capable of suffering from category-absurdity. Some modern theorists of grammar, on the other hand, have claimed that such sentences owe their oddity to a violation of syntactical rules, i.e. they are a species of ungrammatical sentences. Suitably interpreted, these claims need not conflict. For the grammarians distinguish different kinds of syntactical rule, and hence different kinds of violation of syntactical rule. And in such differences the traditional theorist of categories may find, redescribed, the distinction (between the 'ungrammatical' and the 'absurd') which he was concerned to draw.

Let us for the moment consider a restricted or traditional notion of grammar according to which category-absurdity is *not* a species of grammatical fault. Then among the strings of words which, according to this notion, would count as ungrammatical sentences if they counted as sentences at all, we can draw certain non-sharp distinctions. Roughly speaking, we can distinguish between those which, while being certainly ungrammatical, are obviously corrigible and those which are not obviously corrigible. Corrigibly ungrammatical sentences abound in the exercises of schoolchildren translating sentences of their native language into sentences of other languages. They result from ignorance, or failure to bear in mind, for example, the fact that French grammar requires the agreement of adjectives in gender and number with their nouns, while English grammar does not; that English grammar lays down a principle for selecting 'whom' instead of 'which' or conversely in certain relative pronoun positions in which French or Spanish permit an undifferentiated 'que'; that German grammar embodies requirements about the position of verbs in clauses which are equally alien to English, French, or Spanish grammar.

When theorists of categories said that category-absurdity presupposes grammaticalness, they did not mean freedom from obviously corrigible ungrammaticalness. They did not mean that it was impossible to preserve a category-mistake in translation while making a grammatical slip. They meant that category-absurd sentences had to satisfy a certain condition of minimum grammaticalness. They meant that the grammatical classes of sentence-parts or elements supplied – noun-phrases, nouns, verbs, verb-phrases, adjectives, pronouns, prepositions etc. – had to be such, and so disposed, that we could read off the main grammatical relations which were supposed to hold among the parts or elements of the sentence. For only under this condition could we even raise the question whether these parts or elements were semantically such that they could, without category-mismatch, stand in those relations.

I have remarked that modern grammarians are inclined, or half-inclined, to claim for the domain of syntax those restrictive rules the violation of which issues in category-absurdity. Suppose the claim granted. (The question is admitted to be one of convenience in organization of the theory of a language.) Then we must point out that this part of syntax at least must be admitted to have a semantic basis. That the verb 'hit', for example, at least in its basic, literal employments, is restricted to taking expressions for corporeal things as its grammatical objects can scarcely be regarded as a truth independent of the sense of the word.

For this part of syntax the relation is obvious. May not some such relation also hold for that part which bears on the satisfaction of conditions of minimum grammaticalness? The notions of the grammatical classes and those of the grammatical relations are def-initionally interconnected. It may be thought improbable that there are no lines of connection which join this network to broad seman-tic classifications of language-elements. To determine just how and where these lines of connection run is no doubt a matter of the greatest difficulty. But if they run at all – if for example there are certain semantic types of language-element which are *basically* nominal or verbal or adjectival – then their discovery may help us to understand better the place of the notion of category absurdity in philosophy.

To suggest a reason why this may be so, I now introduce the second of the two kinds of consideration I mentioned. It is often remarked that category-absurd sentences, though they resist literal interpretation, frequently lend themselves to figurative interpret-ation. Ryle remarked that many jokes were type-pranks. In the same spirit one might say that many tropes are type-trespasses. Some analogy, some imaginative stretch or more or less remote connection can often be found, or made, to bring the categorially absurd in from the cold of the blankly nonsensical to the wide and welcoming domain of figurative speech. Now philosophers do not often, if ever, produce, in all seriousness, sentences which flatly offend against category-propriety. If they use what are plainly metaphors, as they often do, it is usually as metaphors that they use them; and hence they are not obliged to take them any further than they wish. What is consciously taken up as a figure can, as a figure, be consciously dropped at any point beyond which it would be unwelcome to pursue it. But it is a commonplace that philo-sophers are prone to be influenced in their theorizing by models or pictures or figures of which they are not fully, or at all, conscious as such; to think they are advancing a literally correct account of some phenomenon when they are actually engaged in elaborating, or being puzzled by, features of the figurative mode in terms of which they are thinking about that phenomenon. It is when the theorist is thus engaged, when he is unconsciously committed to this sort of thinking, that the brusque style of making category-points is most appropriate and effective. It has the damaging effect of bringing the concealed figure out into the open. And the effect is damaging because you cannot say 'Thus far and no farther will I go with my figure' when you did not think it was a figure at all, but thought it was the literal truth about the phenomenon in question.

And now to try to bring these two kinds of consideration together.

'Sincerity' is a noun; 'smile' is sometimes a noun; 'the death of Caesar' is a noun-phrase. But the noun 'sincerity', we say, is formed from the adjective 'sincere'; the use of 'smile' as a noun is secondary to its use as a verb; the noun-phrase 'the death of Caesar' is derived from a clause in which the noun 'death' does not figure, though the verb 'die' does. Such thoughts as these are given a more systematic shape in the work of modern grammarians, who distinguish between 'deep' and 'surface' grammatical structure and study their relations under the name of transformations. The operation of revealing deep structure points to certain sentences as having a relatively basic or underived character. These are sentences corresponding to the most deeply embedded sentence-forms in the deep structure of given sentences. If we want to find, as it were, the basic models for (at least some) grammatical relations and classes, it is presumably to such basic sentences that we should look, seeking for general connections between types of element-meaning and potentialities of grammatical role in such fundamental sentence-structures. Here we should find our primitive nominals, adjectivals, adverbials, transitive and intransitive verbals; and our primitive cases of grammatical combinations and relations. Next, we should seek to understand the analogies, partly logical and partly other than logical, which underlie the vast extension in the scope and coverage of those grammatical classes and relations, an extension which involves bringing in new meaning-elements such as have no place in basic sentences as well as allowing for trans-formed or derived forms of elements which already have a place. Thus we might get a grasp of our grammar and, to that extent, of the structure of our thinking.

But we might also get something more, and more relevant to our immediate concerns. We might get some insight into the source of those unconscious models or figures which haunt the philo-sophical imagination and which it is the function of brusquely made category-points to expose. Grammatical relations and classifications which we find in surface grammar are modelled in part on those we find in deeply embedded sentence-forms of deep structure. It is to be supposed that genuine analogies, in part logical, in part semantical, underlie this modelling. But may not the modelling be escorted, even helped on its way, by imaginary analogies as well? May not a deceptive ghost of the semantics of the original nominals, verbals, and adjectivals cling to the emergent nominals, verbals, and adjectivals? The theorists of categories, I repeat, have normally contrasted the grammatical acceptability with the semantic unacceptability of their category-absurd sentences. A proper use of such sentences, I repeat, has been to expose the unconscious figures which plague philosophical thinking. May we not find a clue to the appeal of those figures by asking just how, and why, it is that what makes (critically useful) category-nonsense, makes (at one level) grammatical sense? In looking for the ancestry of the grammatical sense that it makes, we may also turn up the features of the figure which fathers the nonsense it makes.

NOTES

1 'Categories', *Proceedings of the Aristotelian Society*, vol. XXXVIII, 1937–8, p. 189.

2 *The Concept of Mind*, London, Hutchinson, 1949, p. 8.

3 *The Concept of Mind*, p. 16.

4 *The Concept of Mind*, pp. 18, 23.

5 *Dilemmas*, Cambridge Univ. Press, 1954, p. 9.

6 *Dilemmas*, p. 10.

7 *Logical Positivism*, ed. A. J. Ayer, London, Allen & Unwin, 1959, p. 333.

8 The sentence, from 'Categories', runs: 'Two proposition-factors are of different categories or types, if there are sentence-frames such that when the expressions for those factors are imported as alternative complements to the same gap-signs, the resultant sentences are significant in the one case and absurd in the other' (p. 203). One should try importing first '27' and then '37' as complements to the gap-sign in 'She is over . . . and under 33 years old'; or first 'mother' and then 'father' into 'It's not your . . . but your father'; or first 'Green' and then 'Red' into '. . . is a more restful colour than red'.

9 'Categories', p. 200.

10 'Theory of Meaning', in *British Philosophy in the Mid-century*, ed. C. A. Mace, London, Allen & Unwin, 1957, p. 245.

11 *The Concept of Mind*, p. 206.

12 Here and in what follows, 'acceptable' = 'true'; and whether or not 'rejectable' = 'false', 'false' implies 'rejectable'.

13 Cf. in N. Chomsky, *Aspects of the Theory of Syntax*, Cambridge, Mass., M.I.T. Press, 1965, the distinction between 'strict subcategorization rules' and 'selectional rules' (p. 95) and its suggested application in distinguishing types of grammatical 'deviance' (p. 153); also the contrast with 'purely semantic incongruity' (pp. 76–7), of which the examples given are all in fact contradictions.

14 It may be that a satisfactory characterization of the notion of logical subject would rule out such 'subject-expressions'. But I do not wish to discuss this here.

15 See, for example, F. Sommers, 'Predicability', in *Philosophy in America*, ed. M. Black, Ithaca, N.Y., Cornell Univ. Press, 1965, p. 280; and the same author's definitions of α-types and β-types in 'Types and Ontology', *The Philosophical Review*, vol. LXXII, 1963.

16 On the basis of a definition of category-mismatch of predicates to individuals, we can of course easily frame a definition of category-mismatch as between predicates – and hence, derivatively, as between predicates and subject-expressions. Two predicates are mismatched if and only if for every individual to which one is *not* mismatched the other *is* mismatched; i.e. there is no individual such that neither is mismatched to that individual. It is easy to see how category-mismatch between expressions combined in other grammatical relations can be derivatively characterized.

7

WITTGENSTEIN'S 'PHILOSOPHICAL INVESTIGATIONS'

This book is a treatment, by a philosopher of genius, of a number of intricate problems, intricately connected. It also presents in itself an intricate problem: that of seeing clearly what the author's views are on the topics he discusses, and how these views are connected. The difficulty of doing this arises partly from the structure and style of the book. Wittgenstein himself describes the former accurately in the preface: 'The best I could write could never be more than philosophical remarks'; 'Thus this book is really only an album.' It would, however, be a very strong prejudice against this disregard of the ordinary conventions of exposition, which could survive a careful reading of the whole book. Wittgenstein did not gloss his thoughts; but he arranged them. And the gains in power and concentration are great. It might even be thought that there were good reasons why no attempt at all should be made to present his views in a more conventional form. But this could be true only on a very specialized view of the nature of philosophical understanding. In what follows, I try to trace and connect the main lines of his thought; conscious that, at best, the result must involve a great

impoverishment of his rich and complex thinking. I refer to passages
in Part I of the book simply by paragraph number (e.g. 500); to passages in Part II by section and/or page number (e.g. II. xi, p. 200).
Comment and criticism will be interspersed with exposition.

MEANING AND USE

In the first thirty-seven or thirty-eight paragraphs of Part I, which
are concerned with meaning, Wittgenstein is anxious to make us
see 'the multiplicity of kinds of words and sentences' (23). We are
prone to assimilate different kinds. In particular, we are prone to
work with a certain idea of language as consisting of words each
correlated with something for which it stands, an object, the meaning of the word (1). This picture, though philosophically misleading
for all words, is better suited to some than to others. When we have
it in mind, we are primarily thinking of common nouns like 'chair'
and 'bread' and of people's names; even primitive reflection shows
that it does not fit, say, logical connectives. So not only is there a
general tendency to assimilate different kinds of words to each
other; there is also a particular direction which this assimilation
tends to take. Perhaps the general tendency is in part explained by
the fact that words look or sound much alike: from their uniform
appearance on the printed page one would never guess at their diversity of function (11). But there are more complex reasons both for
the general tendency and for its particular direction. The central
point is this: *the picture with which we are inclined to work derives
essentially from the instruction-setting of someone who has
already mastered in part the technique of using the language;* i.e.
from the situation in which someone is being taught the place
of one word, of which he is ignorant, in a way of using language
with which he is familiar (cf. 10, 27, 30, 32). In this situation, the
instructor may well proceed by saying something like 'the word x
means (is the name of, stands for, signifies, etc.) y' where the place
of 'y' is taken by, e.g. 'this', 'this number', 'a number', 'this colour',
'the colour which . . .'; or simply by a synonym or translation of
the word in question. In some, though not all, cases, he may accompany these words by pointing. Or he may just answer the question

'What is y (this, this colour, this thing) called?' by pronouncing the word. These procedures may give us the impression of a relation of a unique kind being established between two items, a word and something else; and the further impression that the essence of meaning is to be grasped by the contemplation of this unique relation. To counter this impression, to remind ourselves that the efficacy of these procedures depends on the existence of a prepared framework of linguistic training, we should bear in mind such points as these two: that an ostensive definition (*many* kinds of words can be taught by indicating situations in which they are in some sense applicable) can always be variously interpreted (28); and that the process of asking the names of things and being told them is itself one language-game[1] among others, and a comparatively sophisticated one.

Two minor comments. (1) Perhaps Wittgenstein does not here sufficiently emphasize the point that the *natural* place for the word 'meaning' and its derivatives in ordinary use is in just such instruction-situations as those referred to. One might get the impression that he was saying: 'In philosophy you want the meaning of the word. Don't look for the mythical, uniquely related term, but look at the use; for *that* is the meaning' (cf. 43). But in view of the natural place of 'meaning', it might be better to say: 'In doing philosophy, it can't be that you are ignorant of the meaning: what you want to know is the use.' (2) Wittgenstein does not seek to give a complete explanation of why, among all the kinds of names there are, it is substance-names that tend to be taken as the model for meaning. A suggestion which can perhaps be extracted from the text is that (*a*) pointing figures largely both in ostensive explanation of words, and in that more primitive training in the naming-game which a child goes through before it actually uses words for any more practical purpose; and (*b*) pointing is more naturally used to discriminate the individual man or horse than any other kind of item. But there remains a question here.

Instead, then, of gazing at this over-simple picture of language, with its attendant assimilations, we are to look at the elements of language as instruments. We are to study their use. Only so can we solve our conceptual problems. Variants on 'use' in Wittgenstein are 'purpose', 'function', 'role', 'part', 'application'. It is not a complaint to say that this central notion is not immediately and wholly clear. The general aim is clear enough: to get us away from our fascination with the dubious relation of naming, of meaning, and to make us look at the speaking and writing of language as one human activity among others, interacting with others; and so to make us notice the different parts that words and sentences play in this activity. But here I inevitably reintroduce one of the variants: 'the parts they play'. Perhaps seeing what sorts of things count as *differences* of use will help one to get clear about the central notion. And here it will seem that there are differences between differences which Wittgenstein might have made more explicit.

Consider first what he says of different kinds of sentences. He makes the point that a formal (grammatical) likeness may cover a functional difference (21–2). Then (23): 'But how many kinds of sentence are there? Say assertion, question, and command? – There are *countless* kinds: countless different kinds of use of what we call "symbols" "words" "sentences".' There follows a list of activities which involve the use of language. When we look at the items in the list, it becomes clear that the shift from 'kinds of sentence' in this question to 'kinds of use' in the answer was an important one. The list includes, for example, as separate uses, the activities of reading a story, play-acting, and translating from one language to another. The sentence 'It was raining' might occur in the course of any one of these activities; as it might in a factual narration. It would be absurd to speak of different *sentences* here, let alone of different kinds of sentences. We *might* speak of different uses of the sentence, though it would be better to speak of different linguistic activities in each of which the sentence occurred. Similarly, I suppose, reading aloud a story containing the sentence would involve a different use from copying the story out; reading aloud a translation of a story from reading aloud (*a*) an original, (*b*) a translated factual narrative in all of which the sentence occurred; and there is also the special use involved in sending an old man to sleep by reading aloud from a translation of a play. Surely distinctions are needed here to save the whole notion from sliding into absurdity. Such points as the following call for attention: sometimes there is a formal (grammatical) distinction to correspond to (not to coincide with) a 'difference in use'; sometimes there is not (in what cases would it be more or less natural to have one, and why?); sometimes the existence of a formal distinction would be self-defeating. There is a class of interrogative sentences (sentences of which the standard use is to ask questions); there is no class of translators' sentences; there *could be* no class of copyists' sentences.

Consider next the point that we cannot in general talk about the functions or uses of *words* in the same sort of way as we can talk about the functions or uses of sentences.[2] (Of course, a word may *sometimes* function as a sentence.) To suppose that we could would be like supposing that we could talk of the function of a numeral in the same way as we could talk of the purpose of a calculation; or discuss a gambit and a piece in the same terms. We might imagine a very simple language A, in which a limited number of sentences could be formed from a limited number of words; and a second language B, containing no distinction of sentences and words, but consisting of unitary expressions such that every sentence of A could be translated into a unitary expression of B. Then it might be the case that every remark we could make about a use of a sentence in A would also be true of a use of an expression in B. We could also discuss the uses of the *words* of A; but there would be nothing to be said on this subject in the case of B. What perhaps causes confusion here is that very often when we (and Wittgenstein) discuss the use of *words* of certain classes, what we are concerned with is the *criteria* for their correct application; and this discussion is the same as the discussion of the conditions in which it is correct to use a *sentence* of a certain kind, namely, the sentence which says that we have here a case of what the word in question describes.

The fact that Wittgenstein is content to leave this central notion of use so vague is a manifestation of his reluctance to make distinctions and classifications which are not of direct assistance to the fly in the flybottle (309). Underlying this reluctance is a general, and debatable, doctrine of the nature of philosophy: to which I shall refer later.

Towards the end of these introductory paragraphs there enters one of the main themes of the book (33–6). Wittgenstein imagines an objection to the view that understanding an ostensive definition requires a mastery of the language. Someone might say that all that is necessary to this understanding is for the learner to know what the teacher is *pointing to* or *meaning* or *attending to*, when he makes his gesture – e.g. to the shape or to the colour of the object. Wittgenstein does not deny this; but points out that though there may be characteristic experiences (e.g. feelings) of 'meaning' or 'pointing to' the shape, which the learner might share with the teacher, their occurrence is not sufficient to make the situation one of 'meaning the shape'. Not just because they do not always occur. Even if they did it would still depend on the circumstances, the setting, on what happens before and afterwards, whether the case is one of intending or interpreting the definition in such and such a way. Seeing this is helped by seeing that there are in fact many things which may occur at the time, and none which must. It is in such cases, however, that we are apt to feign a *special* experience or mental act or process to answer to such a description.

This single topic, of *meaning* or *understanding something* by, say, a gesture, a word or a sentence, is the most persistently recurrent in the book. It is easy to see why. It is a place where two major preoccupations overlap, where two principal enemies may join hands. These enemies are psychologism in the philosophy of meaning, and the doctrine of special experiences in the philosophy of mind. Against them stand Wittgenstein's ideas. To grasp a meaning is to be able to practise a technique; while 'meaning, understanding something by a word' is itself a prime instance of those psychological expressions which seem to refer to something which happens at a point, or over a short period, of time, and may indeed do so; but, when they do, it is to something which gains its significance and its claim to its special title from what stretches before and after the point or the period.

But the main discussion of psychological concepts is deferred until the end of a further discussion of language and logic.

LANGUAGE, ANALYSIS, AND PHILOSOPHY

(38–137)

The general over-simple picture of meaning which Wittgenstein examines at the beginning of his book takes an intenser, tauter, form in a certain special doctrine of the *real* names of a language. This doctrine Wittgenstein now discusses; and the discussion broadens into a general repudiation of the set of philosophical ideas and ideals, roughly indicated by the title of 'logical atomism'. He begins with a consideration of two related notions: the idea of the genuine names of a language, and the idea of the simple indestructible elements of reality which can only be named, not described or defined, and which are the meanings of the genuine names. These are the primary elements referred to by Socrates in the *Theaetetus*, and are identified by Wittgenstein with Russell's 'individuals' and his own 'objects' of the *Tractatus* (46). Both ideas are subjected to destructive criticism and diagnosis in 39–59. First Wittgenstein attacks the notion of the word of which the meaning is the object it applies to: he instances the ordinary proper name and distinguishes between its bearer and its meaning (40); in this case, too, the meaning is the use (41–3). (Wittgenstein here gives the wrong reason for objecting to the identification of the, or a, meaning of a proper name with its bearer, or one of its bearers. If we speak at all of the meaning of proper names, it is only in quite *specialized* ways, as when we say that 'Peter' means a stone, or 'Giovanni' means 'John'. This is not an accident of usage, but reflects a radical difference between proper names and other names. But here, as elsewhere, Wittgenstein neglects the use of 'meaning'.)

The antithesis 'simple-composite' is next examined and shown to have application only in a particular context, and to have different applications in different contexts: the *philosophical* question whether something is composite or simple is only too likely to lack a suitable context and hence a sense (47). Next (48–9) a simple model-language is constructed which might be held to answer to the specifications given in the *Theaetetus*; an arrangement of coloured squares is 'described' by an arrangement of letters, one letter for each square, the letters varying with the colour of the squares. We might perhaps say, in the context of this language-game, that the 'simple elements' were the individual squares. But then the assertion that the simple elements can only be named, not described, is at best, perhaps, a misleading way of saying that in the case of an arrangement consisting of one single square, the description consists of a single letter, the name of the coloured square; or of saying that *giving* a name to an element is different from *using* the name to describe a complex. Wittgenstein next considers the doctrine of the indestructibility, the necessary existence, of elements named by genuine names: the doctrine that the very meaningfulness of the name guarantees the existence of the item named. He is rightly not content to rely on a general repudiation of the notion of meaning-as-object, but produces answers to arguments in the doctrine's favour, and further explanations of its sources. The interest of the answers is weakened by the indescribable badness of the arguments (cf. 55, 56, 57). The explanations remain. If I understand them rightly, they run as follows. (1) We are inclined to get muddled over sentences like 'Turquoise exists'. This might be used to mean 'There are things which are turquoise' – an ordinary empirical proposition, which could be false – or 'There is such a colour as turquoise' (i.e. ' "Turquoise" does have meaning as a colour-word'). Taken the second way, it is again an empirical proposition, this time about a word. The muddle begins when we both take it this way and at the same time inconsistently take it as a proposition *using* the word 'turquoise' with the meaning it has, and thus as saying something about the colour, turquoise. Then we seem to be saying something necessary (for a word couldn't be used with, i.e. have, a meaning, and not have one), and also seem to be saying something about the colour, viz., that it necessarily exists (58). Wittgenstein does not remark that this account might apply to the abstract-noun form of *any* descriptive word (e.g. healthiness), and not merely to those which philosophers are prone to take as the names of ultimate elements. Perhaps this account should be regarded simply as a supplement to the other (2) which is summed up in the epigram, 'What looks as if it *had* to exist is a part of the language' (50). If it were a necessary part of the activity of using a word 'W' that we, say, consulted a sample of W, then we might say that a sample of W must exist in order for the word to have meaning. From this *recherché* possibility, I take it we are to move to the truism that we could not teach a word by naming a sample unless there were a sample to name (cf. 50), and to join this to the reflection that there are at any rate some words which it is tempting to suppose could not be learnt except by means of an ostensive definition. Then we have the makings of a tautology which might be misconstrued as an assertion of metaphysically necessary existence.

The doctrine of elements is obviously connected with the belief in *analysis* as the inevitable method of philosophical clarification: the belief that the philosophical elucidation of an ordinary sentence is achieved when it is replaced by another, which makes explicit the complexity of the proposition expressed and reflects exactly the form of the fact described (91). This belief is an illusion, engendered by confusions about language and logic, and to be dispelled only by a clear view of the actual functioning of language. How exactly does the illusion arise? (Here Wittgenstein's answer has a kind of passionate obscurity which it is difficult to penetrate.) In logic, which is at once completely pure, exact, and general, we seem to have the clue to the essential nature of thought and language, and with this, the clue to the general *a priori* order of the world, of things empirical (97). For do not thought and language mirror the world? (The *thought* that it is raining is the thought *that it is raining*: the propositions fit the facts (95–6).) Somehow the exactness and order of which logic gives us the idea must (we think) be hidden in every, even the vaguest-looking, sentence of ordinary language: the *sense* of each must be definite. Logic shows us in advance what the structure of language and the world is – so this structure must be found hidden, to be revealed by analysis, in what we actually say (98 *et seq.*). Wittgenstein does not suggest that what philosophers have called 'analysis' is, in fact, useless. Sometimes 'misunderstanding concerning the use of words, caused, among other things, by certain analogies between the forms of expression in different regions of language . . . can be removed by substituting one form of expression for another' (90). But this fact itself contributes to the illusion that there is 'something like a final analysis of our forms of language, and so a *single* completely resolved form of every expression' (91).

To dispel this illusion, we are to give up looking for the essence of language and instead are to look at what is all the time before our eyes: the actual functioning of language. Then we see that linguistic activities are as diverse as all the things which we call 'games', and which are so called not because of any single common element, but because of 'family resemblances' – a 'complicated network of similarities, overlapping and criss-crossing' (66). (The sub-class of linguistic formations that we call 'propositions' is also just such a family. We are apt to think we have a clue to the general nature of the *proposition* in the idea of *whatever is true or false*. But one of these ideas cannot be used to elucidate the other: they move too closely together, they share each other's ambiguities (134–7).) Wittgenstein here makes an ingenious double use of his examination of the word 'game'. He not only uses the concept 'game' to cast light on the concept 'language' by means of direct *comparison*: games form a family, and so do the various activities which come under the general description of 'using language'. He also uses it as an *illustration*, to cast light on language in another way: by showing the parts which the notions of rules, and of exactness of meaning, play there. Thus the application of the word 'game' is not limited by any precise boundary; though a boundary could be fixed for a special purpose. We could say it was an *inexact* concept, that there was an indeterminacy in the rules for its use. But the important thing to notice is that this does not detract from its usefulness for ordinary purposes (and for extraordinary purposes, special rules can be devised). So that it would not even be *correct* in general, to speak of inexactness here; for 'inexact' is a word of dispraise, signifying that what is so-called falls short of a standard required for some particular purpose (88); and here no such special purpose has been specified. Moreover: (1) in whatever detail we give the rules for the use of a word (or for the playing of a game), cannot we always imagine a case in which there might be a doubt as to whether the rule applied to this case or not; and (2) is there not always the possibility of someone's not knowing how to interpret the rules or the explanations we give him of them, or the explanations of those explanations? The point Wittgenstein is making here is that the demand for absolute precision in the rules (a fixed meaning) or for absolute finality in their interpretation, their explanation, is senseless. What determines whether there is enough precision in the rules, or a sufficient explanation of them, is whether the concept is used successfully, with general agreement (84–7).

(One of the illustrations which Wittgenstein uses here is unfortunate. He wishes to say that I could use a proper name 'without a fixed meaning', without its losing its usefulness; 'asked what I understand by "N" ', he says, I might adduce various descriptions some of which I might later be prepared to abandon as false of N (79). Of course, I never should be asked *what* I understand by, but *whom* I mean by, 'N'; and in answering, I should not be defining 'N', but identifying N.)

With what conception of philosophy is this revised view of the nature of language associated? The key to the solution of our problems still lies in their source, viz., language itself. But we are not to try to improve on, to tamper with, language; only to describe its workings. For the confusions we are troubled by arise not when language is doing its work, but when it is idling, on holiday; it is when we consider words and sentences in abstraction from their linguistic and non-linguistic contexts that they seem to conceal a mystery and invite a myth. So we are to 'assemble reminders' of obvious facts about their uses; not at random, nor yet systematically; but on each occasion with some particular purpose in view, the purpose of dispelling some particular confusion. And to make clear the ways in which words actually function, it will sometimes be helpful to consider ways in which they do not, but might, function; invented language-games will be useful objects of comparison with actual language-games (109–33).

Many philosophers would agree with much of this: it is difficult not to share the conception of philosophy held by the first philosopher of the age. Yet there are at least two very different directions in which it may seem unduly restrictive. First, there is the idea that the *sole* purpose of the distinctions we draw attention to, the descriptions we give of the different ways in which words function, is to dispel particular metaphysical confusions; and, associated with this, an extreme aversion from a systematic exhibition of the logic of particular regions of language. Now, even if we *begin* with a therapeutic purpose, our interest might not exhaust itself when that purpose is achieved; and there can be an investigation of the logic of sets of concepts, which starts with no purpose other than that of unravelling and ordering complexities for the sake of doing so. The desire to present the facts systematically here becomes important in proportion as therapeutic aims become secondary. The other direction might be suggested by what Wittgenstein himself says of certain metaphysical doctrines such as solipsism. The inventor of such a doctrine has discovered 'a new way of looking at things' – something like 'a new way of painting . . . or a new kind of song' (401). It is surely over-puritanical to hold that, just because the claims made for such new ways were too large, we should be concerned solely with preventing ourselves from seeing the world afresh. We might make room for a purged kind of metaphysics, with more modest and less disputable claims than the old. But one does not need to have an equal sympathy with both these possibilities in order to ask: could not the activities we call 'doing philosophy' also form a family?

MEANING AND UNDERSTANDING

(see first 132–242, 319–26, 357–8, 431–6, 454, further references are given later in this section.)

Wittgenstein next reverts to the themes of *meaning* and *understanding* something by an expression – a theme announced, but not developed, at the end of the introductory paragraphs (33–6). The main sections which he devotes to this topic are of great brilliance and clarity. He begins with the point that the fundamental criteria for whether someone has understood an expression lie in the application which he makes of it. Of course, he may correctly be said to 'grasp the meaning in a flash'. A picture or a paraphrase may come before his mind; he may produce them to us. But neither picture nor paraphrase dictates the use that is to be made of it: they can be *variously* applied, and if we are inclined to forget this, it is because we are inclined to think of only one application. So the production of the picture or paraphrase, though normally (and rightly) enough to satisfy us, is not the final test: *that* resides in the application. Now this may seem acceptable enough so long as we are considering the criteria we employ for someone else's understanding. But do we not often and correctly say of *ourselves*, when, e.g. someone is trying to teach us how to develop a series, things like: 'Now I understand!', 'Now I can go on!'? It is obvious that we are not here applying to ourselves the criterion of application: we seem to be reporting something which 'makes its appearance in a moment'. No doubt there usually is some momentary experience: e.g. a formula for the series may occur to us, or we may just experience a feeling of release of tension. But, though in certain cases, a remark such as 'The formula has occurred to me' might have the same force, serve the same purpose as 'Now I understand' etc., it will not do to say that in general these expressions have the same meaning (183). In any case it is clear that *the understanding* is not to be identified with any such characteristic experience. (This will seem only too clear; and is the point at which we are tempted to look for a special experience.) If we ask what, *in the eyes of others*, 'justifies' me in using the words 'Now I understand' etc., what shows my use of them to be 'correct', it is not the occurrence of the experience, whatever it may be, but the circumstances under which I have it (e.g. that I have worked with these formulae before, that I now continue the series, etc.) (153–5). This obviously does not mean that the words 'Now I can go on!' are short for a description of all these circumstances, or that they mean 'I have had an experience which I know empirically to lead to the continuation of the series' (179); my certainty that I shall be able to go on is not a matter of induction (cf. 324–8). What we need (here I interpret a little) is to look at such first-person utterances in a radically different way from the way in which we look at the corresponding third-person utterances: to see them not as reports about myself for giving which *I* have to apply criteria, but rather as 'exclamations' (323) or 'signals' (180, p. 218), natur- ally and appropriately made or given in certain circumstances. Such an exclamation could even be compared with 'an instinctive sound' or 'a glad start' (323). Failure to perform successfully after the signal had been given would not necessarily mean that it had been incorrectly given. In some cases (e.g. if there had been an unforeseen interruption or disturbance) we should accept the plea: 'When I said I knew how to go on, I did know' (323).

Two minor comments. (1) Wittgenstein does not enlarge on the suggestion given by the word 'signal'. One might take as a typical case that in which a teacher turns from the blackboard, proffers the chalk to the class with the question 'Who can go on?'. Here the answer '*I* can' would have the same function as a silent acceptance of the chalk. (2) Wittgenstein's continual use of phrases like 'gave him the right to say', 'made it a correct use of', 'justified him in saying' in connection with these first-person utterances might tend to obscure a little his own doctrine. The essential point is that a person does *not* have (or need) grounds or reasons (does not apply criteria) for saying correctly that he himself understands, in the sense in which others must have them to say it of him. Of course, he may himself have, or lack, reasons or justifications in another (a social) sense.

Grasping the meaning (understanding it) should be compared with intending the meaning (meaning it). The two are connected in this way. We may be inclined to think that the purpose of the explanations we give (of, e.g. the rule for the development of the series) is really to get the learner to catch hold of something essential, the meaning we *intend* (210); and that the correct application he then makes of the rule is somehow a consequence of his catching hold of this essential thing. And here we have the idea of the mental act of *intending, meaning* this expression of the rule in a certain way, as somehow anticipating and predetermining all the steps of its application before they are taken. Or the connection may be approached in another way. The criterion for the learner's having understood the rule aright is his application of it. But not *any* application (anything that could possibly be represented as an application of the expression of the rule) will do. It must be the *correct* application. But what are the criteria for correctness? Here again one is inclined to answer that the correct application is the one that was meant: and this answer may once more give us the picture of all the steps being somehow covered in advance by the act of meaning. This idea is *very* compelling. For does not the *sense* of the rule (of the expression) determine what is to count as the correct application of it? What does the determining here is not just the words or the symbols themselves. They are dead, inert (432, 454); they could be applied, and applied systematically, in indefinitely numerous different ways. And the same goes for any paraphrase or picture (433), the substitution of one expression or symbol for another: 'interpretations (in this sense) by themselves do not determine meaning' (198). It is natural to suppose that only the intention, 'the psychical thing', can do that. Natural, but of course wrong (or at least misleading). The criterion for the correct application of the rule is *customary practice* (199–201); the customary practice of those who have received a certain training; the way we are taught to use the rule and do always use it. It is, too, in the existence of this customary practice, and nowhere else, that we may find the way in which the steps are 'determined in advance', and the way in which a certain application is 'meant', or 'intended' by the ordinary instructor who has mastered that practice. (Of course; for 'the rule determines this application' means 'the rule is not correctly understood unless used in this way'.) What gives us the illusion of some other mysterious determinant is the fact that, having received a certain training, we find it so *utterly natural* to make a certain application of the expression. We draw the consequences of the rule *'as a matter of course'*; and cannot understand how anyone can make a wholly different application of the expression. (' "But surely you can see . . .?" That is just the characteristic expression of someone who is under the compulsion of a rule' (231).) Of course, in the instructor-pupil situation, explanations are in place; but the purpose of the explanations is to get the pupil to do as we do, and find it equally natural. 'Explanations come to an end somewhere'; then we just act. But equally, of course, 'the pupil's capacity to learn may come to an end'.

Among resistances to his view Wittgenstein notes the tendency to fall back on the words 'the same': the tendency, e.g. to say 'But when we explain a rule to someone by giving him examples of its application, all we want him to see is that he is *to do the same* in other cases'. In answer to this, Wittgenstein points out that the idea of a single, generally sufficient criterion of 'what is the same' is nonsense. The criteria for 'doing the same' in *the case of a particular rule* are just the criteria, whatever they may be, for the correct observance of that rule. The concepts of 'rule' and 'identity' are as closely related to each other as the word 'proposition' to the phrase 'true or false'. (See 185, 208, 215–16, 223–7.)

Now although Wittgenstein, in the sections here discussed, is directly concerned mainly with the topics of meaning or understanding something by an expression of a rule, what he says is taken by him to have much wider implications about language in general. These implications give the meaning-use equation a new significance, of the utmost importance in relation to the topics of experience and sensation which he next discusses. Roughly speaking: what he says about obeying what we would ordinarily call 'rules' is applied to obeying what philosophers are apt to call 'the rules for the use' of all expressions, whether or not they are the expressions of rules. Obeying a rule is conforming to an agreed common practice; 'it is impossible to obey a rule "privately" ' (202). The emphasis is on the *agreed common practice* in the use of expressions, and this carries with it, in cases where it is appropriate to speak of criteria, the existence of *agreed common criteria* for their application. Wittgenstein notes that this in its turn demands the existence of general agreement in *judgments* (242). The great importance of these points emerges rapidly in what follows.

Before turning to Wittgenstein's discussion of his next topic, it is in place to notice some of the further things he says about 'meaning something by an expression'. To this he reverts at intervals, in a rich succession of examples, arguments and suggestions throughout the rest of the book (see especially 503–10, 525–34, 540–6, 592–8, 607, 661–93, II. vi, II. xi, pp. 214–19). As before, the main doctrine attacked is the doctrine that what gives an expression, in use, its meaning and its life, is the user's special experience, or act, of meaning something by it. I select some principal points.

(*a*) One of the sources of the doctrine is the difference we feel between using words in an ordinary, and in an abnormal, context (e.g. repeating a sentence mockingly, or as a quotation, or in elocution practice, etc.). Aware of a difference of feeling in these latter cases, we are apt to suppose it consists in the absence of the normal experience of meaning what we say. Just so might we suppose, until we remember the facts, that everything that does not feel strange, feels familiar (592–8, 607; cf. also, on 'being influenced', 169–70).

(*b*) In II. vi (cf. also 592), Wittgenstein analyses brilliantly the idea of a special atmosphere or feeling carried by each particular word. (So some philosophers have spoken, for example of an 'if-feeling'.) Whatever feeling-accompaniment the reading or uttering of a certain word may have, it is only *as so accompanying the word* that we are tempted to invest it with this special significance. Any such feeling or sensation might occur in a different context and not be recognized at all. But a feeling or atmosphere which loses its identity (its identity as, say, the 'if-feeling') when separated from a certain object, is *not* a special feeling or atmosphere associated with that object at all. Contrast it with a genuine case of separately identifiable but closely associated things. Here a different association would shock and surprise us.

(*c*) Wittgenstein does not deny that a sense can be given to the notion of *experiencing* the meaning of a word. (See II. ii and II, xi, pp. 214–16. Cf. also 526–34.) This phrase might reasonably be used in connection with many experiences which we do have, and which profoundly affect our *attitude* to language. Among these are: finding the *mot juste* after rejecting a number of candidates; reading with *expression*; saying a word again and again until it seems to 'lose its meaning'. In particular Wittgenstein notes the game of pronouncing a word like 'March', now with one, now with another of its meanings. We can comply with the instruction to do this, and can perhaps report a different experience of the word. But this very game shows how unimportant the experience is in relation to meaning the word now in this way and now in that in the ordinary course of events; for then we may not be able to report any such experience. In general, the word 'meaning' may be said to acquire a secondary use in connection with all these experiences which are of such significance in relation to the way we *feel* about our language. But this use *is* secondary. Words could still have their meanings, language be used as a means of communication, in the absence of these phenomena.

(*d*) The most important of these later discussions (661–93, and pp. 216–17) is concerned with meaning in the sense it has in such a question as 'Whom (which one) did you mean?', i.e. with an intended reference as opposed to an intended sense. But there are close analogies between the two. When, with reference to an earlier remark, I say 'I meant him' I refer to a definite time (the time at which I made the remark); but not to an experience which I had at that time. There may sometimes be characteristic accompaniments, looks, movements of attention; but these are not what 'meaning him' consists in. Compare 'I meant him' with the phrase 'I was speaking of him'. What makes it true that I was speaking of him is the set of circumstances in which the original remark was made, and in particular, the general set or direction of my actions, of which the explanation ('I meant him') is itself one. What is apt to confuse us here is that of course I do not discover whom I meant by studying those circumstances. But nor do I report an indubitable special experience. It is rather (here I interpret a little) that in giving the explanation of whom I meant I continue a certain chain of actions; as I might, in pointing things out on a complex diagram, discard a blunt pointer in favour of a finer one, more serviceable for my purpose. Or I might *dis-continue* that chain of action, think better of it; and substitute another name; and then I shall be said to have lied. The question *not* to ask is: 'How do I know whom I meant?' For I have no *way* of knowing, I apply no criteria. (Wittgenstein suggests that the words 'know' and 'doubt' are both out of place here. But of course, one can in fact be said to forget whom one was speaking of, and thus to be in doubt, to be 'not sure'; and then to remember. But this is an unimportant qualification; for Wittgenstein discusses elsewhere the question of *remembering* one's intentions.)

PAIN AND PERSONS

(see 142, 243–315, 350–1, 384, 390, 398–421, II. iv, II. v)

Studying the sections in which Wittgenstein deals with sensations, one may well feel one's capacity to learn coming to an end. Wittgenstein's case against saying that the phrases 'meaning/

understanding something by an expression' stand for or name special experiences seems to me thoroughly made out. But even the significance of this denial comes into question if it then appears that no word whatever stands for or names a special experience. (Experiences which characteristically accompany 'I understand!' are not to be identified with understanding. Try substituting 'I am in pain' and 'pain' in the appropriate places here.) Wittgenstein seems to me to oscillate in his discussion of this subject between a stronger and a weaker thesis, of which the first is false and the second true. These may be described, rather than formulated, as follows. (I attach no importance to their descriptions: their significance must emerge later.) The stronger thesis says that no words name sensations (or 'private experiences'); and in particular the word 'pain' does not (cf. 293). The weaker thesis says that certain conditions must be satisfied for the existence of a common language in which sensations are ascribed to those who have them; and that certain confusions about sensations arise from the failure to appreciate this, and consequently to appreciate the way in which the language of sensations functions. The oscillation between the two theses is to be explained by the fact that the weaker can be made to yield to the stronger by the addition of a certain premise about language, viz., that all there is to be said about the descriptive meaning of a word is said when it is indicated what *criteria* people can use for employing it or for deciding whether or not it is correctly employed.

The stronger thesis is first developed by an attack on the idea of a private language (243 *et seq.*). By a 'private language' we are here to understand a language of which the individual names (descriptive words) refer solely to the sensations of the user of the language. He may be imagined as keeping a record of the occurrence of certain sensations. The main point of the attack is that the hypothetical user of the language would have no check on, no criterion of, the *correctness* of his use of it. We might be inclined to say that his memory provides a check. But what check has he on his memory? Suppose in the case of one particular word he keeps on misremembering its use. What difference will it make? There will be no way in which he can distinguish between a correct and an incorrect use.

So the idea of a correct use is empty here: and with it the idea of such a langauge. Now the interesting thing about the attack is that Wittgenstein presents it as if it applied only or peculiarly to the idea of a private language in which all the descriptive words were supposed to stand for sensations. But of course, if it has any validity at all, it has an equal validity for the case of a private language (here this means 'a language used by only one individual') in which the words stand not for sensations at all, but for things like colours or material objects or animals. Here again the individual will have no external check on the correctness of his use of the names. (It is no good saying that he can, in this case, though not in the case of the sensation-language, make himself a physical dictionary, e.g. a table with names opposite pictures. Wittgenstein's own arguments in other places are here decisive. The interpretation of the table depends on the use that is made of it.) But if this is so, then Wittgenstein's arguments would at most tend to show that the idea of a language *of any kind* used only by one person was an absurdity: and this conclusion would have no special immediate relevance to the case of sensation.

But it is clear that Wittgenstein intends his arguments to have special relevance to this case. So let us look at the differences between the two supposed private languages. We may suppose (following Wittgenstein) that in the case of the first private language, the one for sensations only, there are no particular characteristic overt expressions of the sensations, manifested by the hypothetical user of the language. Now we introduce observers, studying the behaviour and surroundings of the language users. The observer (B) of the user of the second langauge observes a correlation between the use of its words and sentences and the speaker's actions and environment. The observer of the user of the first language does not. Observer B is thus able to form hypotheses about the meanings (the regular use) of the words of his subject's language. He might in time come to be able to speak it: then the practice of each serves as a check on the correctness of the practice of the other. But shall we say that, before this fortunate result was achieved (before the use of the language becomes a *shared* 'form of life'), the words of the langauge had no meaning, no use? And if we do not say this of the case where this result can be achieved, why should we say it of the hypothetical case where it cannot? In each case, while the language is used by one person alone (let us say as in one of Wittgenstein's examples, to record occurrences), the meaning of the words is a matter of the customary practice of the user: in each case the only check on this customary practice is memory. But (it might be said), the hypothesis that someone was using a language of the first kind could never be tested. But what is to count as a test here? Suppose he also mastered the ordinary common language, and then *told us* that he had been (or was still) using a private language. It is also *just* worth asking, in connection with some of Wittgenstein's arguments here: do we ever in fact find ourselves misremembering the use of very *simple* words of our common language, and having to correct ourselves by attention to others' use? – Wittgenstein gives himself considerable trouble over the question of how a man would *introduce* a name for a sensation into this private language. But we need imagine no special ceremony. He might simply be struck by the recurrence of a certain sensation and get into the habit of making a certain mark in a different place every time it occurred. The making of the marks would help to impress the occurrence on his memory. One can easily imagine this procedure being elaborated into a system of dating. (The purpose of these remarks is to indicate the place the sensation-name might play in the private language-game.)

Another of Wittgenstein's main arguments is basically a variant on the first. He notes two associated points, which one is not inclined to dispute: (1) 'the expression of doubt has no place in the language-game' (288), i.e. in the language-game with 'I am in pain';[3] and (2) 'what I do (when I say "I am in pain") is not to identify my sensation by criteria' (290). Wittgenstein seems to think that these facts can only be accommodated if we regard 'I am in pain' as an *expression* or manifestation of pain, alongside such natural expressions as crying or groaning, but of course, one which, unlike these, is the result of training (244, 288, etc.). So regarded, 'pain' ceases to appear as the name or the description of a sensation. If we do *not* so regard it, then we shall require criteria of identity for the sensation; and with these there would enter the possibility of error (288). (Here one is, of course, reminded of the discussion of understanding. There are criteria of understanding, as of pain, which we apply in the case of others. But a man does not apply them to himself when he says 'I understand' – and his saying this is to be compared with an exclamation, a glad start, not a report of a mental occurrence.) Wittgenstein here seems to me to be in a muddle: the weaker thesis is being muddled with the stronger. What he has committed himself to is the view that one cannot sensibly be said to recognize or identify anything, unless one uses *criteria*; and, as a consequence of this, that one cannot recognize or identify sensations. But of course this is untrue. Consider cases where the rival pull of 'expression' or 'manifestation' is weaker or non-existent. Consider, for example, tastes; and such phrases as 'the taste of onions', 'a metallic taste'. Here we have one thing (a taste) associated with another (a material substance), but quite certainly recognizable and identifiable in itself. Only, of course, one does not use *criteria* of identity for *the taste*. If the question 'What is the criterion of identity here?' is pushed, one can only answer: 'Well, the taste itself' (cf. 'the sensation itself'). Of course, the phrases by which we *refer* to such tastes involve allusions to what can be seen and touched; for we speak a common language. But we do not identify the taste by means of the associated substance by allusion to which we name it. Consider also that we discriminate and recognize different particular pains (I do not mean pains in different places) – aches and throbs, searing and jabbing pains, etc. In many cases, there are not, or not obviously, different characteristic natural expressions of pain to correspond to these differences in quality. The phrases by which we name these particular pain-experiences are commonly analogical; and this too for the reason that we want a common language.[4] All the time here Wittgenstein is driving at the conditions that are necessary for a common language in which pain can be ascribed to persons, the consequent need for *criteria for the ascription* of pain, and the effects of this upon the use of the word 'pain' of our common language. Hence his obsession with the *expression* of pain. But he errs through excess of zeal when this leads him to deny that sensations can be recognized and bear names. Rather the case is that these names must always contain in a more or less complex way, within their logic, some allusion to what is not sensation, to what can be seen and touched and heard.

Why is this? The answer illuminates the nature of Wittgenstein's mistake, and also the great extent to which he is right.

(1) To deny that 'pain' is the name of a (type of) sensation is comparable with denying that 'red' is the name of a colour.

(2) It is just the difference between the ways colours and pains enter into our lives that accounts for the fact (i) that we call the latter and not the former sensations (or, alternatively, that accounts for the very special status we assign to sensations); it is just this difference that accounts for the fact (ii) that we *ascribe* pains to those who suffer them and not colours to those who see them; and which accounts for the fact (iii) that *without* criteria for ascribing pains to persons, we could have no common language of pain. Finally, it is because our common language-game must be that of ascribing pains to persons that symptoms, expressions, of pain assume such overwhelming importance.

(3) Fact (iii), misunderstood, is reflected (upside down) in all the usual philosophers' confusions about sensations; and, over-emphasized, is reflected (rightside up, but obscuring the rest of the picture) in Wittgenstein's.

To understand at least part of what is meant by 'the difference between the ways colours and pains enter our lives', it will be help-ful to consider some unrealized possibilities. Let us suppose first that we feel pain only and always under the condition that our skin is in contact with the surfaces of certain bodies. (Cf. Wittgenstein's 'pain-patches' (312). But he does not exploit this fully.) The pain begins and ends with the contact. Then our pain-language might have a logic wholly different from that which it does have. Instead of ascribing pains to sufferers, we might ascribe painfulness to sur-faces, much as we at present call them rough, smooth, hard, soft, etc. Another possibility is this. We say things like 'It's hot in here', 'It's cold out there', and so on, ascribing temperatures (I do not mean in degrees Fahrenheit or Centigrade) to regions. Let us suppose that any person felt pain if and only if every other normal person in the same region (which could be the size of a room or a continent) at the same time also felt pain. Then we might ascribe painfulness to regions instead of pain to persons; saying, e.g. 'It's painful today', or 'It's painful in here'. The point of both examples is that in each case we should have as *impersonal* a way of describing pain-phenomena as we have of describing colour-phenomena. But of course the incidence of physical pain is not like this. The causes of pain are often internal and organic. Even when pain is caused by contact, it generally requires a special kind of contact rather than contact with any special kind of thing; and it generally does not cease when contact ceases. If you have a pain and I come to the place where you are, or touch or look at what you are touching or looking at, this will not in general result in my having a pain. As Wittgenstein not infrequently points out, it is such very obvious general facts of nature which determine the logic of our concepts. I may put the point very roughly as follows. A set of people together in certain surroundings will be in general agreement on 'what it looks like here, what it feels like (to the touch) here, what it sounds like here'. In this possibility of a general agreement in judgments lies the possibility of a common impersonal langauge for describing what we see and hear and touch (cf. 242). But there is no such general agreement as to whether or not 'it's painful here', as to what it feels like (as we misleadingly say) *within*. In the absence of general agreement in judgment, a common language is impossible; and this is why a common impersonal pain-language is impossible. But if (to speak absurdly) we are prepared to make our pain-language a language for ascribing pain to persons, then we have something (i.e. people's pain-behaviour) which we see and hear, and on which, in consequence, general agreement in judgment is possible. Because of certain general facts of nature, therefore, the only possible common pain-language is the language in which pain is ascribed to those who talk the language, the criteria for its ascription being (mainly) pain-behaviour. And because of *this* fact it is necessarily empty and pointless (I will *not* say meaningless) either (*a*) to speculate about the ascription of pain to anything which does not exhibit behaviour comparable in the relevant respects with human behaviour (i.e. the behaviour of those who use the concept), or (*b*) to raise generalized doubts about other people's experience of pain, or about one's own knowledge of this. It is the above points which I take Wittgenstein essentially to be making. (He sees (142) that, as things are, the possibility of the language-game rests on there being characteristic expressions of pain.) But the way in which he makes them is, in part at least, misleading. For from none of these facts does it follow that 'pain' is not the name of a sensation. On the contrary. It is only in the light of the fact that 'pain' is the name of a sensation that *these* facts are intelligible; or, better, to say that 'pain' is the name of a sensation is (or ought to be) just to begin to draw attention to these facts. One could say: that pain is a sensation (or, that sensations have the special status they have) is a *fact of nature* which dictates the logic of 'pain'.

This outline is of course extremely crude. What a proper treatment of the topic above all requires is extensive and detailed *comparisons* between the different types of sensible experience we have.

THOUGHTS AND WORDS

(316–94, 427, 501, 540, 633–7, II. xi, pp. 211, 216–23)

Wittgenstein's treatment of this topic has close connections with his account of 'meaning/understanding something by an expression'; and presents certain analogies with the account of pain. It should first be noted that Wittgenstein is not primarily concerned with certain rather specialized applications of the word 'thinking' which are apt to come first to mind. We sometimes contrast the thinker and the active man; or may speak of having spent a fortnight's holiday without having a single thought. But Wittgenstein is not especially concerned with the thoughts which come only to the reflective. Again, we sometimes use 'thinking' in the sense of 'thinking out how to do something', or 'solving, or trying to solve, a problem', when the problem may indeed be as practical a one as you please. But Wittgenstein is not especially concerned with the thinking that overcomes difficulties. His concern is not restricted in either of these ways. He is quite as much interested in the most ordinary case of 'having a thought' or 'thinking something', in the sense in which, for example, someone who, talking neither at random nor insincerely, says that *p*, may be said to have had the thought that *p*, or to think that *p*, or to have said what he thought. The close connection between Wittgenstein's discussions of 'meaning something' and 'thinking' should now be clear. For if a man satisfies the criteria for meaning a sentence in a certain way (and is not insincere in uttering it), then he also satisfies the criteria for having thought something and said what he thought. So much of the argument on the former topic bears directly on the latter.

There is a certain once common view of the nature of thinking against which Wittgenstein's arguments are mainly directed. It is this. Thinking or having a thought is a special event or process which may accompany and be expressed in speech or writing or relevant action, and may also occur in the absence of these. No one can ever know what another's thoughts are in just the way he knows what his own are; for each man is directly cognisant only of his own internal processes. Wittgenstein's general counter-thesis runs as follows. It is true that having a thought is not to be identified with any particular outward process of speech or writing or action; nor with inner speech or other imagery. The having of a thought is not the occurrence of any of these; but nor is it any other occurrence. It is the occurrence of one of these in a certain context, in certain circumstances. To see what sort of context, what sort of circumstances are relevant here, one must consider what criteria are used in ascribing thoughts to people. A man's actions may show his thought (cf. 330), or his remarks may tell it; but if a monkey imitated the actions, or a parrot repeated the words, we should not ascribe the same thought to the monkey or the parrot. The difference does not lie in what went on inside them, but in the difference between the rest of their behaviour. Of course, a man does not, in telling his own thoughts, apply to himself the criteria for ascription of thoughts which he applies to others. But neither, when he says what he is or has been thinking, does he report on any concurrent or antecedent inner process. It is rather that he takes, or continues, a certain line of linguistic action, much as he might take or continue, in other circumstances, a certain line of non-linguistic action; and of course, he might 'think better of it', *change* his line.

It is quite clear and very important that Wittgenstein does not deny the existence of those occurrences, whether observable, like an exclamation, or unobservable, like what we call a flash of insight, or inward speech, by reference to which we may *date* the occurrence of a thought. What he is most concerned to stress is the fact that these occurrences do not owe their significance or their claim to the titles they bear, to their own peculiar nature or that of some psychical accompaniment; but to their place in a general pattern of actions and events. The concept of thinking demands such a general pattern as a setting for the occurrence of thoughts. In this, which I shall call his hostility to the doctrine of immediacy, Wittgenstein is surely right. Another factor in his treatment of thinking which is, I think, quite distinct from this, and also more questionable, might be called his hostility to the doctrine of privacy. It is because of this factor that I speak of analogies with his treatment of pain. I shall try to illustrate this from some of the things he says about inward speech, i.e. about saying something to oneself in imagination. (I would emphasize that the hostility to the doctrine of privacy is not of peculiar importance in connection with *thinking*. It has more general application. It is merely that it can be very clearly illustrated by some things that Wittgenstein says in the course of his discussion of thinking.)

II. xi, pp. 220–3, are largely concerned with telling or confessing what one 'has been saying to oneself in one's thoughts'. Wittgenstein says: (1) that what I say to myself in my thoughts is hidden from others only in the sense in which my thoughts are hidden from one who does not understand the language in which I speak out loud (pp. 220, 222); and (2) that when I tell another what I was saying to myself, or acknowledge that he has guessed aright, I do not describe what went on inside me: I do not tell what I was thinking from inspection of the inner process (p. 222). Now it seems to me that Wittgenstein is here equivocating with 'what I say to myself'; and that his motive for doing so is his hostility to the idea of what is not observed (seen, heard, smelt, touched, tasted), and in particular to the idea that what is not observed can in any sense be recognized or described or reported. The equivocation is made possible by the fact that 'what I was saying to myself in my thoughts' can mean either 'what I was thinking' or 'what words were going through my mind'. Now it is true that in saying what I was thinking, I do not report on 'what went on within me' (p. 222). In just the same way I do not tell what I am imagining by inspecting my image (II. iii). But also in just the same way I do not, in the case where I am talking or thinking aloud, discover what I am or have been thinking by listening to my words or their echo. As far as this goes, audible and inner speech are on the same level. (This fact indicates both the respect in which remark (1) above is justified and also the respect in which it is false.) They are on the same level in another way too. I may tell what I was saying to myself, not in the sense of telling that I was thinking, but in the sense of reporting what words were going through my mind. And here 'what went on within me' is just as much to the point, as 'what went on audibly' is when I am asked not to say what I meant when I spoke aloud, but to *repeat my words*. Of course, the difference between *these* two cases is that there is, and can be, no check (except the general reliability of my short-term memory) on my report of what words were going through my mind, whereas there can very well be a check on the correctness of my repetition of my audibly spoken words. But only a prejudice against 'the inner' would lead anyone, on the strength of this difference, to deny the possibility of the first kind of report. Only the same prejudice would lead anyone to deny that I can sometimes say something by way of description of my experiences of having imagery, as well as describing to people what I am imagining. (Having a confused and jumpy or intermittent image is not the same as imagining something as confused and jumpy or intermittent.) It is very likely true that some have not distinguished describing or reporting such experiences from telling what one is thinking, or describing what one is imagining. That a fact can be misconstrued is not, however, a reason for denying it. It is also true that when we describe 'private' or 'inner' or 'hidden' experiences, our descriptions of them (like our descriptions of their status) are often *analogical*; and the analogies are provided by what we *do* observe (i.e. hear, see, touch, etc.). This is in itself an important fact. It throws light once more on the conditions necessary for a common language. One could almost say that it is this fact which Wittgenstein is often stressing, often in a perverse way. But a description is none the worse for being analogical, especially if it couldn't be anything else.[5] Moreover, some of the analogies are *very good ones*. In particular the analogy between saying certain words to oneself and saying them out loud is very good. (One can even be unsure whether one has said them out loud or to oneself.) The analogy between mental pictures and pictures is, in familiar ways, less good.

Perhaps what is really operating here is the old verificationist horror of a claim that cannot be checked. Elsewhere in his treatment of thinking, Wittgenstein manifests the more intelligible aversion from a hypothesis or supposition that cannot be checked (344, 348–9).

STATES OF MIND AND INTROSPECTION

(572–87, II. i, ix. x; also 437, 465)

Wittgenstein writes on expectation, hope, belief, wishes, grief and fear. As in other cases, the main hostility is to the doctrine of immediacy. Expectation, hope, grief are forms of human life, each with many variations. What the subject of these states is at any given moment doing or experiencing gets its significance, its importance, from its surroundings (583–4), its context of situation and behaviour. The isolated occurrences could not claim these names. The falsity of the doctrine of immediacy is indeed, in some of these cases, a great deal more evident than it is in the cases of thinking or understanding. For a man may be said to expect or to believe or to be grieving over something when no thought of that thing is in his mind. There is therefore an *a fortiori* character about the non-immediacy of the states that these words name.

Among the criteria that we use for the ascription of certain of these states to another person, the *verbal* behaviour of the subject of them assumes an overwhelming importance. Wittgenstein in fact suggests that a necessary condition of the ascription of, e.g. hopes, wishes and some beliefs to a subject is the subject's mastery of a language for the *expression* of these (see II. i, ix and 650). His reason for this is clear. A creature's non-linguistic behaviour may certainly provide adequate criteria for the ascription of *some* states;

but where descriptions of states take on a slightly higher degree of complexity, it may be difficult or impossible to imagine what sort of complication of non-linguistic criteria would be adequate in the case of beings incapable of speech. ('We say a dog is afraid his master will beat him; but not, he is afraid his master will beat him to-morrow.') In the sections on thinking Wittgenstein placed an analogous and obviously connected restriction on the ascription of thoughts. It seems that one ought here to distinguish between the thesis that there are certain *kinds* of state (say, wishing or hoping) which cannot even in their simplest forms be ascribed to beings without the power of linguistically expressing them; and the weaker thesis that there are more complex forms of certain kinds of states (wishing, believing, hoping) which cannot be ascribed to beings without this power. The weaker thesis seems to me obviously true. Still more obviously, the stronger thesis must, on *one* interpretation, be false. Words like 'wish' and 'hope' could never acquire a use at all unless there were *some* circumstances or range of circumstances, other than that of their being uttered, in and because of which it was correct to use them; and since wishes and hopes are ascribed to others, these circumstances must include *criteria*, must include the observable. Wittgenstein's general principles here refute his particular thesis. I may, however, very likely be mistaken in ascribing the stronger thesis in this form to Wittgenstein. His position may rather be the intermediate one that *some* linguistic capacities are required in the subject to whom wishes and hopes are ascribed, not the specific linguistic capacity for the conventional expressions of wishes and hopes. So amended, the doctrine cannot, of course, be refuted in this way.

What in general of the roles of first-person utterances about states of mind? Wittgenstein here draws an admirable distinction between those first-person utterances which are correctly called reports of the results of introspection, or descriptions of states of mind, on the one hand, and those which are only misleadingly so called (and only so called by philosophers), on the other. We can *come to conclusions* about our own hopes, fears, expectations, even beliefs; and in doing so we use much the same criteria as we use in coming to conclusions about others, though we may (or may not) have certain advantages in our own case. But first-person utterances about states of mind are more commonly not of this kind, but of another: not conclusions about, but conventional expressions of, states of mind, taking their (special) place among the other criteria which are used in ascribing them. I think Wittgenstein does not perhaps give quite enough weight to the *very* special nature of this place, that he tends to exaggerate a little the degree to which, or the frequency with which, the utterances are, so to speak, forced from us. We use them very often pretty deliberately, and to inform; to show others where we stand, what we may be expected to do and for what reasons. And this may safely be admitted – without either returning to the doctrine of reported special experiences, or advancing to the absurdity that *all* such utterances are *conclusions* about ourselves – just so long as we acknowledge, what Wittgenstein elsewhere examines, the nature of our certainties about own deliberate behaviour. The utterance of 'I am embarrassed/amazed/ shocked/confident/very glad', etc. may be a social *act* (by this I mean something comparable with a polite greeting, a move to help someone, an offer of resistance, etc.); it may be a piece of deliberate self-revelation (compare exaggerating a *natural* facial expression) or an explanation of one's behaviour; it may be simply an embarrassed (amazed, etc.) *response*; it may be a conclusion about oneself, based on introspection (and only in this case does the question how one knows, arise); or it may be some, though not *any*, combination of these. I am not suggesting that Wittgenstein would dispute this diversity of function. On the contrary, much that he says (cf. especially II. ix on 'I am afraid') tends to emphasize it. It is rather that in his anxiety to stress the difference between most uses of these sentences on the one hand, and descriptions based on observation on the other, he tends perhaps to minimize their aspect as *deliberate exhibitions* of states of mind.

Immediately after the discussion of 'I am afraid', Wittgenstein reverts briefly to 'I am in pain' (p. 198). These words 'may be a cry of complaint and may be something else'. It looks as if he were almost prepared to acknowledge here that they may be just a report of my sensations. Pain is not, like grief, a pattern of life. And a report can *also* be a complaint; or a request.

VOLUNTARY ACTION AND INTENTION

(611–60, II. viii, II. xi, pp. 223–4)

What Wittgenstein says on these difficult topics is immensely suggestive and interesting – but elusive and incomplete. He begins
with a brilliant short account (611–20) of our temptation, under the
pressure of such a question as 'How do you raise your arm?' and of
obvious analogies, to think of willing as a special act of which the
phenomenal features of ordinary actions are consequences; a very
special act, for the obvious difficulties of this model then force us to
think of it not as an act which we perform, but as one which just
occurs, of the will as 'only a mover, not a moved'. Then, abruptly,
the problem is stated: '. . . what is left over if I subtract the fact that
my arm goes up from the fact that I raise my arm?' This is sunk in
the other question: 'How do you know (when your eyes are shut)
that you have raised your arm?' The answer is 'I feel it', and this
answer is correct, but misleading. For it suggests that you recognize
the special feelings (the kinaesthetic sensations) *and can tell from
recognizing them* that their constant accompaniment, the raising
of the arm, has occurred. And this is wrong. In fact, the certainty
that you have raised your arm is itself a criterion of recognizing
the feeling here (625). It is important to note two things that
Wittgenstein is *not* saying. He is not saying that one would have
this certainty in the absence of any feeling, or in the presence of an
unaccustomed feeling. It is no doubt *because* of the kinaesthetic
sensations that I know; but it is not *from* them that I tell (II. viii).
Nor is he saying that I could never (say, if suitably stimulated) be
mistaken about this (624). Here is a case where I know, but don't
have a *way* of knowing, of telling. Now he reverts to the former
question, and suggests: 'voluntary movement is marked by absence
of surprise' (628). As a *sufficient* condition (he neither says nor
denies that he means it as one), this will not do. Experience of
involuntary movements in certain circumstances might lead me to
be quite unsurprised by their occurrence. The answer suggested by
his own remarks about knowing, may be more useful. Voluntary
movements are characterized by a certainty of their having been

made, which neither has *nor needs* a ground; though it may both have and, in another sense, need a cause. It is still far from clear that we have a sufficient condition; for this seems true of many compelled or involuntary movements of parts of the body. But for the purposes of Wittgenstein's enquiry, I do not think a sufficient condition is required. For his purpose, I think, is to throw light from 'knowing what one has done' on 'knowing what one is going to do (intends)' and on 'knowing what one *was* going to do (intended)'. For there is no more reason to suppose that we need a *way* of knowing, of telling, in these cases than in that one. Of course, an announcement of a present intention, or a recalling of a past unexecuted intention is helped by, arises naturally from, the situation 'in which it is (or was) embedded'. But we do not read off or infer our intentions from these situations, any more than we tell what limb-movements we have just made from recognition of the accompanying sensations. (Nor in announcing or recalling our intentions do we report a current or remembered special experience. Look for this and it vanishes (645–6).) The point is that knowing what we intend to do is no more mysterious than knowing what we are going to do. (We as often make announcements of intention in the form 'I shall . . .' as in the form 'I intend to . . .'.) And a man may very well know what he is going to do (*be able to say*, if he is asked or if it should otherwise become desirable), and do it, without having raised the question to himself at all, without indeed having thought about it. The purpose – or one purpose – of announcing intentions is obvious: others have an interest in knowing what we will do. Remembering and telling a past unfulfilled intention is a less obvious case. An intention might be unfulfilled because I abandoned it or was interrupted or forestalled, etc.; or because my action failed of its effect. In no such case am I reporting something else that happened at the time. (This is particularly clear where my telling could be described as 'telling what I nearly did'.) It is rather that I exhibit *now* a response to the past situation; and my purpose in doing this may be to reveal to my auditor 'something of *myself*, which goes beyond what happened at the time' (659).

Evidently this topic – of doing and intending – could be pursued into refinements and elaborations which Wittgenstein, with his fixed polemical purpose, neglects. But rarely has a subject been treated so powerfully and suggestively in so few pages.

SEEING AND SEEING AS

(II. xi, pp. 193–214)

By means of a series of examples and comments, Wittgenstein seeks to bring out some of the complexities of the concept of seeing. The cases he mostly considers are very special ones; and it is consequently difficult to see just how far his conclusions reach. One thing at least which gives under the strain of his examples is the doctrine of the purely sensory given on the one hand, and our interpretation of it on the other, as two ever-present but distinguishable elements in visual perception.

The examples of which Wittgenstein writes are examples of 'the "dawning of" (noticing of) an aspect'. Sometimes when we look at a thing we suddenly *see* it *as* something different from what we saw it as before, while also seeing that it has not in any way changed. Easily the best cases of this are provided by certain schematic pictures or diagrams: but we may also, e.g. suddenly recognize a face, or suddenly see its likeness to another. In none of these cases is it to be supposed that we 'get a better (or different) view'. These cases, then, are to be sharply distinguished from those in which we suddenly see something because, say, a light has been switched on, or a screen removed. They are also to be distinguished from cases in which a man is able in certain ways to *treat*, say, a figure as a such-and-such or as a picture of a so-and-so, but does not have the experience of its suddenly assuming for him the aspect of a such-and-such or of a picture of a so-and-so. The difference from the first of these contrasted cases is that when a man *sees* something *as x* and then *as y*, there is a perfectly good sense in which it looks the same to him as it did before: viz., that drawings showing it as it looked to him before and after the change of aspect would be indistinguishable. The difference from the second contrasted case is that a man on whom an aspect dawns is not merely prepared to make different applications of what he sees, but also sees it differently, has the 'visual experience' of a change of aspect.

Wittgenstein notes an ambiguity in 'seeing as', which it is important to mention since it emphasizes the special character of the experience he is concerned with. Suppose we have a visually ambiguous object such as Wittgenstein's duck-rabbit – a picture which can be seen as a picture of a duck or again as a picture of a rabbit. Then a man who never has the experience of the change of aspects, the dawning of an aspect, may nevertheless be said by those who know of its visual ambiguity to see it as, say (a picture of) a rabbit. So a person may in an unimportant sense see something as something without having the experience in which Wittgenstein is interested. In neither sense is something which is not visually ambiguous – say, a conventional picture of a lion – normally said to be 'seen as' anything.

Why is the experience of the dawning of an aspect of such particular interest to Wittgenstein? He suggests that its importance resides in an analogy with 'experiencing the meaning of a word' (p. 214). Perhaps we might say that when an aspect of a figure dawns on us, we are 'experiencing an interpretation of the figure'. What we have here is something instantaneous, a visual experience; but it is also true that a *logical* condition of our having the experience is our being capable of making such-and-such applications of the figure, of reacting to it in certain ways, of *treating* it as what we *see* it as (p. 208). If we are to describe the experience correctly, we cannot isolate a 'pure visual element' in it and say that that and that alone is the momentary experience (cf. p. 193); we can describe the experience correctly only by referring to what does not relate to the moment. (Wittgenstein is helped in making this point by the fact that the figure in one sense presents exactly the same visual appearance – does not look different – before and after the dawning of the aspect.) We have here, Wittgenstein says, a modified concept of experience, of seeing.

What Wittgenstein is essentially opposed to is the conjunction of the three propositions: (1) that we have here (*a*) a pure sensory element, and (*b*) an interpretation (a tendency to treat what we see in certain ways); (2) that (*a*) and (*b*) are simply associated or conjoined; and (3) that (*a*) alone is the visual experience proper. What may at first seem odd is not this opposition, nor the remark that we have here a modified concept of experience (contrast for example with pains), but the remark that we have here a modified concept of seeing (209). For surely ordinary instantaneous visual experiences, such as we have when the light is switched on and we suddenly see the room and its contents, can also be correctly described only by a description which entails our possession of concepts of certain kinds, and which thus refers beyond the moment. So in what way is the concept of seeing *modified* in the special case of seeing as? I think the *difference* between the cases, which leads Wittgenstein to speak of a modification of the concept, is the presence in the case where the light is switched on of just such an instantaneous change in the way things look, in the visual appearance of things, as is absent from the case where the aspect changes. But if this is right, it is not very happy to speak of a modification of the concept of seeing in a way which suggests that a certain feature which is common to both seeing and 'seeing as' is peculiar to the latter.

CONCLUSION

Wittgenstein has penetrating and illuminating things to say on other subjects: for example, identity and difference of meaning, meaninglessness, negation, induction, dreams, and memory. But the topics which I have selected are those which receive most extensive treatment. On these I have tried to summarize and criticize his main arguments and conclusions, aware that much of the power, vividness and subtlety with which, by means of example, comment and epigram, these conclusions are presented, must in this way be lost. For this there is no remedy but study of the book itself.

Three cardinal elements in his thought, as presented in this book, may perhaps be epitomized in these quotations:

(1) 'To imagine a language is to imagine a form of life' (19) and 'What has to be accepted, the given, is – so one could say – forms of life' (p. 226).

(2) 'What is happening now has significance – in these surroundings. The surroundings give it its importance' (583).
(3) 'An "inner process" stands in need of outward criteria' (580).

The first may serve to remind us of a general prescription for doing
philosophy: to understand a concept, a word, put the word in its
linguistic context and the whole utterance in its social context and
then describe, without preconceptions, what you find; remembering
that each word, each utterance, may figure in *many* contexts.

The second epitomizes what I earlier called the hostility to the
doctrine of immediacy. It has analogies with the first. Just as a word
gets its significance from the context of its use, so those elements of
our experience which we are tempted to isolate (or, failing this, to
fabricate) and make the self-sufficient bearers of certain names get
their significance too from their setting, from the form of life to
which their titles allude.

The third, though it contains much that is true, contains also
the germ of mistakes. It epitomizes the hostility to the doctrine of
privacy. For the worn and dangerous 'outward' and 'inner' we may
substitute 'shared' and unshared'. Then what is right and wrong in
Wittgenstein here begins from the insight that a common language
for describing and reporting requires general agreement in judgments. So for a (descriptive) word or phrase to belong to a common
language, it is essential that *the occasions on which it is right to
apply it should provide shared experiences of a certain kind*, the
existence of which is connected with the rightness of applying the
word. The experiences need not be connected with the rightness of
applying the word or phrase as *criteria* for its application. No one
has *criteria* for something's looking red, though this is something
on which we commonly agree. (Wittgenstein is perhaps misled
here by temporarily confusing criteria which justify one in applying a word or phrase with criteria which justify one in saying that it
is correctly applied. That there is a distinction is clear from much
else that Wittgenstein says. For *every* expression of a common
language (I speak here of non-analogical uses) there must exist, in
the common practice of the use of the expression, criteria for
determining whether a given use of it is correct or not. This will be

so even where the expression in question has no descriptive use at all. So the existence of criteria for the correctness of the use of an expression does not entail that using it correctly is applying it on the strength of certain criteria. Wittgenstein would agree that the entailment does not *generally* hold; and there is no reason for thinking that it holds in the *special* case of descriptive or reporting uses of expressions. Moreover it could be independently argued that it *could* not hold here.) Now, when a word is not applied on the strength of shareable experiences, Wittgenstein is inclined to say that it is not applied in the way of report or description at all, but is used in some other way, is something else: e.g. a response, the habit of which is acquired by training, an action, a signal and so on. Sometimes, often, this is right: it is right in just those cases where the relevant shareable experiences count as criteria in the full, *logical* sense of that word. But there are other cases for which, taken as a general rule, it is wrong. For sometimes a person applies a word or phrase not on the strength of shareable experiences but on the strength of non-shareable experiences, and *is* publicly reporting or describing those experiences; and this he is enabled to do either by the existence of shared experiences which count as signs (criteria in the weaker sense) of the occurrence of the unshared experiences (the case of 'I am in pain'), or by the adoption or invention of analogical modes of description, where the analogy is with share-able experiences (e.g. reporting the words that pass through my mind).[6] What misleads Wittgenstein here is, I think, partly the belief that criteria are always essential to a report or description, a belief in its turn based, perhaps, on the confusion, mentioned above, between criteria for application and criteria for correctness; and partly the fear of legitimizing certain metaphysical doubtings and wonderings. As for these, they are, if you like, senseless: but in their own way, and not in any other. They are pointless and unreal and you can do nothing with them (unless you strip them of their form and use them to point a contrast); and that is condemnation enough.

Right or wrong, Wittgenstein's particular doctrines are of the greatest interest and importance. But the value of the book as a model of philosophical method is greater still. (Here I do *not* refer to idiosyncrasies of style and form.) It will consolidate the philosophical revolution for which, more than anyone else, its author was responsible.

NOTES

1 Wittgenstein uses this phrase to refer to any particular way, actual or invented, of using language (e.g. to a particular way of using a certain sentence, or a certain word); and also to 'the whole consisting of language and the actions into which it is woven' (7).

2 Cf. G. Ryle, 'Ordinary Language', *The Philosophical Review*, vol. LXII, April 1953, pp. 178–80. Perhaps Professor Ryle puts too much weight on the fact (if it is a fact) that we do not speak of the 'use' of sentences. Certainly we use them. But it is at any rate true that there are some things we might mean by 'the use of a word' which we could not mean by 'the use of a sentence'; and the other way about.

3 Even this is not quite true as it stands. There is no place for one kind of doubt, the kind that might be expressed in 'Am I interpreting the facts of this situation aright?' But there is sometimes place for another kind, which might be expressed in 'Does this quite deserve the *name* of "pain" '?

4 The fact that there are characteristic natural expressions of pain but not (or not obviously) characteristic differences between natural expressions of different kinds of pain (I do not mean different degrees or locations) is the explanation of the fact that the descriptions of the different kinds tend to be analogical, whereas the word 'pain' is not analogical. See below.

5 If one were *very* anxious to appease here, one *could* say they were only 'descriptions' in an analogical sense. But I think this would be being over-anxious.

6 Of course (*a*) the antithesis 'shared' and 'unshared' which I have used here, is a shorthand no more immune from misunderstanding than any other; and (*b*) I do not suggest that it represents a sharp division: tastes, for example, might count as an intermediate case, since one has to do something rather special to get them shared on a given occasion.

8

SELF, MIND AND BODY

One of the marks, though not a necessary mark, of a really great philosopher is to make a really great mistake: that is to say, to give a persuasive and lastingly influential form to one of those fundamental misconceptions to which the human intellect is prone when it concerns itself with the ultimate categories of thought. So today, more than three hundred years after the death of René Descartes, philosophers struggling with one of these fundamental misconceptions think of it under the name of Cartesian dualism. Not that they all think of the doctrine in question as a misconception. The doctrine has its defenders. Indeed if it did not represent a way of thinking about mind and body which has a powerful intellectual appeal, it would not be worth struggling against. There is little point in refuting errors which no one is inclined to make.

In this article I want to try to bring out the force of one way, which has received some attention in recent English philosophy, of demonstrating the, or a, central error in Cartesian dualism. First, we need a reasonably clear statement of the dualist position to work on.

It seems an obvious and uncontentious point that the sorts of things which we can truthfully say about ourselves and other human beings are very various, that they form a very mixed bag indeed. Thus we can and do ascribe to one and the same individual human being things as various as actions, intentions, sensations, thoughts, feelings, perceptions, memories, physical position, corporeal characteristics, skills or abilities, traits of character and so on. A person or human being, as a subject of discourse, typically collects predicates of all these kinds. Now a Cartesian dualist is one who holds that this way of talking about people, though convenient and perhaps essential for practical purposes, tends to disguise rather than display the real nature of a human individual. We should first recognize, he thinks, that of these various predicates some refer directly to the states of consciousness of a person, some refer directly to his bodily condition and some refer in a more or less indirect and complicated way to both at once. But recognizing this is no more than a step in the right direction. It is not enough to acknowledge that a person has two sides to his nature and his history, a mental or conscious side and a material or corporeal side. For really the history of a human being is not the history of one two-sided thing, it is the history of two one-sided things. One of these things is a material object, a body; the other is an immaterial object, a soul or mind or spirit or individual consciousness. These are totally distinct kinds of thing, with totally distinct kinds of properties and states. None of the predicates which properly apply to bodies (like having a certain weight or size or colouring) properly apply to minds; and none of the predicates which properly apply to consciousnesses (like having a certain thought or experiencing a certain sensation) properly apply to bodies. During the lifetime of a human being, two of these things, one of each kind, are peculiarly intimately related; but the intimacy of their union does not count against or diminish the essential independence of their nature.

Now if the Cartesian were right in this, it seems that it should be possible in principle to lay down at least the general outlines of a new and more metaphysically revealing way of talking about people than that which we find practically convenient. This new way of talking would reflect, in a dualism of grammatical or linguistic subjects the dualism of real or metaphysical subjects which the Cartesian finds conjoined in the human individual. If we assembled all the statements which in our ordinary way of talk-ing have the name of one man as their grammatical subject, and reconstructed them in a Cartesian grammar, then for each state-ment there would be three possibilities of reconstruction: either the grammatical subject of the new statement would be the designation of a body or part of a body or it would be the designation of a mind or consciousness or the original statement would be analysed into two separate statements, one of them about a mind and one of them about a body.

It might seem at first that the germs of an 'improved' or Cartesian style of speech about people were already present in our ordinary style of speech about people. For included in our ordinary style of speech is a lot of perfectly intelligible talk in which we explicitly ascribe predicates to people's bodies (or parts of them) and also a lot of perfectly intelligible talk in which we explicitly ascribe predi-cates to people's minds or even consciousnesses. So it might look as if our ordinary habits of thought and speech already contained an implicit, though incomplete, acknowledgement of the truth of Cartesianism.

However, it is clearly not enough for the Cartesian to point to our habit of talking about people's minds and bodies as well as about people, as if this were conclusive evidence for his thesis. The difference between the Cartesian and his opponent is a difference of view about the *relation* between the concept of a person on the one hand and the concept of a person's mind on the other. The anti-Cartesian holds that the concept of a person's mind has a secondary or dependent status. The fundamental concept, for him, is that of a human being, a man, a type of thing to which predicates of *all* those various classes I distinguished earlier can be ascribed. To talk about the mind of a man is just a way of talking about a man, in respect of certain sorts of things that are true of him. Just so we can talk of the *surfaces* of tables as well as of tables, of the *score* in a football match as well as of a football match. But we recognize that the concept of a surface is dependent on the concept of a material object, that the concept of a score is dependent on the concept of a game. Similarly, the anti-Cartesian holds, the concept of a mind or consciousness is dependent on the concept of a living person.

But the Cartesian cannot admit this dependence. He must hold that the notion of an individual consciousness or mind is perfectly intelligible apart from the notion of a person whose mind or individual consciousness it is. He cannot admit that the idea of a mind presupposes that of a person; he must hold, on the contrary, that a dualistic *reduction* or *analysis* of the idea of a person is in principle possible or intelligible.

Let us consider more carefully what would be necessary in order for a Cartesian reduction to be successfully carried through. We begin with statements of which the subjects are the designations of people and the predicates are of the various kinds already mentioned. The Cartesian thesis requires that these be replaceable in principle with sentences of which the subjects are either the designations of minds (consciousnesses) or the designations of bodies. Hence it seems to require too that the predicates of our original sentences should either be already equivalent to consciousness-predicates or to body-predicates or be capable of being analysed into a body-predicate component and a consciousness-predicate component. Moreover the Cartesian reduction-sentences, it seems, must be genuinely, and not merely apparently, reductive. Consider, for example, the statement that John is writing a letter. 'Writing a letter' seems to be one of those predicates which must be split up into a mental component and a bodily component; but it would seem unsatisfactory to try to isolate the mental component by means of some such a sentence as 'His mind was going through the mental processes involved in writing a letter'. For this leaves it open to the anti-Cartesian to say that the concept of such a mental process is dependent on the concept of writing a letter; and that writing a letter is essentially not something that a mind does or something that a body does, but something that a person does.

It seems, then, that there might be very considerable difficulties in effecting a genuine reduction of person-predicates to a mental component and a bodily component. And many of these difficulties are very clearly indicated in some work in recent British philosophy, notably in Professor Ryle's book, *The Concept of Mind*, and in Wittgenstein's posthumous *Philosophical Investigations*. Yet I think that a convinced Cartesian might be comparatively unmoved by this kind of difficulty. He might agree that there were good reasons why our language was unequipped with, and perhaps was bound to remain unequipped with, the resources necessary for a genuine reduction of all such predicates as these to a mental component and a bodily component, and yet maintain that it was really quite obvious that all such activities as writing a letter really did involve both mental processes and bodily processes; and it would be hard to deny that on this point he was right in some sense, even if not in quite the sense he supposed.

What would move the Cartesian much more, I think, would be a clear demonstration that there was something wrong, not on the predicate side, but on the subject side, with the idea of a Cartesian reduction. We have already remarked that it is not sufficient for the Cartesian to appeal to the fact that we do intelligibly talk about people's minds and people's bodies. The anti-Cartesian thesis is not the thesis that there are no such things as minds, but that the concept of an individual mind or consciousness is only to be understood as logically derivative from the concept of an individual person. It is up to the Cartesian to show that this is not so, to show that we can make perfectly good sense of the idea of an individual mind without making that very idea dependent upon the idea of an individual person. Hence it is a prima facie awkwardness for the Cartesian that when we ordinarily talk about people's minds or consciousnesses, we do so by way of referring to the people whose minds or consciousnesses they are. Thus if we say 'Mary's consciousness was entirely occupied by the thought of how becoming her dress was', the grammatical subject of our statement is certainly the designation of an individual mind or consciousness. But we succeed in designating the consciousness only by way of designating Mary; and Mary, happily, is not simply a consciousness; she is not only *thinking* about the dress, she is *wearing* it.

It is easy enough for the Cartesian to meet this difficulty in a formal way: that is, to give examples of expressions designating consciousnesses which don't formally depend on designating people. One general form of substitute-designation might go something like this: 'The consciousness which stands in a peculiarly intimate relation with the body in such-and-such a place'. Another general form might run something like this: 'The mind which is at such-and-such a time occupied by such-and-such thoughts and feelings'. But we simply don't know whether, by the use of such forms, we achieve a reference to a mind which is genuinely independent of reference to a person, until we know the answer to a further and most important question: viz., what justifies us in using the little word 'the' – implying reference to a single one – before 'mind' or 'consciousness'.

It is here that we come – at last – to the central difficulty in Cartesianism. If we are to talk coherently about individual consciousnesses or minds, or about individual items of any kind whatever, there is one thing at least which we must know. We must know the difference between *one* such item and *two* such items. We must know, that is, on what principle such items are to be counted. And this means further – if they are supposed to be items capable of lasting through a period of time – that we must know how to identify the *same* item at different times. In general we have no idea what a *so-and-so* is unless we have some idea what *a* so-and-so is. If we have no idea of how the notions of numerical identity and difference apply to individual consciousnesses then we really have no clear concept at all of such items.

Now the anti-Cartesian is able to satisfy this requirement for having a coherent concept of an individual mind or consciousness. Since he regards this concept as secondary to, or derivative from, that of an individual person, he can advance the following simple rule: *one* person, *one* consciousness; *same* person, *same* consciousness. His recipe for counting individual minds is to count people; for him the identification of a mind presents no greater (and no less) a problem than the identification of a person. He does not have to pretend that the question as to what the criteria of personal identity are is an easy or straightforward question. But he can properly point out that we have, and know how to use, adequate criteria for ordinary cases; and that we can perfectly intelligibly discuss how our criteria should be interpreted or adapted for any extraordinary cases which we might encounter or imagine.

But how does the matter stand on the Cartesian philosopher's view? It is essential to his view that the application of the notions of identity and numerability to souls (consciousnesses) should *not* be determined by their application to persons. (The determining must be the other way about.) But then how *is* the application of these notions to souls or consciousnesses to be determined? Suppose I were in debate with a Cartesian philosopher, say Professor X. If I were to suggest that when *the man*, Professor X, speaks, there are a thousand souls simultaneously thinking the thoughts his words express, having qualitatively indistinguishable experiences such as he, the man, would currently claim, how would he persuade me that there was only one such soul? (How would each indignant soul, once the doubt has entered, persuade itself of its uniqueness?) There is another, more familiar difficulty, about the identity of a soul from one time to another. If the concept of the identity of a soul or consciousness over time is not derivative from, dependent upon, the concept of the identity of a person over time, then how is it determined? What do we mean by 'the same consciousness' if not 'the same person's consciousness'? Some philosophers, like the British empiricist, Locke, used to suppose that an adequate account of the identity of a consciousness through time could be given in terms of memory alone; but the failure of such accounts is a commonplace of philosophical criticism which I will not repeat. Other philosophers refer, or used to refer, to a Pure Ego or soul-substance, as if this exempted them from having any idea what it *meant* to speak of *the same one* from one time to another. To them one may reply, in a rough paraphrase of Kant: if you're allowed to invoke that hypothesis whenever you like, without being required to elucidate the principle of its application, what is to prevent me from introducing a rival hypothesis, also unelucidated: wherever you say there's one continuing soul-substance, I say there's a whole series of them each of which transmits its states and the consciousness of them, to its successor, as motion might be transmitted from one to another of a whole series of elastic balls.

The dilemma is roughly, this. Either the concepts of identity and difference of individual human consciousnesses are derivative from the concepts of identity and difference of individual people (human beings, men and women) or they are not. If they are, then our ordinary style of talking about human beings is not even in principle reducible in the way in which the Cartesian must hold that it is. If they are not, if a Cartesian reduction is in principle possible, then it must also be possible to make *independently* intelligible what is meant by identity and difference of human consciousness. But there is not the slightest reason for thinking that this can be done.

What, then, is the source of the Cartesian delusion? Well, no doubt it has several sources. But I think a particularly important one is a certain experience of intense looking within, or introspective concentration, of which most of us are capable and which certainly seems to have been characteristic of Descartes' own meditations. One is tempted to say in such moments that one has direct experience of oneself as a conscious being. And this may be a harmless thing to say. But it may put us on the path of illusion. Let us see how it can do so.

The ordinary personal pronouns and possessives, including 'I' and 'my', are used in ordinary inter-personal communication for the purposes of personal reference. If the speaker says 'I', his or her hearers know what man or woman is meant. But when we reflect philosophically on the type of introspective experience I have just described, we can quite easily get into a kind of daze about the meaning of 'I' and '*my*'. We can say to ourselves things like '*I* am aware of *myself* now' or 'This is how it is with *me* now' and say such things with the conviction of their expressing absolutely indubitable fact. And then perhaps we may begin to feel that we don't have to *explain* the notions of identity and difference as applied to the soul, for we have *direct experience* of the individuality and identity of the soul, experience which might be expressed in remarks like these. And no doubt an experience of some kind *is* expressed in such a remark. But, really, if we make this kind of *claim* about it (i.e. that it is direct experience of the individuality and identity of the human soul), then we are trying to have things both ways: we are trying to keep the immediacy and indubitability of the experience and at the same time to keep the ordinary referential force of 'I', the word that the individual *man* uses to refer to himself. We are tricking ourselves by simultaneously withdrawing the pronoun from the ordinary game and yet preserving the illusion that we're still using it to play the ordinary game. And it should be easy to see this, since Kant exposed the illusion; yet, as Kant also remarked, the illusion is powerful. Perhaps a way to get at it is this. All the immediacy and indubitability of experience which seem to go with the use of 'I' and 'me' in such remarks as I've just quoted could be preserved while re-expressing the remarks in some such form as '*This* is a conscious experience' or 'The soul having this experience is conscious of itself as having *this* experience'. Then it would be apparent where the limits of immediacy and indubitability fall; it would be apparent that there is nothing in the experience itself to rule out the suggestion that there might be a thousand exactly similar experiences occurring in association with the same body – hence a thousand souls simultaneously associated with that body – and equally nothing to rule out the suggestion that the, or each, soul having such an experience is just one evanescent member of such a temporal series as Kant spoke of – hence, perhaps, a thousand souls the next moment. If this suggestion is to be ruled out, it must be on grounds extraneous to the experience itself. But the fact that this is so is masked by the use of 'I' and 'me' – expressions which, even while they seem in this context to shake off, yet surreptitiously invoke, the ordinary criteria of distinctness and identity of persons. For when *a man says* 'I', then there speaks *one* identifiable man: he can be *distinguished* as *one* by ordinary criteria and *identified* by ordinary criteria as, perhaps, Professor X, the Cartesian.

The fact is that a Cartesian and an anti-Cartesian alike, and anyone else who wants to be taken seriously on the subject of the soul, wants his doctrine to have the consequence that a perfectly ordinary man, in the course of a perfectly ordinary life, has just one soul or consciousness which lasts him throughout. There is only one way of guaranteeing this consequence; and that is to allow that the notions of singularity and identity of souls or consciousnesses are conceptually dependent on those of singularity and identity of men or people. But if we allow this, we must reject a Cartesian conception of the soul.

The arguments I have used to bring out a central incoherence in the doctrine of Cartesian dualism are arguments of a partly logical, and partly epistemological, character. They turn essentially on the notions of the identity, and of the identification, of particular things. The importance of these notions, both in the present connection and in others, has recently received a fair measure of acknowledgement in English philosophy. But, as my references to Kant have shown, these arguments are not essentially novelties, any more than is the recognition of the importance of these notions. The progress of philosophy, at least, is dialectical: we return to old insights in new and, we hope, improved forms.

9

AESTHETIC APPRAISAL AND
WORKS OF ART

We have the words, *assessment, appraisal, evaluation, criticism, judgment.* No doubt their senses are different. But I do not want now to distinguish between them. I want to consider instead one way in which we distinguish, within the application of each, between different *kinds* of assessment, appraisal or judgment. For some of these kinds we have special names: we speak of moral or logical or aesthetic appraisal, criticism or judgment. More often, perhaps, we speak of judging a thing from such-and-such a point of view, or by such-and-such standards, or of judging it as a so-and-so. Thus things may be judged by military or financial standards; from the soldier's, the plumber's or the economist's point of view; a thing may be judged as a piece of plumbing, as an investment, as a work of art or as a concert-hall. It is not redundant when we are assessing something, say an X, to precede our verdict with the phrase, 'as an X'; to say 'As an X, it is good, fair, bad'. It is not redundant, for there are many points of view from which anything can be assessed; and it is an important fact that we can sometimes make our point of view clear by using the ordinary classificatory name for a thing, by speaking of judging it as an X, where 'X' is that name.

Can anything clear and general be said which will distinguish, among these kinds of assessment, the aesthetic? We should note, first, that the word 'aesthetic' perhaps has normally a narrower use than we at least half-wish to make of it in asking the question. It would be odd to say, 'He didn't really judge it as a painting; he judged it from a narrowly aesthetic point of view.' But it would not be odd to say, 'He judged it from a narrowly aesthetic point of view; he didn't really judge it *as a novel* at all.' In spite of this, we are inclined, or half-inclined, to think of our question as a question about a kind of assessment that includes judging a novel as a novel as well as judging a painting as a painting. If, on the other hand, someone said, 'He was judging it from a purely aesthetic point of view; he wasn't judging it as a game of football' (or 'as a contribution to the discussion' or 'as a piece of engineering'), then we should be less inclined to make reservations about the implied contrast. So we claim to be interested in a kind of assessment which certainly includes judging a painting as a painting, and perhaps includes judging a novel as a novel, but does not seem to include judging a game of football as a game of football, a contribution to a discussion as a contribution to a discussion or a piece of engineering as a piece of engineering. But though our kind of assessment does not seem to include these kinds, these kinds might be said by some to include our kind. And, whether this is said or not, we certainly want to say that the aesthetic is a kind of assessment which *can* be made of what is in fact a game of football, a contribution to a discussion or a piece of engineering. And the question then arises: is there such a kind of assessment? Or – since there *are* whatever kinds of things we like, and we can draw lines where we choose – can anything clear and general be said about the nature of this kind of assessment?

The reasons for answering 'No' seem very strong. For in what direction should we look for something clear and general? The traditional directions seem unpromising, the results of following them inspire a kind of disgust. Following one of these traditional directions consisted in asking: what is there common and peculiar to the objects of which we make a favourable assessment of the kind concerned? But we do not expect a helpful answer to this; for the items and kinds of items of which we may make an aesthetic assessment are nearly as diverse as the items and kinds of items there are. They are not quite as diverse as this. It would be very precious for anyone to say that he found predication or disjunction aesthetically admirable (though I have heard a logician say that he found quantification aesthetically admirable). But most of what we find or make, whether concrete like a lily-pond or abstract like a proof, can be so assessed.

Following another traditional direction of search consisted in asking: when we enjoy something of which we make a favourable assessment of the kind concerned, what is there special about our response to, our experience of, the thing? But the looking within, which this encourages, is, for good reasons, out of fashion. *Can* we detect a special experience which always accompanies this kind of enjoyment and no other? And, if we could, would *its* presence be what made it *this* kind of enjoyment?

A third and less debilitating line of enquiry might seem to exist: viz., in an examination of the kinds of language we typically use in articulating assessments of the kind concerned. And certainly there are plenty of questions about these uses of language: but the profitable ones seem more limited and departmental than the general question of the general distinction between aesthetic assessment and other kinds. In relation to this question, the apparently limitless elasticity and variety of the vocabulary of criticism are merely daunting.

So scepticism about the possibility of a clear and general answer to the general question is natural. And if challenged to explain why we nevertheless are here inclined to speak of one kind of assessment the sceptic has a reasonable answer, which runs, or might run, like this. Many of the kinds of assessment we make are such that there is no particular relation between favourable assessment of a thing and *enjoyment* of that thing. But for some ways of praising, there is a very close, though not an invariable, connection between assessing something favourably and enjoying it. This is the case with what we call aesthetic appraisal and aesthetic enjoyments. Further, there are certain obvious analogies and contrasts between different kinds of enjoyment. One can enjoy a game, argument or dance one takes part in, and say at the end: 'That was a good game (argument, dance)'. One can also enjoy a game or a dance one watches or an argument one listens to or reads, and again say at the end, 'That was a good game (argument, dance)'. There is an analogy between the members of this second group of enjoyments and appraisals; and a contrast between the second group and the first. In general one can find a contrast between the enjoyment of what one reads, listens to, looks at or tastes on the one hand, and, on the other, the enjoyment of the activities of work, play and exercise in which one takes part; though the two kinds of enjoyment may be mixed. Suppose we call the former 'spectator-enjoyments' and the latter 'participant-enjoyments'. Then aesthetic enjoyments take their place among spectator-enjoyments. But they have no very *definite* place there. What happens, perhaps, is this. Certain spectator-enjoyments are easily discriminable by the fact that a certain single sense is appealed to; say, the eye or the ear. Suppose we regard these two as aesthetic enjoyments *par excellence*. Then, especially when we come to say what it is about the objects of our spectator-enjoyments that we enjoy, we find ourselves finding analogies between the objects of very different spectator-enjoyments. Not all objects of spectator-enjoyment are equally joined by these links of analogy to the objects of aesthetic enjoyment *par excellence*. Some (say, exhibitions of bear-baiting) are not joined at all; some (say, cheese, regarded as an object of taste) by very few links; some (say, mathematical proofs or philosophical arguments) by links of analogy which, though perhaps not weak, may seem insignificant in comparison with points of contrast; some, (say, poetry) by very strong links indeed. Objects not directly linked to the centre may be linked to it by other objects so linked. The existence of this network of analogy then generates the illusion that there is one definite and distinctive *kind* of enjoyment, and one definite and distinctive *kind* of appraisal, viz., the aesthetic. When we are said to be enjoying or admiring something from an aesthetic point of view, all this can in fact mean is that in saying what it is about the object of our spectator-enjoyment that we enjoy, we find ourselves on one of the indefinitely numerous, indefinitely extendable lines which make up this network of analogy. The attempt to find a more definite meaning than this, the attempt to describe the general nature or essence of aesthetic enjoyment or appraisal, must always be futile, must always end in promoting one impossibly stretched analogy to the status of a theory, or in fabricating a special experience, or in some other wearisome error.

Perhaps this scepticism is right. I am at least half-inclined to think that it is. But I am also half-inclined to think that it is not, half-inclined, that is to say, to favour a more positive account. I certainly do not claim that this account is original; only that it is, from time to time, worth reconsidering. For there seems to be a feature of aesthetic judgment, repeatedly but obscurely stressed by writers on the subject, which might contain the possibility of a general distinction; a distinction which does not relate to some special character of the objects of aesthetic enjoyment nor to some special experience of enjoying, but is, rather, a formal, or logical, distinction. The feature I have in mind was effectively stressed by Professor Hampshire in an article published some years ago.[1] He set in extreme contrast two classes of judgments: moral judgments of action and critical judgments of art. To the former, he said, general rules and principles are essential; to the latter, quite irrelevant. He meant, I think, that it is quite meaningless and empty to praise a man's character or express moral approval of one of his acts without having reasons of a certain sort – of such a sort that giving the reasons would involve mentioning, in terms not themselves evaluative, generally applicable criteria of excellence in men or rightness in acts; whereas judgment in aesthetic matters is not thus wedded to non-evaluative descriptions of general features of the thing judged. Of course, this does not mean that nothing can be said in amplification and support of an aesthetic 'This is good'. But either what is said in amplification and support is not non-evaluative, as when we amplify our judgment by the use of further evaluative words, such as 'masterly', 'brilliant', 'original', etc.; or it is not general, but consists essentially in drawing attention to particular features or parts of the object praised, and their relations to each other in the object. Typical sentences from Hampshire are: 'The canons of success and failure . . . are . . . internal to the work [of art] itself'; 'Virtue and good conduct are essentially repeatable and imitable, in a sense in which the work of art is not'; '[The] purpose [of the critic] is to lead people . . . to look at precisely this unique object, not to see the object as one of a kind, but as individual and unrepeatable.' Another writer on aesthetics, Miss Macdonald, made similar assertions in an earlier article.[2] She said: 'Every work of art is unique and in the last resort, perhaps, can be judged by no standard but its own'; and again, 'Works of art are unique. Their performance cannot be repeated, even by the artist.'

The remarks I have quoted, and others like them by other writers who stress the individuality of the work of art, and the non-conceptual character of aesthetic appreciation, have this in common: that they seem true, but mysterious. One wants to ask *why* we can have no general principles of art in just the sense in which we have general principles in morals. Why are there no general descriptive criteria of excellence in the aesthetic sphere, such as there are not only in the sphere of moral behaviour but, it seems, in every other sphere in which we make assessments at all? One wants also to ask in what special sense the work of art is unique, individual, unrepeatable. Perhaps it is a tautology that there are no general descriptive criteria of aesthetic excellence, and, if so, this might provide just the logical distinction we want to make; but, if so, the tautology needs expanding a little. The two questions, 'Why are there no general descriptive criteria for aesthetic appraisal?' and 'In what sense is the work of art unique (individual, non-repeatable)?' are closely connected. We should remember that the general names we give to things allude to a kind of assessment; and the concepts 'work of art' and 'aesthetic assessment' are logically coupled and move together, in the sense that it would be self-contradictory to speak of judging something *as a work of art*, but not from the aesthetic point of view. So there is point in trying to clarify the notion of aesthetic appraisal *via* the notion of the work of art, even though things other than works of art may be objects of aesthetic appraisal.

First I must make a simple point about the logical status of works of art. Sometimes a distinction is made between, say, pictures and statues on the one hand, and literary and musical compositions on the other. The work of art in the first group of cases is sometimes said to be a concrete physical *particular*; while the work of art in the second group of cases is to be classified logically as a *type*, as something which, while not itself a particular physical phenomenon, can be embodied on different occasions in different particular physical phenomena. One and the same word can be spoken or written many times, one and the same flag (the Union Jack) can flutter simultaneously from many mast-heads. Individual literary or musical compositions are to be thought of as related to particular copies or renderings of them as the type-word and the type-flag are related to their particular embodiments in utterance or cloth. Now there is of course a genuine distinction between pictures and statues on the one hand and, at least, musical compositions on the other, a distinction which partly accounts for the form of this supposed further distinction; we might express it shortly by saying that pictures and statues are essentially such that the one original can be looked at again and again, while musical compositions are essentially such that they cannot be enjoyed again and again unless they are reproduced again and again. But this does not warrant distinguishing between the former as particulars and the latter as types. One is tempted, presumably, to make the distinction in this form by the merely contingent fact that we are, for all practical purposes, quite unable to make reproductions of pictures and statues which are completely indistinguishable, by direct sensory inspection, from the originals. If this practical limitation did not exist,[3] then the originals of paintings and works of sculpture, like the original manuscripts of poems, would not as such have any but a sentimental value, and, perhaps, a technical-historical interest as well; we should be able to speak of the same painting being seen by different people in different places at one time, in just the way in which we now speak of the same sonata being heard by different people at different times in one place. As far as the deeper logic is concerned, therefore, there is no reason for regarding the members of some classes of works of art as essentially particulars, rather than types. All works of art, certainly, are individuals; but all are equally types and not particulars.

Miss Macdonald, whom I quoted as saying 'Works of art are

unique. Their performance cannot be repeated, even by the artist', goes on to amplify these remarks as follows: 'In this they seem to differ from certain other performances in which what is produced, though numerically different, may be qualitatively exactly similar. This is not a mysterious fact about works of art, but follows, I think, from the way in which we use the term "work of art".' Now if the statement that works of art cannot be both numerically different and qualitatively exactly similar is meant to elucidate the special sense in which the work of art is unique (and the sentence which follows suggests that it is), then it is plainly inadequate. For this remark, though it is true of works of art, is, to speak roughly, true of all types whatsoever and is indeed part of what may be said in elucidating the logical idea of a type. English sentences, electrical circuits, motor-cars, etc. all have this in common: that if we are speaking of the types, and not the particular instances of the types, then we cannot allow that there are numerically distinct but exactly similar sentences, circuits, cars, etc. So Miss Macdonald's explanation, if it is intended as such, of the special uniqueness of the work of art, will not do as it stands.

Perhaps, however, her explanation can be replaced by another which is more helpful, and may correspond more closely to her intentions than what she actually says. Suppose we were asked to consider two motor-car types or two wireless-set types, and to assess them from a certain point of view: say, from the point of view of performance, or from that of their suitability for a particu- lar purpose. Suppose even that we were simply asked to assess them *as* motor-cars or *as* wireless-sets. We might make lists in non-evaluative terms of all and only the features of each which were relevant to this appraisal; and the two lists might be identical. An important consideration in appraising the wireless-sets might, for example, be high selectivity: but it would not matter in detail how the high selectivity was secured in each case, so long as no other relative advantage accrued to one of them from the difference in the detail of design. There may be qualitative differences bet- ween two types without there being any qualitative differences which are relevant to the kind of assessment actually being made, even when that assessment is of the kind alluded to by the ordinary classificatory name of the thing concerned. This may also be true of works of art, so long as they are *not* being assessed *as* works of art, i.e. from an aesthetic point of view. If what is wanted for a certain purpose is a picture of certain dimensions representing horses in a naturalistic manner, there may be several which answer equally well. In contrast with these examples, it seems a clear tautology that there could not be two different works of art which were indistinguishable in all the respects relevant to their *aesthetic* appraisal. (By a 'respect relevant to aesthetic appraisal' I must emphasize that I do not mean anything which has an evaluative name; but I do mean something on account of which evaluative names are applied.) But there could very well be two different type-arguments, type-motor-cars, type-sentences which resembled one another in all respects relevant respectively to their logical, mechanical or grammatical appraisal. To use a fashionable phrase, the *criterion of identity* of a work of art is the totality of features which are relevant to its aesthetic appraisal. So the work of art has not merely the qualitative uniqueness which any type logically possesses; it has a further kind of uniqueness when viewed as an object of a certain kind of appraisal, the kind which its name alludes to. Perhaps I could also express the point in this way: the only method of describing a work of art which is both entirely adequate for the purpose of aesthetic appraisal, and does not use evaluative language, is to say 'It goes like this' – and then reproduce it. And, of course, this is not a method of *describing* at all.

This perhaps answers, though still obscurely, the question 'In what sense is the work of art unique?'; and it goes a part, but only a part, of the way towards expanding the putative tautology that there can be no general descriptive criteria for aesthetic assessment. Certainly, it goes no more than a part of the way. For, it might be said, I have spoken of *respects* and *features* of works of art, on account of which evaluative names are applied; and even if the totality of aesthetically relevant features individuates a work of art, cannot individual respects or features, or sets of them, be shared by different works of art and hence provide a basis for general criteria? But to this I should reply that the words 'feature' and 'respect' are misleading here, just because they make us think of aesthetically relevant features as like shareable *properties* and *qualities*. There *is* a sense in which such features can be shared: it is illustrated by the fact that one poem can incorporate or quote a line from another, and by the fact that one poem or picture can be a *version* of another. But there are no aesthetic merit-conferring *properties*, with non-evaluative names. When you draw attention to some feature on account of which terms of aesthetic evaluation may be bestowed, you draw attention, not to a property which different individual works of art may share, but to a part or aspect of an individual work of art. There is ordinarily a distinction between individuals (whether types or particulars), and the properties directly on account of which we make assessments of the individuals; a distinction related, presumably, to the kinds of interest in objects which these assessments reveal. But this distinction seems to break down for the case of aesthetic assessment of the work of art. If this is true, then the impossibility of general descriptive criteria of aesthetic excellence follows as a consequence. (At most, we could regard each individual work of art itself, as type, as a general rule for the production of its own particular instances.) But why it is true, if it is true, is hard to say. One might suggest, as above, that the ordinary distinction between individuals and their merit-conferring properties reflects certain features of those interests and aims which show themselves in *non*-aesthetic assessments; and that these features are simply absent from the kind of interest we display when we make aesthetic assessments – so different is the aesthetic attitude from other attitudes. To make this out in detail would, if it were possible, be hard. I do not propose to try. But a way to begin would, evidently, be to turn our question and ask, not: 'Why does the distinction between individuals and merit-conferring properties break down for the case of aesthetic appraisal of works of art?', but 'Why does the distinction play the role it does in our non-aesthetic assessments?' Why is the moralist concerned with shareable properties of different particular actions, the dietary adviser with shareable properties of different types of food, the writers of *Which?* with shareable properties of different types of motor-car or washing machine? These questions at least remind us that an aesthetic interest in an individual is not any kind of practical interest, not an interest in anything it can or should do, or that we can do with it, not even an interest in specific responses (say, excitement or stupefaction) which it will produce in us. (If it were this sort of interest, there could indeed be general rules and recipes.)

The suggestion is, then, that scepticism about the possibility of a general account of the nature of aesthetic appraisal is to be answered, if at all, by exploiting a justified scepticism about the possibility of general descriptive criteria for aesthetic appraisal. Thus the peculiarity of this way of assessing is that when we have a class of objects of which the name, 'works of art', marks them out as primarily to be assessed in this way, then there cannot be numerically distinct members of the class, or parts of these members, which yet share all the features relevant to this kind of assessment. Further it is suggested that what underlies this fact is the fact that, as far as works of art are concerned, the idea of an aesthetic merit-conferring *property* is a mistake, a misapplication of a distinction which does not apply at all in this sphere. This suggestion would be merely confirmed by the fact, if it is a fact, that the idea in question might have application in some cases of things other than works of art of which we may make aesthetic assessments. For instance, it seems that two motor-car types might be aesthetically indistinguishable (I do not mean just of *equal* merit, but identical in aesthetically relevant respects) and yet be numerically two, as containing, say, different mechanical features; and here we might perhaps think of their *appearance* as a shared property. The word 'property' is in order this time just because we individuate the objects not as works of art but as motor-car types.

Finally, it may help to make the central point a little clearer, if one contrasts what I have called aesthetically relevant *features* of works of art with different kinds of what can certainly be called shareable properties of works of art. First we have those characteristics whose names are not non-evaluative, but already incorporate an evaluative judgment. Thus different works of art can resemble one another in ways which we mark by such words as *witty, delicate, economical* and so on, into all the immense and largely figurative vocabulary of praise or dispraise. And works of course can share *these* qualities without quoting passages from one another or

207

even belonging to the same form. Then we have technical properties: being contrapuntal, being written in hexameters, having consonant rhymes, and so on. But it is not on account of these features *as such* that aesthetically evaluative names are bestowed. Then there are names for the types of response the works tend to evoke: *stimulating, tranquillizing,* etc. (The behaviour of these words in this connection is, of course, distinctive: they are used not quite as a doctor uses them in talking about drugs.) Then there are names of, roughly, styles, again applied over different forms: baroque, classical, gothic. But to name the style is not to make an aesthetic evaluation, nor to supply a sufficient basis for evaluation of any individual exemplar of the style. So, then, the objects primarily of aesthetic assessment have plenty of shareable properties: there are plenty of ways in which we find general resemblances between them. But, in naming these, we do not name, in non-evaluative terms, those features directly on account of which we make aesthetic judgments of the individual bearers of those properties; for either these names of shareable general properties are themselves evaluative, or, if they are not, then, in applying them, we leave our listeners in the dark as to what evaluations to make of the individual works to which they are applied.

NOTES

1   'Logic and Appreciation', *Aesthetics and Language*, ed. W. Elton, Oxford, Blackwell, 1954.
2   'Distinctive Features in Criticism of the Arts', *Proceedings of the Aristotelian Society*, supp. vol. XXIII, 1949.
3   There are comparable cases to which it does not apply. We should think of lithographs, etchings and bronzes as well as paintings and chiselled stone.

10

IS EXISTENCE NEVER
A PREDICATE?

My aim in this paper is a very modest one. I want to discuss the doctrine that existence is not a predicate, in connection with two particular classes of utterances. The discussion of both types of case will seem at first to harmonize well enough with this doctrine. But at the end I shall try, certainly not to *confute* the doctrine, but to unsettle it just a little, to show that it must be taken in a slightly less simple way than we might be inclined to suppose.

I begin by considering spoken or written utterances of sentences containing the singular names of fictional or mythical characters as these occur in the actual telling of the story or recounting of the myth. In approaching the discussion of these, I shall make a certain assumption regarding a different class of utterances, namely those in which definite identifying reference is made to actual historical individuals. I shall take it as understood that the existence of the individuals referred to in such utterances is presupposed, rather than implicitly asserted, in the making of such utterances.

Evidently, when fictional or mythical names are used in the kinds of utterance I mentioned – i.e. in the telling of the story, the recounting of the myth – one is not, in so using them, making successful identifying references to historical particulars, to actual men or gods. Yet the predicates attached to such names may be, it seems, of just the same general sorts as are attached to the designations of men in true-or-false statements in which men are identifyingly referred to. There was a time when some philosophers felt the need to produce analyses of sentences containing such fictional or mythical names, analyses which would, for example, have the character of straightforwardly true-or-false reports of what was to be found in certain books. Apart from such obvious stumbling-blocks as the fact that this form of analysis could scarcely be applied to those sentences in which the fictional names made their first appearance, we may well now feel that any such programme of analysis was unrealistic. Even more unrealistic would be any account of such sentences which represented them as all false on the ground that they implied false existence-claims, or which denied them a truth-value on the ground of reference-failure on the part of the singular terms. (We may indeed deny them – or some of them – a truth-value; but not on *this* ground.)

What makes any thorough-going account of any of these kinds seem unrealistic is the recognition that, in the case of sentences containing such names, we typically have uses of language which are quite simply *different* from those uses involved in the important business of stating, or trying to state, empirical facts. They are themselves many and various, these different uses; but we can say that many of them cluster round the central notion of telling, or re-telling, a story. The linguistic forms of these uses of language are taken over, complete, from the fact-stating uses; and the linguistic *functions* of the fact-stating uses are, as it were, reproduced, story-wise, within the story-telling uses. One of the functions there reproduced is that of identifying reference, often, though not only, performed by the use of names; only, of course, the reference is to characters in the story, not to people in the world. Where you have identifying reference, you have also presuppositions of existence; only, of course, the presuppositions of existence are, like everything else in this realm of discourse, governed by the unspoken rubric – '*in the story*'. Of course, I am here saying nothing new, but simply sketching a general, and a special, reminder. In general, it is undesirable to treat sentences belonging to one way of using language as if they embodied attempts – attempts which straightforwardly fail or tortuously succeed – to use it in another. In special, there is no reason to deny that story-telling uses of language may have their own style of identifying reference, that fictional names may simply be used to refer, story-wise, to fictional characters.

However, when we say 'Don Quijote is a fictional character', we clearly aren't using 'Don Quijote', *story-wise*, to refer to a fictional character. That Don Quijote is a character in a story is not part of the story of Don Quijote. Nor is it part of the legend of King Arthur that King Arthur is a legendary king. In general, we have here a set of occurrences of such names which do not seem straightforwardly amenable to the treatment I have just suggested. Logicians, with their characteristic parsimoniousness of examples, have generally picked from this set the single phrase, 'did not exist', or, rather, the less likely 'does not exist', and concentrated their attention on it, together with its working partner, 'exists' or 'did exist'. King Alfred existed, King Arthur did not; Bucephalus exists, Pegasus does not. Just as we cannot say, of the negative forms, that the names are being used, story-wise, to make identifying references to fictional characters, so we cannot say, of the affirmative forms, that the names are being used, in the manner of ordinary factual discourse, to make identifying references to horses or men. A story-wise identifying reference carries a presupposition of story-wise, as opposed to factual, existence. An identifying reference in one of the language-games of factual discourse carries a presupposition of factual, as opposed to story-wise, existence. Where what follows the name, as in my examples, is a serious and substantial affirmation or denial of factual existence, we cannot coherently cast the name for either of these roles. Consequently, we cannot coherently construe 'exists' as functioning predicatively *relatively to the name taken as having either of these roles*.

There are, one might say, two types of classical solution here, two classical models for interpreting our sentences. For the sentence, 'King Arthur never existed', one model is provided by such a sentence as 'There is no king of Britain who even roughly answers to the descriptions associated with the name "Arthur" in Arthurian legend'. The second model gives us something like 'The concept "King Arthur" is not instantiated'. (There are variations on the second model.) The first model replaces 'exists' with a quantifier and the name with a complex general term in 'predicative position'.[1] The second model offers us a definite singular term in 'referential position',[1] but one which refers to a concept, not a character; and replaces 'exists' with, or construes it as, a predicate-expression signifying a property of concepts, viz., being instantiated.

Must we accept such models as these (or accept them for *every* such case)? The exercise I want to propose is that of inquiring whether we could not find another model which would preserve a predicative role for 'exists' *without* casting the subject-expression for the somewhat ungrateful role of singular term referring to a concept. This is, perhaps, a slightly pedantic (scholastic) exercise. But there seems to be life in it. A recent article in *The Philosophical Review*[2] was devoted to denying that such a thing could be done in these cases. In any case there is always something to be said for poking a stick into a dogma.

I approach the question obliquely, by raising the topic of my second class of utterances. We are to forget, for the moment, about definite singular terms. Presuppositions of existence are not confined to them. I want, adapting freely from G. E. Moore's discussion of tame tigers,[3] to remind you of some things he pointed out and to point out some others which he didn't. The sentences

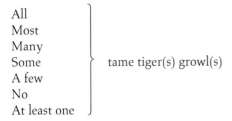

All
Most
Many
Some   } tame tiger(s) growl(s)
A few
No
At least one

are all perfectly in order. But if we replace in each sentence the word 'growl' (or, in the case of the last, the word 'growls') with the word 'exist' (or 'exists'), we obtain a curious result. All the resulting sentences *except the first two* seem perfectly, or at least reasonably, natural; the first two, on the other hand, sound extremely odd. And this result is connected with the result of another test in which 'all' and 'most' seem to behave differently from the other quantifying adjectives (as we may call them) in our list. The following sentences all seem straightforwardly satisfactory and natural, viz.:

There are $\begin{Bmatrix} \text{many} \\ \text{some} \\ \text{a few} \\ \text{no} \end{Bmatrix}$ tame tigers

There is at least one tame tiger

whereas the sentences

There are all tame tigers
There are most tame tigers

don't seem to make sense *in this series* at all. To make any sense of them, it seems that we should have to interpret 'There are' in a quite different sense from that which it can comfortably bear in the longer list; we should have to construe 'There' as a real demonstrative adverb of place and not as simply an integral part of the construction 'There are/is'.

The explanation of these facts seems to be somewhat as follows. Suppose the existence of tame tigers to be something which the parties to a speech situation know or believe or are prepared to assume to be the case; minimally, something which a speaker believes, and assumes his audience to be prepared to assume. Then the question may be raised, to what extent and in what proportion tame tigers, say, share the habits of ordinary tigers. Do they, for example, growl? The answer may be that they all do; or that some of them do; or that a few of them do – and so on. The sentences I first listed could all serve as answers to that question. Even if they are not actually serving as answers to such a question, they call for a similar background of belief or assumption. There is here a (weakened and partial) parallel to the use of singular expressions with the function of identifying reference. We may express it by saying that the sentences in question are most naturally taken as asserting, *with regard to the member of a class the existence of members of which is presupposed,* that all, most, some or a few etc. *of them* exhibit a certain characteristic. Let us speak, for short, of *a class the existence of members of which is presupposed* as a *presupposed class.* Then the quantifying adjectives, as used in my first list of sentences, indicate, though in some cases very roughly indeed, how far the speaker is prepared to go in ascribing a certain characteristic to the members of a presupposed class.

In the existential sentences, on the other hand, the quantifying adjectives, where they work at all, work differently. There is a difference between indicating (roughly) how big a slice of the membership of a presupposed class one is prepared to affirm to possess a certain characteristic and indicating (roughly) how big one is prepared to affirm the membership of a non-presupposed class to be. And in this difference lies the reason why some of the quantifying adjectives can be used for both jobs and some only for one.

The difference might be illustrated graphically.

(1) Represent a presupposed class by an already drawn circle; and then represent the ascribing of a property to some part of its membership by the shading of some part of its area. We may suppose the instructions for *this* use of the quantifying adjectives to go somewhat as follows. (The vagueness of some of the instructions reproduces the vagueness of the words.)

For 'no'	leave the circle unshaded
For 'at least one'	draw one short stroke
For 'a few'	draw a few short strokes in a small area
For 'some'	shade a rather larger area
For 'many'	shade a sizeable area
For 'most'	shade more than half the total area
For 'all'	shade the whole area

(2) For the existential case, on the other hand, there is no circle

already drawn. Instead we are to draw one (or to refrain from drawing one!). We find we can issue (usually vague) instructions for some of the quantifying adjectives in *this* use; but not for others. Thus we could say:

For 'no'	refrain from drawing a circle
For 'at least one'	draw as small a circle as you can
For 'a few'	draw a circle a few times the area of the smallest you can
For 'some'	draw a somewhat larger circle
For 'many'	draw a quite sizeable circle

But there is no way at all of continuing this series which would give us a representation of 'most' and 'all'. For them we must have, whereas for the others we don't seem to need, an already drawn circle.

This method of graphic representation has, of course, no particular importance in itself. It is only *one* method of bringing out (even perhaps slightly exaggerating) the difference between the two jobs which the quantifying adjectives perform in the two types of case, so that we can see clearly that, and why, all of them can perform one of these jobs while only some of them can perform the other. But seeing this helps us to see something more. It helps us to see how the oddity or non-oddity of the sentences embodying the quantifying adjectives is connected with the doctrine that existence is not a predicate; or, more exactly, with the doctrine (1) that the verb-form 'exists' (or 'exist'), while it cannot be denied to be a predicate in the sense of grammar, nevertheless is not, or does not signify, a predicate in a logical or functional sense of the word, and (2) that the grammatical subjects of this verb are not true logical subjects. Moore never really stated *what* the connection between the example-sentences and this doctrine was. But if the essence of predication is the ascribing of something to an individual, or to some, none or all of a class, where the existence of the individual or of members of the class is presupposed (or has been *antecedently* affirmed or implied), *then* we can see the connection. The doctrine seems to follow at once and the example-sentences serve simply to cast, we might say, Moore light upon it. From them, and our explanation of them together, we can extract a test, understanding its rationale. The test will go like this. Given a grammatical subject and predicate, then it is a necessary condition of their counting as a *logical* subject and predicate respectively that if the grammatical subject admits of starting off with *any* of the quantifying adjectives, then it should admit of starting off with them all (with, where necessary, i.e. where 'at least one' is involved, a change from singular to plural or vice versa).

So far we have a neat and tidy theory. Let us see if we can upset it. Consider the following example. I enter a room in which a discussion is going on. I hear what sound like ordinary personal names being freely used and person-predicates used in connection with them. I quickly come to the conclusion that the discussion is primarily about fictional characters. I hear the names Anna and Pierre and Emma and Julien Sorel and recognize the characteristics and incidents alluded to as belonging to the appropriate stories. Also, the speakers occasionally refer to themselves. One says she wouldn't have done what (say) Pierre did in his. However, a lot of other names occur which I can't, as it seems to me, *place* in their appropriate stories. Tolstoy's Anna is being compared with an Ann, and Tolstoy's Pierre with a Peter, whom I can't identify. At this point I intervene and say: 'I know who Anna and Pierre, Emma and Julien are, but what stories do these other characters come in?' And to this I receive the unexpected reply: 'They don't come in any stories. *Most* of the people (characters) we're talking about actually *exist*.'

Another example. A child asks to look at a book, actually the Classical Dictionary, and I hand it to him, saying: 'A good proportion of the characters listed are mythical, of course; but *most* of them *existed*.' (Or conversely.)

What are we to say about the proposed test in the light of these examples? Are we to say that the examples simply show that the proposed test gives only a necessary, and not a sufficient, condition of our having genuine subjects and predicates? We might; but why should we? Why shouldn't we say that what the examples do is simply to draw attention to certain cases in which the verb *is* used as a predicate? Somebody might object: 'This won't do at all. The appeal of the test lay in the fact that it made a certain sort of sense. The *point* of it was that where the quantifying adjectives "most" and "all" could be comfortably employed, they were typically employed in a certain way, i.e. in a way, which presupposed the existence of members of the subject-class. The whole point was, wasn't it, that you had a genuine subject and predicate just in the case where existence was presupposed. But no case where existence is explicitly *asserted* is a case where existence is *presupposed*. Yet your example-cases are cases where existence is explicitly asserted. So you can't simply admit a predicative use of "exist" in these cases without implicitly giving up the rationale of the test.'

The reply to this objection is that it is confused. We can still retain the principle that where the quantifying adjectives are used in the way in which 'most', unlike 'some', is always used, the subject-class is a presupposed class. Only we have to pause to consider what this class is. In the example under consideration it is the class of *characters being talked about*. And the peculiarity of such a class is that it may be, and in the case under consideration actually is, radically heterogeneous; even, if you will permit the expression, ontologically or metaphysically heterogeneous. In using 'exist' here we really are saying that most of the members of this heterogeneous class belong to one of its sub-classes as opposed to another. Why shouldn't we say, then, that 'exists' really does work as a predicate here; and that so also would, in such a context, 'fictional', 'legendary', 'mythical', 'imaginary', 'made-up' on the one hand – and 'real' or 'historical' on the other?

Now if we can work this trick for some sentences whose subjects admit quantifying adjectives, can we also work it for sentences whose subjects are definite singular terms? I think perhaps we sometimes can. We can't work it in quite the same way, of course, making our point *via* the quantifying adjectives. But we can work it on the same underlying principle. King Alfred did exist, King Arthur did not. We have only to see the names as serving to identify, within the *heterogeneous* class of kingly characters we talk about – a class which comprises both actual and legendary kings – a particular member of that class in each case; and then see the predicate as serving to assign that particular member to the appropriate sub-class. Thus 'exists' appears as a predicate and not as a predicate of a concept; but as a predicate of some, and not of other, members of the heterogeneous class. What, on this model, we shall have to regard as presupposed by the use of the name in each case is not the existence in history of an actual king with certain actual characteristics, or the existence in legend of a legendary king with certain legendary characteristics, but rather the existence-in-history-or-legend of an actual-or-legendary king with certain actual-or-legendary characteristics.

But now, we might ask, have we anything other than a case of theory, elaborating itself in the void, out of touch with the facts? Is there any reason for saying, in any actual case of the use of definite singular terms with 'exists' or 'doesn't exist', that *this* model supplies the right way of looking at what is said, as opposed to one of the other models I mentioned? Well, at least one might be more inclined to say this in some cases than in others: cases, for instance, where the singular term comes up in contexts like those provided by my two examples. Or, in the case of a child, his head filled with names and stories, who asks: 'Did King Alfred exist? Did King Arthur? Did Jesus? Does God?', we might think both of his questions and (if we are sympathetic) of our answers in this way. No doubt there are occasions enough when the model doesn't fit at all. But we might also consider whether we are obliged to *oppose* the models (theoretical accounts) to each other in every case. Must we suppose that at least and at most one model will fit each case? I am inclined to think that we take our models too seriously, if we suppose this, and have too little regard for the pleasant fluidities of thinking.

NOTES

1   The phrases are Quine's.
2   W. Alston, 'The Ontological Argument Revisited', *The Philosophical Review*, vol. LXIX, 1960.
3   'Is Existence a Predicate? II', *Proceedings of the Aristotelian Society*, supp. vol. XV, 1936.

11

ON UNDERSTANDING
THE STRUCTURE OF
ONE'S LANGUAGE

Action-ascribing sentences are susceptible of adverbial modification of such a kind that a proposition expressed by a sentence so modified entails any proposition obtained from it merely by shearing away some or all of the modifiers. Different theories are current which purport to explain our grasp of the structure of these entailments. In general there is a contrast between a theory, like Professor Davidson's,[1] which explains these relationships by reference to well-understood logical structures represented as underlying the surface forms of action-ascribing sentences, and any theory which finds an explanation closer to the surface of ordinary language by recognizing a more complicated basic syntax than a Davidsonian theorist is prepared to allow for. A theory of the second sort might deserve the name of an 'Adverbial Theory'. Indeed I shall pretend that we have to do with some particular theory of this sort, which I shall call *the* Adverbial Account, to be set over against the Davidsonian Account.

This contrast between theories obviously points to a question of considerable depth and generality – a question which relates not simply to Davidson's analysis of action-sentences but to any theory whatever which seeks to explain our general understanding of types of sentence and our general grasp of types of logical relation by reference to a true or underlying logical structure which differs more or less radically from the superficial grammatical form of the sentences in question. If this claim to explain is made, we must surely take it seriously and ask what it involves; and not just assume that the answer to this is obvious or that we know it perfectly well. For it is not at all obvious and really, when we look into it, seems to involve a great mystery – or, alternatively, the making of highly unplausible or quite unverifiable claims.

So what exactly is involved in such a claim? (I shall call it the 'explanation-claim'.) Let us try to get at the answer to this by contrasting the type of claim in question with something much more modest. A philosopher first points to the well-understood semantics of a language with the grammatical structure of the predicate calculus. He then points out that by quantifying over actions etc. we can frame Davidsonian action-sentences, and also that our understanding of the logical relations of these sentences is explained by our grasp of the semantics of any language which exhibits the grammatical structure they manifestly possess. Finally he points out that we can see very well that our ordinary action-sentences are equivalent to Davidsonian action-sentences: i.e. that given any pair of ordinary action-sentences, S_1 and S_2, such that S_1 entails S_2 (and this relation is an instance of the kind we are concerned with) then we can frame a pair of Davidsonian sentences, DS_1 and DS_2, such that DS_1 is equivalent to S_1 and DS_2 is equivalent to S_2 and DS_1 entails DS_2; and our grasp of *this* entailment relation (i.e. the entailment of DS_2 by DS_1) is explained by our grasp of the semantics of any language possessing the grammatical structure of the predicate calculus.

Now these are interesting things to point out, and they are not things that are in dispute. But simply to point them out evidently falls a long way short of making the claim that our ordinary grasp of the class of logical relations such as the entailment of S_2 by S_1 is *explained* by these facts. The claim is expressed by saying (1) that sentences of the form of DS_1 and DS_2 exhibit the true or underlying structure of sentences of the form of S_1 and S_2, and (2) that it is because this is so that we understand the logical relations of sentences of the form of S_1 and S_2. We still do not know quite what this means. Contrast it, whatever it means, with yet another modest claim: if our ordinary action-sentences had the manifest form of sentences of the DS type, then our grasp of their logical relations (or those of the kind we are currently interested in) could be easily understood and explained as just one instance (or class of instances) of our general grasp of the semantics of any language with the grammatical structure of the predicate calculus. This wistful hypothetical, however, makes no pretence of explaining our understanding of the logical relations between action-sentences as we find them.

Could the explanation-claim come to this: it is *because* we grasp or understand our ordinary action-sentences *as* equivalent to DS sentences (with *their* well-understood semantics) that we have the general understanding we do have of the logical relation of our ordinary action-sentences? Now it may be that this interpretation of the explanation-claim can itself be understood in more than one way. Indeed I rather think this is the case; and on one way of understanding the explanation-claim, it is exposed to a type of reaction or challenge it is not exposed to on another way of understanding it. By looking first at reactions of this type, we may come to be better placed later on to see how the claim might be understood in a different way which is not exposed to this type of reaction.

So let us look first at a very impatient reaction. What is the evidence, one might ask, for the view in question? Surely such evidence as there is is all against it. For ordinary speakers of the language understand their action-sentences and grasp their logical relations very well without ever having dreamed of DS sentences; and when they are introduced to these unfamiliar objects, some time may have to be spent and explanations gone through before they can be got to understand DS sentences and hence to see the equivalences in question. So understanding our ordinary action-sentences as equivalent to DS sentences is not even a condition, let alone an explanatory condition or underlying ground, of our understanding of the logical relations of our ordinary sentences. It may be said that this is far too crude an interpretation of the claim: that the claim refers to underlying general capacities: that it is only because we have the *capacity* to see our ordinary action-sentences as equivalent to DS sentences (when the latter are introduced and explained to us) that we have the general under-standing we do have of the logical relations of our ordinary action-sentences. But to this the impatient reply is again obvious. Of course this capacity and this understanding may be expected to go together; for if the two forms of sentence are indeed equiva-lent and we understand them both, we may be expected to appreci-ate their equivalence: our not doing so would count against our truly understanding one or the other. But no reason whatever has been given to invoke one capacity (the generally unrealized because generally untested capacity to appreciate the equivalences) to explain our possession of the other (the generally realized cap-acity to grasp the logical relations of ordinary action-sentences). One might just as plausibly, indeed far more plausibly, invoke our ordinary understanding of the logical grammar of ordinary action-sentences to explain our capacity to appreciate the possibility of Davidsonian equivalents.

Let us put these impatient reactions on one side for the moment and consider what appears to be a subtler difficulty. Suppose it were the case that our understanding of the relevant logical relations among ordinary action-sentences (call them SS sentences – the first 'S' for 'surface') is somehow dependent on the fact that, in some as yet unclarified sense, we do indeed understand them as equivalent to corresponding DS sentences, understanding of the corresponding logical relations among which is explained by the semantics of the predicate calculus. Then we have another problem of explanation on our hands: viz., the problem of explaining our general grasp of the logical relations of mutual entailment between SS sentences and the corresponding DS sentences. Evidently the semantics of the predicate calculus cannot be invoked to solve *this* problem. Equally evidently it will not be satisfactory to appeal to an intuitive grasp of these equivalences. For if that were satisfactory, there would have been no problem in the first place and we could simply have appealed to an intuitive grasp of the logical relations among SS sentences.

How might the reply to this objection go? I imagine that it might go like this. There is a limited set of what might be called transformation or translation rules in accordance with which any SS sentence can be represented as derived from the corresponding DS sentence, and any DS sentence as recoverable from the corresponding SS sentence. The fact that the ordinary speaker of the language understands his SS sentences as equivalent to the corresponding DS sentence is to be explained by crediting him with a 'tacit' or 'implicit' mastery of these rules. His mastery of these rules must be supposed to be a part of his acquisition of the language. Credit him both with a mastery of these rules and with a grasp of the semantics of the predicate calculus, and the task of explaining what was to be explained is completed.

I said the objection to which this is a possible reply was to be a subtler, a less impatient, objection. But you will see that it really leads simply to a more thorough and careful statement of the impatient reaction. We have a theory which sets out to explain our ordinary grasp of a set of relations which we might represent like this:

$$I \quad \begin{array}{c} SS_1 \\ \downarrow \\ SS_2 \end{array}$$

The theory proceeds by crediting us with mastery of sets of rules and relations which we might represent like this

$$II \quad \begin{array}{c} SS_1 \rightleftarrows DS_1 \\ \downarrow \\ SS_2 \rightleftarrows DS_2 \end{array}$$

where the horizontal arrows represent our translation or transformation rules and the vertical arrow represents relations which result from the well-understood semantics of the predicate calculus;

the theory then claims that our mastery of system I is explained by our mastery of system II.

The simple objection is that the DS sentences of system II are for the most part relatively unfamiliar objects and that, on the evidence of verbal behaviour, many ordinary language-speakers show a perfectly competent mastery of system I but would require a certain amount of instruction to get the hang of system II; so it cannot be the case that mastery of system II is a condition of, let alone the explanation of, mastery of system I. If it is said that this is to misinterpret the notion of 'mastery' of a system, and that what is meant is a kind of implicit mastery the existence of which is quite consistent with the facts just mentioned, the retort must be that the claim has now become quite mysterious and unverifiable. If it is now said that the claim is not at all unverifiable, that part of what is meant is simply that one could not show competence in system I unless one were *capable* of mastering system II (i.e. learning to make the translations and inferences of system II), then this claim (or part of the claim) must be conceded as at least plausible; but the further claim that *actual* mastery of system I is *explained* by *potential* mastery of system II remains both unsupported and mysterious.

Here, then, is a profound and surely important difference between any explanation in general semantico-syntactical theory which, like our supposed adverbial account, applies pretty directly to the surface structure of our sentences, and any explanation which, like the Davidsonian account of action-sentences, appeals to an underlying structure differing more or less radically from the superficial grammatical form of the sentences in question. An explanation of the latter kind, it seems, has to face a certain kind of challenge, as to what exactly it is claiming and how these claims are verified; an explanation of the former kind, whatever other challenges it has to face, does not have to face just this kind of challenge. This is not to say that such a challenge, when it has to be met, can never be met successfully. Nor is it to deny that our theoretical understanding of our grasp of the semantic-syntactic structure of sentences of a certain class may be assisted by the production of paraphrases, or more or less equivalent sentences, of a different grammatical structure, even when no claim that the latter make manifest the true or underlying structure of the former can be sustained.[2] Nevertheless the contrast I have drawn does carry weighty implications for those concerned with the systematic semantics of natural languages; concerned (I quote Davidson) to 'elicit in a perspicuous and general form the understanding of logical grammar we all have that constitutes (part of) our grasp of our native tongue'. It really diminishes the attractions of any programme, like the general Davidsonian programme, which is committed in advance to explaining our grasp of all truly structural semantic relations in terms of a very restricted set of underlying structures, viz., those of the predicate calculus. By the same token it encourages the use in our explanations of a wider range of (more specific) categories than those merely of individual name, individual variable and predicate; and of the ideas of kinds of combination over and above that of simple predication plus sentence-composition and quantification.

If this is truly the way to proceed, then it is futile to lament the fact. Of course it may be natural to do so, in so far as the logical grammar of the predicate calculus stands before us, clearly articulated, a model of clarity and intelligibility.[3] If we cast ourselves adrift from it, what guidelines have we except a vague sense of what categories and combinations are fundamental in our thinking and our discourse? But things are not quite as bad as this. We have checks on our vague sense of the appropriate in the degree of success we achieve in elaborating a plausible theory: and checks on plausibility which linguists and psychologists can combine to supply.

But is it not after all possible that this doctrine of challenge – the challenge to the theory of underlying structure which the Davidsonian account seems to fail to meet – rests on a misunderstanding? If there is any possibility that this is so, then it is important to investigate that possibility. And I think it might be held that it *is* so.

Consider again one of our ways of formulating the claim to explain. It ran: it is *because* we understand our ordinary action-sentences as equivalent to DS sentences (with their well-understood semantics) that we have the general understanding we do have of the logical relations of our ordinary action-sentences. Now this formulation, it might be held, is ambiguous. It *can* be interpreted, as just now it was, as claiming that our understanding of our ordinary action-sentences depends on, and is explained by, our having knowledge or mastery, in some sense, of translation-rules relating SS to DS sentences etc.; and, so understood, it is at best unplausible, at worst totally mysterious. But it can be read quite differently. It might be read as implying rather that the difference between the formal arrangement of parts in an SS sentence and the formal arrangement of parts in a DS sentence is, in a sense, a quite superficial difference; somewhat as the difference between indicating which is the subject and which is the object of a transitive verb by word order, as in English, or by case-inflection, as in Latin, is a superficial difference. What is fundamental in the latter case is that, in any language containing two-place non-symmetrical predicates, there must be some provision for indicating the order of the two elements in an ordered pair. It does not matter what the provision is: we understand the related forms just so long as we understand them as doing just this. (Only philosophers, or logicians, would express the condition of our understanding the forms in this way; nevertheless this technical description is a perfectly correct general description of the condition of our understanding such forms.)

If this comparison holds good, it will be seen that there is a sense in which we cannot understand our SS sentences at all without understanding them as equivalent to DS sentences. Not that we need have dreamt of DS sentences: the sense is closer to that in which a man might be said not to understand 'Brutus is wiser than Caesar' unless he understood it as equivalent to 'Caesare Brutus sapientior'. And the point will be that to understand the logical grammar of SS sentences is to see their actual formal arrangements as indicating certain combinations of semantic or meaning-elements, precisely those combinations of precisely those elements which are indicated, by means of different formal arrangements, in the corresponding DS sentences. Our ordinary language-speaker satisfies this condition *directly*: we don't have to credit him with mastery of translation-rules etc. (with mastery of system II) any more than we have to credit the man who understands 'Brutus is wiser than Caesar' with the ability to write out the equivalent in the style of logical notation, or in Latin.

SS sentences, then, and corresponding or equivalent DS sentences are alike in indicating, by different formal arrangements in each case, precisely the same combinations of precisely the same elements. Moreover they do so – and this is how the challenge is avoided – equally directly in each case, though not equally perspicuously. The difference between an SS sentence and its DS equivalent – and this is also the reason for bringing DS sentences into the picture at all – is that the elements in question and their modes of combination are simply *more clearly represented* by the formal arrangements employed in a DS sentence. For practical purposes the differences do not matter. Each way of indicating what elements are combined in what way may be as good as the other, and indeed what is in one sense the less clear way may be the better, e.g. the more economical of breath. But for theoretical purposes the DS form is preferable for the reason just given. By looking at the DS sentences we can see straight off how the semantics, the logical grammar, of our action-sentences is already taken care of in the predicate calculus. This is not obvious from looking at the ordinary forms, though in fact it *is* taken care of in just the same way.

(Now there is no danger of misunderstanding, we can reintroduce system II, translation-rules and all. We do not have to think of this as something that the ordinary speaker has mastered in any ordinary sense; or in any extraordinary sense either. It is just a devious way, useful for theoretical purposes, of representing the fact that he directly understands his SS sentences as indicating just those combinations of just those elements which they do, in their theoretically unperspicuous way, indicate.)

I think this defence or reinterpretation successfully meets the challenge it has so far been confronted with in the sense that the theory as now presented is not exposed to that challenge. But it is exposed to another. By hypothesis, we have available an alternative account (the Adverbial) of the elements and modes of combination involved, according to which these elements and combinations are not at all unperspicuously represented by the formal arrangements of SS sentences as they stand. And why, indeed, should they be? True, the Adverbial Account has something to explain: viz., the possibility of the equivalent, structurally different, DS forms. This problem can be solved with the help of a theory of nominaliza- tion and attendant predication: a theory which squares with our unreflective sense that the forms which figure in DS sentences are grammatically derivative forms. The Davidsonian account, on the other hand, on its present interpretation, has what looks like a much less tractable problem to face: the problem of explaining the striking lack of perspicuousness of our ordinary forms of action- sentences. One who holds the Davidsonian position dogmatically can perhaps afford to view this problem fairly lightly: it exists, but it need not worry us overmuch. But for one who holds the position non-dogmatically, who is prepared to envisage the possibility of a theory of structural semantics which is not confined *a priori* within these narrow limits, there must seem to be a serious worry here.

But by now another and uneasy impression may begin to gain ground. It may begin to seem as if the whole issue is unreal. For it may begin to seem that we could finally settle it only if there were something to appeal to, extraneous to the forms of language itself, to decide what the basic categories of semantic element and modes of their combination were. It seems almost as if we wanted to ask: *forms of language* – natural or artificial – *apart*, is the underlying semantic element expressed by 'kiss' (or 'kill' or 'kick') really apt for entry into predicative combinations as a two-place predicate (of agents and objects) or as a three-place predicate (of actions, agents and objects) or as a one-place predicate (of actions) usually in conjunction with a three-place predicate (of actions, agents and objects)? And this may seem absurd.

But the situation is not really so bad; for two reasons.

(I) The general question regarding semantic categories and modes of combination is this: given a natural language as we have it – and our understanding of it – what is the simplest *realistic* theory of (a) semantic categories and modes of combination, and (b) formal arrangements for expressing the latter, which will cover the facts? It is not really a matter of 'forms of language apart'. Forms of language as we find them must, of course, be considered when we assess our theories for plausibility, simplicity, realism. It is precisely here that the Davidsonian account encounters difficulties, encounters one or another of the challenges above-mentioned.

(2) The second reason is that it *is* possible to bring extra-syntactic considerations, considerations from outside the philosophy of language, from general philosophy, to bear on the question. Davidson's own arguments relating to the philosophy of action, though easily rebutted, are a case in point. And arguments can be produced on the other side. Thus, it could be argued that what underlies the linguistic grammatical fact that actions and events generally (when they are happenings to things) normally appear as individuals as the result of nominalization is the point that actions and events suffer in general from identity-dependence on substances; and that what underlie this in turn are more general facts about our existence in, orientation in and knowledge of, an objective world.

NOTES

1   'The Logical Form of Action Sentences', in *The Logic of Decision and Action*, ed. N. Rescher, Univ. of Pittsburgh Press, 1967.

2   Nor, of course, does the point in any way touch or impinge upon the activities of theorists of language who do not claim to contribute in any way to the explanation of our understanding of the structures of our languages. For instance if you are simply concerned to draw up a set of classifications and rules which will generate the structures recognized in a given language, you may proceed in any way which you find most convenient and economical. Or if, like Quine, your interest is in producing structures which appeal by virtue of their clarity and economy, your concern with ordinary structures may go no further than the concern to produce, where you feel the need of them, intelligible alternatives which satisfy your ideals of clarity.

3   Granted, that is, that we understand the 'basic combination' of predication – but do we?

INDEX

Related titles from Routledge

Scepticism and Naturalism: Some Varieties
Peter Strawson

'If one man were to be singled out as personifying Oxford analytic philosophy over the past thirty years, Sir Peter would be that person. In all these four lectures...he weighs in four traditional arenas of philosophical contention. In one arena the existence of external objects is at stake, in the other the grounds of morality, in a third the status of mentalistic language, and in the fourth the existence of abstract objects.' – *New York Review of Books*

'It is a delight to have this book before us. At a level of considerable abstractness an important idea is put to work in the sure hands of a master to illuminate extremely difficult questions at the centre of philosophy.' – *The Times Literary Supplement*

By the time of his death in 2006, Sir Peter Strawson was regarded as one of the world's most distinguished philosophers. Unavailable for many years, *Scepticism and Naturalism* is a profound reflection on two classic philosophical problems by a philosopher at the pinnacle of his career.

Based on his acclaimed Woodbridge lectures delivered at Columbia University in 1983, Strawson begins with a discussion of scepticism, which he defines as questioning the adequacy of our grounds for holding various beliefs. He then draws deftly on Hume and Wittgenstein to argue that we must distinguish between two types of naturalism – 'hard', or scientific, and 'soft', or humanistic. In the remaining chapters the author takes up several issues in which sceptical doubts play an important role, in particular the nature of transcendental arguments and including the objectivity of moral philosophy, the mental and the physical, and the existence of abstract entities.

Scepticism and Naturalism is essential reading for those seeking an introduction to the work of one of the twentieth century's most important and original philosophers.

This reissue includes a substantial new foreword by Quassim Cassam and a fascinating intellectual autobiography by Strawson, which together form an excellent introduction to his life and work.

ISBN13: 978–0–415–45049–2 (pbk)

Available at all good bookshops
For ordering and further information please visit:
www.routledge.com

Related titles from Routledge

The Routledge Companion to
Twentieth Century Philosophy
Edited by Dermot Moran

The twentieth century was one of the most significant and exciting periods ever witnessed in philosophy, characterised by intellectual change and development on a massive scale. *The Routledge Companion to Twentieth Century Philosophy* is an outstanding and authoritative survey and assessment of the century as a whole. Written by leading international scholars such as Paul Guyer, Dan Zahavi, and Matt Matravers and featuring twenty-two chapters, the essays in this collection examine and assess the central topics, themes, and philosophers of the twentieth century, presenting a comprehensive picture of the period for the first time:

Featuring annotated further reading and a comprehensive glossary, *The Routledge Companion to Twentieth Century Philosophy* is indispensable for anyone interested in philosophy over the last one hundred years, suitable for both expert and novice alike.

ISBN10: 0–415–29936–5 (hbk)
ISBN13: 978–0–415–29936–7 (hbk)

Available at all good bookshops
For ordering and further information please visit:
www.routledge.com

Related titles from Routledge

Ethics and the Limits of Philosophy
Bernard Williams

'Williams's discussions are much to be valued: his explicitness and argumentative ingenuity focus the issues more sharply, and at greater depth, than any comparable work I know... One of the most interesting contributions of recent years, not only to ethics but to philosophy.' – *John McDowell, Mind*

'This is a superior book, glittering with intelligence and style.' – *Thomas Nagel, Journal of Philosophy*

'Remarkably lively and enjoyable...It is a very rich book, containing excellent descriptions of a variety of moral theories, and innumerable and often witty observations on topics encountered on the way.' – *Philippa Foot, Times Literary Supplement*

By the time of his death in 2003, Bernard Williams was one of the greatest philosophers of his generation. *Ethics and the Limits of Philosophy* is not only widely acknowledged to be his most important book, but also hailed a contemporary classic of moral philosophy.

Presenting a sustained critique of moral theory from Kant onwards, Williams reorients ethical theory towards 'truth, truthfulness and the meaning of an individual life'. He explores and reflects upon the most difficult problems in contemporary philosophy and identifies new ideas about central issues such as relativism, objectivity and the possibility of ethical knowledge.

This edition includes a new commentary on the text by A.W.Moore, St.Hugh's College, Oxford.

ISBN10: 0–415–39984–X (hbk)
ISBN10: 0–415–39985–8 (pbk)
ISBN10: 0–203–94573–5 (ebk)

ISBN13: 978–0–415–39984–5 (hbk)
ISBN13: 978–0–415–39985–2 (pbk)
ISBN13: 978–0–203–94573–5 (ebk)

Available at all good bookshops
For ordering and further information please visit:
www.routledge.com

Related titles from Routledge

Philosophy of Language: a Contemporary Introduction, Second Edition
William Lycan

Philosophy of Language: a Contemporary Introduction introduces the student to the main issues and theories in twentieth-century philosophy of language, focusing specifically on linguistic phenomena.

Topics are structured in three parts in the book. Part I, Reference and Referring Expressions, includes topics such as Russell's Theory of Descriptions, Donnellan's distinction, problems of anaphora, the description theory of proper names, Searle's cluster theory, and the causal-historical theory. Part II, Theories of Meaning, surveys the competing theories of linguistic meaning and compares their various advantages and liabilities. Part III, Pragmatics and Speech Acts, introduces the basic concepts of linguistic pragmatics, includes a detailed discussion of the problem of indirect force and surveys approaches to metaphor. Part IV, new to this edition, examines the four theories of metaphor.

Features of *Philosophy of Language* include:

- New chapters on Frege and puzzles, inferentialism, illocutionary theories of meaning and relevance theory
- chapter overviews and summaries
- clear supportive examples
- study questions
- annotated further reading
- glossary.

ISBN13: 978–0–415–95751–9 (hbk)
ISBN13: 978–0–415–95752–6 (pbk)
ISBN13: 978–0–203–93000–7 (ebk)

Available at all good bookshops
For ordering and further information please visit:
www.routledge.com

Related titles from Routledge

Routledge Philosophy GuideBook to
Wittgenstein and the Tractatus
Michael Morris

Written by two leading experts, this is the ideal guide to the only book Wittgenstein published during his lifetime, the *Tractatus Logico-Philosophicus*. Michael Morris makes sense of Wittgenstein's brief but often cryptic text, highlighting its key themes. He introduces and analyzes:

Wittgenstein's life and the background to the *Tractatus*

the ideas and text of the *Tractatus*

the continuing importance of Wittgenstein's work to philosophy today.

Wittgenstein is the most important twentieth-century philosopher in the English-speaking world. This book will be essential reading for all students of philosophy of language and metaphysics.

ISBN13: 978–0–415–35721–0 (hbk)
ISBN13: 978–0–415–35722–7 (pbk)
ISBN13: 978–0–203–00309–1 (ebk)

Available at all good bookshops
For ordering and further information please visit:
www.routledge.com